Ordination Rites
of the Ancient Churches of East and West

Paul F. Bradshaw

Ordination Rites
of the Ancient Churches of
East and West

Pueblo Publishing Company

New York

Design: Frank Kacmarcik

The author and publisher gratefully acknowledge the permission to reproduce extracts from copyright material granted by the following:

Carol Bebawi for her translation of the *Canons of Hippolytus*, which originally appeared in Paul F. Bradshaw's *The Canons of Hippolytus*, Alcuin/GROW Liturgical Study 2 (Nottingham, 1987).

The late Geoffrey Cuming for his translation of the *Apostolic Tradition* of Hippolytus, which originally appeared in his *Hippolytus. A Text for Students*, GLS 8 (Nottingham, 1976).

H. Boone Porter for his translations of Western ordination prayers from his *Ordination Prayers of the Ancient Western Churches*, Alcuin Club Collection 39 (London, 1967).

ISBN: 0-925127-00-0

Printed in the United States of America

Contents

Preface   ix
Abbreviations   xi

PART I: Introduction
1 The Sources   3
2 The Structure of the Rites   20
3 Bishop   37
4 Presbyter   58
5 Deacon   71
6 Deaconess   83
7 Minor Orders   93

PART II: Patristic Texts
Apostolic Tradition of Hippolytus   107
Canons of Hippolytus   110
Apostolic Constitutions   113
Testamentum Domini   117
Sacramentary of Sarapion   122

PART III: Eastern Texts
Armenian   127
Byzantine   133
Coptic   140
East Syrian   156
Georgian   166
Jacobite   174
Maronite   188
Melkite   201

PART IV: Western Texts
Roman   215
Gallican   222
Mozarabic   231
An Ordination Prayer Used in England: The Leofric Missal   236
The Later Composite Rite: The Sacramentary of Angoulême
   237

Appendix A: The Relationship between Eastern Ordination
    Prayers   243
Appendix B: Synopsis of Eastern Ordination Prayers for a Bishop
    245
Select Bibliography of Secondary Literature   249
Notes   252
Index   285

To my wife

PREFACE

The student of early Western ordination rites is in a relatively
fortunate position in that the subject has already been extensively explored, and he or she may therefore build upon the
foundations laid by others. Furthermore, many of the relevant
texts are conveniently assembled in a critical edition, with an English translation, by H. Boone Porter, *The Ordination Prayers of the
Ancient Western Churches* (Alcuin Club Collection 39, London
1967). The student of Eastern ordination rites, on the other
hand, is in a very different situation, since only a handful of
studies exist in this vast and complex field. Most of these cover
only a very limited part of the subject, and hardly any of them
are without some error. Moreover, even the texts themselves are
not easily accessible—either in their original languages or in
translated form. An added difficulty for English-speaking students has been that nearly all the earlier studies of both Eastern
and Western rites have been written in other languages. This
present volume is intended, therefore, to do something toward
ameliorating that situation.

Part I attempts to present the current state of scholarship with
regard to the early practice of ordination in both East and West
and, especially in the case of the East, to correct and extend previous research. The first chapter introduces the principal primary
sources available for such a study, and the second deals with the
elements of the ordination ritual that are common to bishops,
presbyters, and deacons in the various traditions, and hence
seem to form its nuclear structure. The remaining chapters consider the prayers and ceremonies that are proper to each of the
ministerial orders. Parts II to IV make available English translations of the texts under discussion, so that the reader may be
able to follow the argument more easily. The principle adopted
has been to use as far as possible the earliest extant manuscript
of each tradition, and to indicate interesting variants either in
notes or in the introductory chapters. Some of these texts have
appeared in English before, but mostly in works long out of
print, whereas others have been newly translated for this volume. In order to facilitate comparison, the Tudor-style English of
the older translations has been amended.

A particular problem that emerges in such an undertaking concerns which ecclesiastical offices should be included and which omitted. For, in addition to the orders of bishop, presbyter, and deacon, five minor orders ultimately emerged in the West. In the East, on the other hand, only two of these orders, subdeacon and reader, are consistently mentioned, but many of the traditions also have rites for deaconesses, *chorepiscopoi* (i.e., rural episcopal assistants), and other offices, as well as special forms for the ordination of metropolitans and patriarchs. Moreover, the later traditions of both East and West do not distinguish between the appointment of ministers and other forms of ecclesiastical or monastic admission and preferment: all alike tend to be described as ordinations and included in the same collections of rites. Though study of all of these would have value, yet in order to keep this volume to a manageable size, the texts and introductions have been limited to those offices that appear to be of greatest antiquity.

I am grateful to all who have assisted me with my work: to the doctoral students in liturgical studies at the University of Notre Dame who contributed useful insights and suggestions on points of detail—Maxwell Johnson, Jeffrey Kemper, Michael Moriarty, and Edward Phillips—and especially to Grant Sperry-White, who made a new translation of the *Testamentum Domini*; to my colleague Professor Harry Attridge, who translated the Coptic rite for me; to Dr. John Brooks-Leonard of the Center for Pastoral Liturgy, University of Notre Dame, for his advice in the translation of *Ordo Romanus* XXXIV; to Msgr. Hector Doueihi, Director of the Office of Liturgy in the Diocese of St. Maron, USA, for his scholarly comments on and translation of prayers from the Maronite rite; and to the Rev. René Mouret for assistance with the translation of the Jacobite pontifical. A particular debt of gratitude is due to Boone Porter, whose earlier work generated the original idea for the book, and who generously consented to the incorporation within it of adaptations both of the translations of the Western texts that had appeared there and also of the substance of the introductions to them. However, responsibility for any misinterpretation of that material remains mine alone.

Paul F. Bradshaw

ABBREVIATIONS

ALW	*Archiv für Liturgiewissenschaft*
BCES	*Compagnie de Saint-Sulpice: Bulletin du Comité des Etudes*
EL	*Ephemerides Liturgicae*
GLS	Grove Liturgical Study
JTS	*Journal of Theological Studies*
OC	Oriens Christianus
OCP	Orientalia Christiana Periodica
OS	L'orient syrien
PG	J. P. Migne, *Patrologia Graeca*
PL	J. P. Migne, *Patrologia Latina*
RHE	*Revue d'histoire ecclesiastique*
ROC	*Revue de l'Orient chrétien*
SL	*Studia Liturgica*
SP	*Studia Patristica*
TS	*Theological Studies*

PART I
INTRODUCTION

1 The Sources

PATRISTIC

APOSTOLIC TRADITION OF HIPPOLYTUS (pp. 107 – 109)

Although references to different ministerial offices and functions are quite plentiful in the Christian literature of the first three centuries, references to a rite of ordination are almost nonexistent: election and appointment are mentioned, but few details are given as to how these were carried out. For this reason the *Apostolic Tradition* of Hippolytus has assumed crucial importance in providing the only full account of ordination procedure prior to the fourth century.[1] It includes instructions and prayers for the ordination of bishops, presbyters, and deacons, and also directions concerning the appointment of widows, readers, and subdeacons. Virgins and those claiming the gift of healing are also mentioned, but there is no formal appointment for either of these groups: the former simply choose that state of life, and it is said that the facts themselves will reveal the truth concerning the latter.

This early Church order, however, needs to be treated with greater caution than it has generally received. Although it is usually dated c. A.D. 215 and regarded as providing reliable information about the life and liturgical activity of the Church in Rome at this period, a few scholars entertain doubts about its attribution to Hippolytus or its Roman origin,[2] and others have suggested that parts of the original work, and especially the section dealing with ordination, may have been retouched by fourth-century hands in order to bring it into line with current doctrine and practice.[3] In any case, it is dangerous to draw the conclusion that other Christian communities in the third century would necessarily have followed a similar practice to that described here. Furthermore, since the Greek original of the document has not survived, except in the form of a few isolated fragments, it has to be reconstructed from an extant Latin translation and from later Coptic, Arabic, and Ethiopic versions, as well as from the use made of it by compilers of later Church orders, which increases the difficulty of determining exactly what the author wrote.

CANONS OF HIPPOLYTUS (pp. 110 – 112)

This is the oldest known derivative of the *Apostolic Tradition* and freely paraphrases, supplements, and adapts its source so as to make it conform to a new situation. It is thought to have been composed in northern Egypt between A.D. 336 and 340, and, although doubtless originally written in Greek, is now extant only in the form of an Arabic version.[4] Like the *Apostolic Tradition*, it provides for the ordination of bishops, presbyters, and deacons, and gives brief directions for the appointment of readers, subdeacons, and widows.

APOSTOLIC CONSTITUTIONS (pp. 113 – 116)

This late fourth-century document is a composite revision of three earlier Church orders, the *Didascalia Apostolorum*, the *Didache*, and the *Apostolic Tradition*.[5] Its ordination rites are developed from those in the *Apostolic Tradition*, and provide for bishops, presbyters, deacons, deaconesses, subdeacons, and readers. It appears to derive from Syria and is generally thought to be the work of an Arian who was to some extent composing an idiosyncratic idealization rather than always reproducing exactly actual liturgical practice with which he was familiar. Thus, although it may be used cautiously as evidence for the early Antiochene tradition, and its ordination prayers do seem to have exercised some influence upon the Coptic tradition (see p. 9), it appears highly unlikely that all other later Eastern ordination rites "depend more or less directly" upon this source, as Pierre Jounel has claimed.[6]

TESTAMENTUM DOMINI (pp. 117 – 121)

This appears to have been the last of the Church orders derived from the *Apostolic Tradition*, and contains forms for the institution of bishops, presbyters, deacons, widows, subdeacons, and readers. It probably dates from the fifth century and seems to have been composed in Syria. Although originally written in Greek, it is extant only in Syriac, Arabic, and Ethiopic versions.[7] Like the

Apostolic Constitutions, it is doubtful how far it represents actual historical practice.

SACRAMENTARY OF SARAPION (*pp. 122 – 123*)

This collection of prayers has traditionally been regarded as the work of Sarapion, Bishop of Thmuis in northern Egypt and friend of Athanasius of Alexandria, and as having been written *c.* A.D. 350.[8] Bernard Botte, however, has questioned this, and suggested that it may not have been composed until the middle of the next century, but its authenticity has been defended by Geoffrey Cuming.[9] Among its prayers are ones for the ordination of a deacon, a presbyter, and a bishop, in that order, but without any rubrics or other formularies of the rites. P. M. Gy has suggested that these may have been influenced by the *Apostolic Tradition,*[10] but there seems to be no real evidence of any literary dependency. The document makes no reference to forms of institution for any other ecclesiastical offices.

EASTERN

Just as is the case with all other liturgical forms in the East, the ordination rites of the various traditions have undergone a process of development and expansion in the course of their history, and hence in order to attempt to recover their ancient forms and consider their relationship to one another, it is necessary to look not at the texts in current use, but at those that reflect an earlier stage in their evolution. This might seem obvious, and yet one of the principal weaknesses of the comparative study of Eastern ordination prayers attempted by J. M. Hanssens in 1952 was its failure to consider anything other than the fully developed versions.[11] The task is made more difficult by the fact that in some traditions very early manuscripts are no longer extant. Nevertheless, although existing texts of the rites tend to display a considerable variation in the rubrics between one manuscript and another, there is a high degree of stability in the form of the prayers themselves, which in any case are likely to be older than the rubrics, and this encourages the belief that they may have undergone relatively little development from earlier times. As we shall see in later chapters, there is evidence to suggest that the substance of some of the prayers goes back to at least the fourth century, and thus is as old as some of the patristic sources.

The relationship between the rites of the various Eastern traditions is an extremely complex one, and hence it is necessary to resist the temptation to look for a single hypothesis that will explain the connection between the prayers for all of the orders—bishop, presbyter, and deacon, and perhaps even deaconess, subdeacon, and reader as well. This approach contains a fundamental methodological error, and consequently is doomed to fail. One cannot assume that whenever material was adopted by one tradition from another or underwent some metamorphosis, this always happened at the same time and in the same way for each of the orders of ministry, and indeed the evidence of the texts themselves clearly suggests otherwise. Thus the interrelationship of the prayers for each order will generally be discussed individually in the relevant chapter.

ARMENIAN (pp. 127–132)

Armenia was evangelized first from East Syria and later from Cappadocia. The royal house was converted by Gregory the Illuminator (c. 240–332), who was consecrated bishop in A.D. 294 by the Metropolitan of Caesarea in Cappadocia. For a time, the office of Catholicos (Primate) was hereditary in his family and remained subject to the jurisdiction of the Metropolitan of Caesarea, who consecrated each successor, but in A.D. 374 the Armenians repudiated their dependence on the church of Caesarea. In spite of its rejection of the Council of Chalcedon (A.D. 451), the Armenian Apostolic Church was in a state of intermittent union with Constantinople between A.D. 590 and 971, and in the late Middle Ages was in some degree of union with Rome. Its liturgical practices were, therefore, subject successively to Byzantine[12] and Western influences.

In Armenian tradition Sahak ("Isaac," c. 350–428), who was instituted as tenth Catholicos in A.D. 387, is credited with having composed many of its liturgical rites, including the ordination of a presbyter, though that for appointing a reader is said to have been "a memorial to us from St. Gregory."[13] The historian Stephanos Asolik, writing between A.D. 991 and 1019, claimed that John Mandakuni, Catholicos during the last decade of the fifth century, "brought to perfection" the rites for deacon, presbyter, and bishop.[14] The earliest extant ordination rites appear to date from the ninth or tenth century,[15] and include forms for the ordination of a reader, subdeacon, deacon, and presbyter, but not for a bishop. They are relatively simple. In the case of reader and subdeacon there is merely a single prayer; in the case of the deacon, after a proclamation and a bidding, there are two prayers, separated by a litany containing special suffrages for the ordaining bishop and the candidate; the rite for the presbyterate is similar in structure, except that it concludes with a ceremonial robing, a ministry of the word, and a third ordination prayer.

Bernard Botte maintained that these rites were "clearly Byzantine."[16] However, this does not appear to be a fair assessment. Although there is some structural conformity, close verbal parallels are very few indeed, and are restricted to elements that have the appearance of secondary additions, whereas the principal euchology seems to have developed in relative independence. Only in the cases of the reader and the deaconess is there any real resemblance to another tradition, and here it is to the Georgian rather than the Byzantine.

BYZANTINE (pp. 133 – 139)

Since in early times Byzantium was not a major center of Christianity, its liturgical practices were derived principally from Antioch and to a lesser extent from Cappadocia. However, the prestige that it enjoyed as the imperial city later enabled it to influence other local rites of the churches of the East. There are in existence three principal manuscripts that witness to the early history of ordination practice in this tradition. Two of these were included in Jean Morin's seventeenth-century collection of ordination rites:[17] Barberini 336, an Italo-Greek *euchologion* of the eighth century, and Grottaferrata G.b.I, a Constantinopolitan manuscript of the eleventh century. The third is Paris BN Coislin 213, an unofficial transcription of prayer material very similar to the Grottaferrata text made in Constantinople in A.D. 1027.[18]

The first of these is obviously the most important for establishing the primitive form of the rite, but since the others do not stand in direct linear descent from it, it is possible that some features found only in those and not in the Barberini manuscript also date from earlier times, and hence they should not be ignored. Like the Armenian rites, the Byzantine forms of ordination have a simple structure: for bishop, presbyter, deacon, and deaconess, they consist chiefly of a proclamation/bidding and two ordination prayers, separated by a litany; in the case of the subdeacon and reader, there is only a single prayer.

COPTIC (pp. 140 – 155)

After the Council of Chalcedon the Egyptian church formed close links with the Jacobites of West Syria. The liturgical practices of the Coptic Orthodox Church were in part derived from the ancient uses of the Alexandrian tradition, translated from Greek into Coptic, and in part from other sources, and especially from West Syrian influence. The principal manuscripts of its ordination rites are all late, dating from the fourteenth century onward, and provide for the ordination of a reader, subdeacon, deacon, presbyter, *hegoumenos* (i.e., abbot), archdeacon, and bishop. In the case of a metropolitan, the prayer for a bishop from *Testamentum Domini* is added to the rite, and there is also a special form for the consecration of the patriarch.[19]

There have only ever been two printed editions of the Coptic pontifical: the first was produced by Raphaël Tuki at Rome in 1761, and was based on the oldest manuscripts in the Vatican library; and the second, containing the rites from reader to *hegoumenos*, was published by Athanasius, Metropolitan of Beni Suef and Bahnasa, in Cairo in 1959. A Latin translation of the rites for the orders below that of bishop was made by Athanasius Kircher in 1647 and published in 1653.[20] This version was reproduced in Morin's collection of texts,[21] and a Latin translation of the rites for bishop, metropolitan, and patriarch was later published by Eusèbe Renaudot.[22] A Latin version by Antony Scholz, collated with earlier translations, appeared in Henry Denzinger's collection of Eastern rites in 1863[23]; and a text with a French translation was published in a series of articles by V. Ermoni at the end of the nineteenth century.[24] According to Emmanuel Lanne, both Ermoni's text and translation are so defective as to be hardly usable, and the various Latin versions employed by Denzinger should be treated with caution.[25] Fortunately, however, O. H. E. Burmester produced a critical edition of the rite for the patriarch in 1960 and a synopsis of the rest of the rites in English in 1967; and a full text and English translation that he had prepared of those rites was published posthumously in 1985.[26]

Because of the late date of the manuscript sources, the early history of these rites cannot easily be reconstructed. The ordination prayers display no obvious affinity to those of the *Canons of Hippolytus* or the *Sacramentary of Sarapion*, but instead they closely parallel those in the *Apostolic Constitutions*, and are supplemented by material derived chiefly from the Jacobite rites. The similarity to the *Apostolic Constitutions* was noted by P. Antoine in 1931,[27] but was more extensively explored first by Hanssens and later by Lanne. Hanssens argued that the prayers of the Coptic rite were not directly derived from those of the *Apostolic Constitutions*, but that both were descended from ancient Alexandrian practice, developing from the *Apostolic Tradition* (which he believed to have originated in Alexandria rather than Rome).[28] Lanne did not go as far as that, but he did claim that the text of the *Apostolic Constitutions* used here was older than that otherwise known to us, and lacked certain theological additions later made to the prayers.[29] Gy, however, has rightly pointed out that the Coptic version of the prayers may instead have deliberately corrected an Arian original,[30] and hence we cannot draw from that any conclusions about the date when they were adopted by the Coptic tradition.

Until the present century, the Ethiopian Orthodox Church was under the jurisdiction of the Alexandrian patriarch, who always appointed an Egyptian monk to be its bishop and to ordain its clergy. Consequently, it had no ordination rites of its own, but used a translation of the Coptic rites.

EAST SYRIAN (pp. 156 – 165)

Although originally part of the Antiochene patriarchate, Christians in East Syria not only had a strongly Semitic background, but also spoke Syriac rather than Greek and lived under Persian rather than Roman rule. Because of these factors, they largely escaped Antiochene liturgical influence and developed quite distinct practices of their own. After their rejection of the Council of Ephesus in A.D. 431, they followed the Nestorian tradition and were thus effectively isolated from the rest of Christendom as the Assyrian Church of the East. In the fifteenth and sixteenth centuries, some Assyrians linked themselves with Rome and became known as the Chaldean Church.

Both the Assyrians and the Chaldeans share the same ordination rites, the extant manuscripts of which are all very late. The oldest dates from A.D. 1496, and contains only the forms for reader, subdeacon, deacon, and presbyter, though later manuscripts include rites for bishop, metropolitan, patriarch, archdeacon, *shahare* (i.e., a presbyteral or diaconal deputy, chiefly responsible for singing the offices), *chorepiscopos*, and deaconess.[31] There is no critical edition. Texts with Latin translations were published by Morin, by J. S. Assemani, and by J. A. Assemani[32]; an English translation was produced by G. Percy Badger in 1852[33]; a Latin translation was made by J. M. Vosté in 1937[34]; and a French translation of the principal prayers was included in an article by Alphonse Raes in 1960.[35]

According to East Syrian tradition, the rites were the work of the patriarchs Marabas I (*d.* A.D. 552) and Iso'Yab III (649–659), Cyprian, bishop of Nisibis (*c.* 767), and Gabriel, metropolitan of Bassorah (*c.* 884). They have no doubt undergone some later expansion and elaboration, but although they include many prayers of an obviously secondary character, their principal elements can still easily be discerned. Botte believed that this tradition originally had only one formulary that was used with appropriate modification for the episcopate, presbyterate, and diaconate.[36] However, he was referring to the first prayer accompanying the imposition of hands in each of the rites, the form and content of which on the contrary suggest that it is a later addition rather than part of the earliest stratum. It is instead the second such prayer that seems to be the original ordination prayer. This is quite different in each case, and is also found in a shorter, and seemingly earlier, recension in the Georgian tradition.

GEORGIAN (pp. 166 – 173)

The origins of Christianity in Georgia (also known as Iberia), in what is now the USSR, extend back to at least the beginning of the fourth century, if not earlier. Unlike its neighbor Armenia, it did not permanently repudiate the Council of Chalcedon, but eventually formed an autocephalous church in communion with the Orthodox patriachates, as remains the case today. Between the fifth and the eighth centuries, its liturgical practices were strongly shaped by those of Jerusalem.

The only ancient ordination text to survive from this tradition is found appended to the liturgy of St. James in a manuscript that is thought to have been copied in the tenth or eleventh century.[37] The eucharistic rite itself was probably translated into Georgian in the seventh century, and the ordination rite may well be of the same date. It contains virtually no rubrics and hence is little more than a collection of prayers for the ordination of a reader, subdeacon, (arch)deacon, deaconess, presbyter, *chorepiscopos*, and bishop. The episcopate, presbyterate, and diaconate are each provided with a set of three prayers, and Gy believed that these rites had "received in the succession of time the ordination prayer of Jerusalem, of the *Apostolic Constitutions*, and of Constantinople."[38] He is at least partially mistaken: the prayers that he describes as coming from the *Apostolic Constitutions* were not taken from that source but copied from the *Testamentum Domini*; and those that he believes to have similarity to the Byzantine rite are in fact versions of the ordination prayers of the East Syrian rite. These latter appear to provide us with valuable evidence, which is otherwise lacking, as to the form of those prayers at an earlier stage in their development. How, and why, they came to be incorporated into the Georgian rites is a mystery, but it seems likely that the original from which they are derived was in existence prior to the isolation of the East Syrians early in the fifth century.

JACOBITE (pp. 174 – 187)

The Council of Chalcedon caused a division among the Christians of West Syria, the majority separating themselves and forming the Syrian Orthodox Church, generally known as the Jacobite Church, after Jacob bar Addai who reorganized it in the sixth century. Its liturgical foundation was the Greek rite of Antioch, translated into Syriac, together with other authentically Syriac material. The present form of the pontifical is attributed to Michael the Great, patriarch from A.D. 1166 to 1199, and contains rites for the ordination of a cantor, reader, subdeacon, deacon, and presbyter; a form for the institution of an archdeacon; one for use for a *chorepiscopos*, visitor, abbot, or abbess; and a rite for the ordination of a bishop, with variations for a metropolitan or patriarch. A note refers to the older practice of ordaining deaconesses, but the rite for this is not reproduced.[39] When compared to earlier rites, these show evidence of considerable accretion and elaboration. In each of the rites, except that for a reader, which has a distinctive shape of its own, several preparatory and supplementary prayers—almost identical in wording for all of the orders—have grown up around the principal ordination prayer. Nevertheless, the latter can still be clearly discerned.

There are a number of manuscripts of the pontifical, the earliest being Vatican syr. 51, dating from A.D. 1172, and Paris BN syr. 112, dating from A.D. 1239,[40] but no critical edition exists.[41] Morin included in his collection only the rites for deacons, presbyters, and bishops, and these were derived from manuscripts of unknown date that lacked the text of the prayers themselves.[42] The full text of the rite for the presbyterate, with a French translation, was published by R. Graffin in 1896,[43] but unfortunately from a fifteenth-century version interpolated into BN Syr. 112; and a full text of all the rites was printed for the first time at Charfé in Lebanon in 1952, but according to G. Khouri-Sarkis, this too displays significant deviations from the early manuscripts known in the West.[44] Denzinger merely reproduced Latin translations made by Morin and Renaudot from late manuscripts,[45] but J. M. Vosté has published a Latin translation based principally on Vat. syr. 51,[46] and Bernard de Smet a French translation of the rite for the episcopate and patriarchate.[47]

MARONITE (pp. 188 – 200)

The Maronite rite originated among the communities of Christians in Lebanon who formed themselves into an autonomous church during the sixth century, centered around the monastery of St. Maron. In A.D. 1215, as a result of the Crusades, they came into contact with Rome. It is very difficult to establish the early history of their ordination rites, since all manuscripts of the pontifical date from after this time,[48] and the only published modern study was by Pierre Dib in 1919, which consisted chiefly of description of the more recent forms.[49] The earliest known reform of the rites was undertaken by Jeremiah Al-Amchiti, patriarch from 1209 to 1230, but this apparently failed to achieve any stability or uniformity of practice, and a further attempt to produce a standardized pontifical, together with a commentary on the rites, was made by Stephen Ad-Doueihi (1630–1704), patriarch from 1670 onward. He carefully collated earlier manuscripts in this process, and for the first time combined into a single form the texts used by both the bishop and the deacon in the celebration of the rites, which had formerly existed as separate versions containing only the parts for which each was responsible. This work was completed in 1683, and further revisions were made in the eighteenth century.[50]

No critical edition of the manuscripts exists. Morin included in his collection of ordination rites a text of the Maronite services together with a Latin translation, but from a single diaconal manuscript that therefore lacked the ordination prayers themselves.[51] A full text with a Latin translation was later published by J. A. Assemani from a manuscript of A.D. 1728,[52] and the translation was reproduced by Denzinger.[53]

The rites contain a multiplicity of prayers and other formulas for each order, suggesting a long process of accretion. Their closest parallels are, not surprisingly, with the Jacobite tradition, but there are also some resemblances to the Melkite rite (see the next section). One of the prayers in the rite for a deacon is a version of the first prayer in the Byzantine rite, and one of the prayers in the rite for a bishop is the ordination prayer from the *Apostolic Constitutions*. A number of the formularies, however, have no known parallels, but it is not always easy to decide whether they represent an ancient and independent euchological tradition or are later compositions.

MELKITE (pp. 201–212)

After A.D. 451, some Christian communities within the Antiochene patriarchate remained faithful to Chalcedon, and were known as Melkites (though that designation has more recently been used for those from this background who are united with Rome). Not unnaturally, they gradually adopted most of the liturgical practices of the Byzantine tradition. In 1938, Matthew Black published a Melkite manuscript that contained two sets of ordination services for reader, subdeacon, deacon, and presbyter, but not for a bishop or deaconess.[54] Though the first set is in Syriac, it closely parallels the Byzantine rites in the Barberini manuscript, and is more or less identical to an unpublished Syriac manuscript of the fourteenth century in the Vatican (syr. 41). The second, however, is written in a mixture of Christian Palestinian Aramaic and Greek, and is composed of rites of a very different kind. Several prayers are provided for each order: some closely resemble the Georgian texts mentioned earlier and hence encourage the belief that they originated in Jerusalem; others are similar to certain of the Byzantine prayers; versions of others are found in the Maronite rites; while the rest have no clear parallels with any other known texts.

WESTERN

ROMAN (pp. 215 – 221)

The oldest known text containing the classical Roman ordination prayers is the so-called Leonine Sacramentary, an incomplete seventh-century book preserved at Verona. This has the prayers for bishops, deacons, and presbyters, in that order. Surviving portions of the manuscript do not contain any provisions for subdeacons or other lesser clerics.[55] The next evidence occurs in the eighth century. The Gelasian Sacramentary,[56] the more-or-less Gallican book known as the *Missale Francorum*,[57] and various eighth-century adaptations of the Gelasian[58] contain these same prayers, but with a considerable amount of Gallican material mixed in with them. The several manuscripts of the Gregorian Sacramentary in the ninth century contain a purer Roman text.[59] A later chapter of this book has brief prayers for instituting a cleric, a deaconess, a "handmaid of God," and an abbot or abbess. The manner of performing the rites is described in some of the *Ordines Romani*, or ceremonial handbooks, of this period, which in some cases include the text of the ordination prayers as well.[60] The oldest of these, *Ordo* XXXIV, apparently dates from the middle of the eighth century.

GALLICAN (pp. 222 – 230)

The ancient native Christian rites of Gaul developed to a high point in the late fifth and the sixth centuries, declined in the seventh, and were progressively displaced by the imported Roman liturgy during the course of the eighth century. The oldest evidence for ordination practice here is found in an interesting document known as the *Statuta Ecclesiae Antiqua*, perhaps written by Gennadius of Marseilles *c.* A.D. 490.[61] It contains a collection of brief rubrical directions for the ordination of bishops, presbyters, and deacons, and also provides for the appointment of subdeacons, acolytes, exorcists, readers, doorkeepers, psalmists, and nuns. As we shall see in later chapters, these directions appear to have been derived at least in part from the *Apostolic Tradition* and other literary sources, rather than reflecting the traditional customs of the region at the time of their composition. Nevertheless, since most of them were subsequently quoted in the Gelasian Sacramentary, they succeeded in establishing themselves firmly in the Franco-Roman rite from the eighth century onward.

In view of the wide liturgical diversity characteristic of Gaul in this era, it is not unlikely that various regions had local ordination prayers of their own, though only one coherent series of such prayers has survived in existing manuscripts. No purely Gallican text of the material is extant, but it is found combined with the Roman texts in the early eighth century in the *Missale Francorum* and, to a slightly lesser extent, in the Gelasian Sacramentary and the various recensions of it.[62] Evident parallelism with the Mozarabic prayers suggests that it may come from Southwestern Gaul. It consists of appropriate formularies for each of the minor orders, and an address to the people, a bidding, and an ordination prayer in the case of deacons and presbyters. For the episcopate, there is also an address and a bidding, but no ordination prayer as such: all that survives here is an interpolation, seemingly of Gallican origin, inserted in the Roman prayer itself. Although this has commonly been regarded as a remnant of the original Gallican formulary, Bruno Kleinheyer has strongly argued that another oration found in later pontificals (see the section after the next) is in fact the true prayer that once belonged to this collection of texts.[63]

MOZARABIC (pp. 231–235)

The ancient national liturgy of Spain, the Mozarabic or Visigothic rite, originated in the same period as the Gallican. Indeed, in many respects Gallican and Mozarabic are merely regional variations of a single liturgy. Spain differed from Gaul, however, in that at an early date a much greater liturgical consistency was achieved throughout the nation. The prayers were composed in much better Latin, and were more carefully copied. The completeness of the Mozarabic liturgy, and the geographical isolation of Spain, kept it relatively free from Roman liturgical influence for a long period, and indeed the services remained in widespread use on the peninsula until the eleventh century.

The texts of the ordination rites were entirely unknown to modern scholarship until 1886 when Dom Marius Férotin discovered at Silos a copy of the *Liber Ordinum*, or book of occasional offices, which he published in 1904.[64] It contains forms for ordaining presbyters and deacons, for admitting clerics and monastics, and for appointing a sacristan, librarian (or chief scribe), subdeacon, archdeacon, chief cleric, archpresbyter, abbot, and abbess. Unfortunately, it does not include the form for ordaining a bishop, and little evidence exists for this rite apart from a brief and partial description in the writings of Isidore of Seville.[65] Although the native biddings and ordination prayers probably date from the sixth century—the classic period of Visigothic creativity—the rites have subsequently been embellished and have absorbed material of Roman and Gallican origin. The volume itself dates from the eleventh century, and unlike the earlier Western texts, both the prayers and the rubrics for the rite are now combined in a single order of service.

AN ORDINATION PRAYER USED IN ENGLAND (p. 236)

Among the ancient Latin ordination prayers, there is one that survives alone, without accompanying biddings, collects, or rubrics. This is a long oration for a bishop, which appears in several medieval English pontificals. It is found first in the so-called Leofric Missal, a liturgical book used at Exeter in the Anglo-Saxon era.[66] It occurs, however, in a portion of the codex believed to have been written in Lotharingia early in the tenth century.[67] In the latter part of the same century, at the famous scriptorium of Corbie in northern France, it was copied in the Sacramentary of Ratold.[68] Evidently, it did not find subsequent favor on the Continent, but it recurs regularly in English orders, including the Benedictional of Archbishop Robert, a late tenth-century codex from Winchester,[69] and the Pontifical of Magdalen College, a manuscript of the second half of the twelfth century,[70] which represents another recension of it. Later medieval books exhibit many minor variations.[71]

What is its origin? On the basis of its style and manner of thought, it groups itself naturally with the Gallican family of texts, which is to say that it may come from Gaul or Spain, or even northern Italy. Antonio Santantoni has contended for an Hispanic origin,[72] but as we indicated earlier, Kleinheyer has put forward the claim that it is in reality the prayer for a bishop that once accompanied the other extant Gallican material.[73] As is the case with other principal liturgical compositions from these areas, the sixth century is the most plausible date for its composition, but it may be even older. Its most remarkable characteristic, however, is the close parallelism between its thought and that of the analogous prayer of the *Apostolic Tradition*. This would thus appear to be one of several points at which that forgotten document somehow exerted an influence on the liturgical rites of the Western churches.

THE LATER COMPOSITE RITE (pp. 237 – 242)

The later development of Western ordination rites is not the object of this study. Nevertheless, since almost none of the surviving liturgical books of Latin Christendom antedates the eighth century, the more ancient rites have to be reconstructed largely from books in which a later process of elaboration is already under way. It is important, therefore, to have some understanding of the course that this later development took.

The elaboration of the rites was encouraged at the outset by the situation in Gaul. As the ancient Gallican rite deteriorated, it was displaced by the Roman. The Roman ordination prayers, however, were of a rather obscure character and they were unable totally to dispossess the native forms. Hence a composite rite emerged. It is first encountered in the Gelasian and *Missale Francorum*, and recurs in the so-called "Gelasians of the eighth century." The general pattern was for there to be first one or more biddings or exhortations (Roman, Gallican, or both), one or more collects, and then the Roman ordination prayer. In the case of presbyters and deacons, this was followed at once by a Gallican bidding and ordination prayer. Thus, in effect, an ordinand received the rites of both traditions one after the other. In the case of a bishop the situation is a little more complicated: as we have seen earlier, the Gallican material interpolated into the Roman ordination prayer may comprise the substance of the original Gallican oration, or, as Kleinheyer has argued, that prayer may have disappeared from most later rites and be found only in certain English pontificals.[74]

Meanwhile, there had developed the custom of anointing the hands of a new presbyter. By the middle of the eighth century, the Frankish king was also being anointed at his coronation, and the anointing of bishops soon followed. Moreover, since the vestments worn by the clergy during the liturgy had now lost their relationship to formal secular dress and had acquired a sacral character, their bestowal on the ordinand also became a liturgical act. The rites of the Sacramentary of Angoulême, dating from the last years of the eighth century, offer an excellent illustration of this process, with the ancient Roman and Gallican forms standing in juxtaposition, and new material emerging.[75] In this book, as in other later sources, the forms for bestowing the minor orders come first, and then those for the diaconate, presbyterate, and episcopate—thus reversing the more ancient arrangement.

At the end of the eighth century, an exemplar of the Gregorian Sacramentary was obtained by the Emperor Charlemagne from Pope Hadrian. This introduced into the North a new and slightly different recension of the Roman prayers, free from all Gallican interpolations. Ironically, however, the Roman prayers themselves, with their ornate references to the Old Testament priesthood, encouraged the very tendencies most characteristic of the Gallican rite. The old Roman prayers had been intended, in the age of the Fathers, to be understood in a mystical and metaphorical sense. In the barbarian North, on the other hand, they were taken more literally, and the reference to "the dew of heavenly unction" in the prayer for a bishop was now thought to refer to a physical anointing, which soon intruded itself into the Gregorian rite at this point. During the course of the ninth century, the new Roman rite, as performed in Gaul, began to receive those Gallican additions that had been appended to the Gelasian rite a century before.

Although the details of later ordination rites varied from place to place, this composite pattern crystallized into what has been called the "Romano-German Pontifical of the tenth century." The order followed in this style of book, or analogous arrangements, became normal throughout Western Christendom. With the displacement of the old Mozarabic rite, it became current in Spain. Norman influence carried it to Britain, and as the Western Church expanded eastward, it was borne into central Europe. The same occurred in Northern Italy, and our oldest text of the

Milanese ordination rites is simply a variant of the Gregorian forms, embellished with the anointings and the usual Gallican additions. Moreover, in the eleventh century, this pattern was also largely accepted in Rome itself.

2 The Structure of the Rites

Amid all the diversity of the various ordination rites of East and West can be discerned a number of elements that are found in many or all of the traditions and that seem to point to a basic pattern of practice followed in the early centuries of the Church's history with regard to the appointment of bishops, presbyters, and deacons. These common features will be examined here, and those that are distinctive of each order will be treated later. The same elements recur in some, but not all, rites for deaconesses, indicating the ambivalence felt with regard to the status of that office, and in some traditions they are extended even to the minor orders. These will be noted in their respective chapters.

THE CONTEXT

According to the *Apostolic Tradition* (p. 107), the appointment of a new bishop took place within the regular Sunday liturgical assembly of the community in which he was to exercise his ministry, and immediately after his ordination, he presided over the celebration of their eucharist, thus fulfilling among them the liturgical role proper to his order. Although it is not made explicit, it is probable that the ordinations of presbyters and deacons were done in a similar manner. This practice, however, was not maintained by the later traditions, but instead ordinations tended to be performed in the centralized location of the diocesan or metropolitan cathedral, where several candidates from different places might be ordained at one time. This development is reflected in the introductory formularies in a number of the later rites, which not only mention the candidate's name, but also specify the church where he is to serve. This reference may be intended as no more than just a means of identifying each individual, but may also be a conscious expression of the rejection of "absolute" ordinations by the early Church: one could not be ordained simply as a bishop, presbyter, or deacon in the universal Church, but had to be appointed to a specific, vacant ministerial role within a particular Christian community.[1]

While ordinations thus ceased to take place in the context of the local community, later traditions did maintain the custom of the rite being performed on a Sunday or major festival in the case of the episcopate, but not always in the case of the presbyterate or diaconate, though they did normally continue to be located within a eucharistic rite, in which the newly ordained fulfilled the liturgical role of their order. Sunday ordinations were preserved more in the East than in the West, because there the celebration of the eucharist was restricted to Sundays and major festivals. Even so, there were still exceptions to this rule: in the Byzantine tradition (and apparently the Melkite, too), the diaconate could be conferred on a day when only the Liturgy of the Presanctified was celebrated, since the diaconal function could equally be exercised there; and in the East Syrian tradition, both the presbyterate and the diaconate might be conferred outside the context of a eucharist.

Letters written by Pope Leo I in the middle of the fifth century indicate that, while he was aware that other churches did not always adhere to the custom of Sunday ordination, it was never theless the practice at Rome.[2] He implies, however, that the ordinations there actually took place on Saturday evening, which was regarded as the beginning of Sunday, in order that the preparatory fasting required of both the ordainers and the ordinands[3] might not be unduly prolonged. From at least the time of Pope Gelasius I (A.D. 482–496), if not sooner, the ordinations of presbyters and deacons, and sometimes of bishops, too,[4] were performed at the Saturday vigil mass of one of the four Ember seasons (the December one being preferred), since these were regular times of fasting for the Roman Church.

There was some variation within the different traditions with regard to the precise point within the eucharistic liturgy at which ordination to each of the orders took place, and also with regard to the particular liturgical functions exercised by the newly ordained. These matters will be considered further in the relevant chapters.

THE APPROBATION BY THE PEOPLE

The evidence of the *Apostolic Tradition* and other early sources suggests that in the third century, ordination to the episcopate, presbyterate, and diaconate comprised two distinct but related actions: firstly, the election of the candidate; and, secondly, prayer for the bestowal of the gifts needed to fulfill the particular ministry. In both these actions, the local Christian community played a major part. Indeed, in the earliest ordinations to the episcopate, it is likely that the procedure was conducted entirely by the local church, and there are some signs to suggest that this may even have been the case in the original version of the *Apostolic Tradition*, and in third-century Alexandrian practice.[5] Elsewhere in the third century, however, according to other evidence, and especially that of Cyprian of Carthage, a candidate for the episcopate required the approval both of the local church and also of the neighboring bishops. It was this, rather than any theory of sacramental transmission, that led to the presence and involvement of the latter in the rite of episcopal ordination. In the case of the presbyterate and diaconate at this time, the right of nomination seems to have rested with the bishop, but he did not normally act without the advice of the clergy and people.[6]

The important place accorded to the election of a candidate for ordination should not be understood as pointing to some notion of the ideal of democracy in early Christianity, nor, at least at first, to the principle that a congregation had the right to choose its own ministers. Nor was it seen as in any way opposed to the divine calling of a minister, but on the contrary it was understood as the means by which God's choice of a person for a particular ecclesiastical office was discerned and made manifest. As both early Christian writings and the prayers in the rites themselves make clear, it was always considered that it was God who chose and ordained the ministers through the action of the Church.[7] There was thus no dichotomy between actions "from below" and "from above." The Church's discernment of the divine choice might even override an individual's own lack of a sense of vocation, as happened, for example, in the case of both Ambrose of Milan and Augustine of Hippo, and it contrasts with more modern views of the primacy of the "interior call."

As time went by, however, the ritual of prayer and the imposition of the hand came to be thought of as the "real" act of ordination, and, consequently, as the means by which the gift of the office itself was bestowed on the candidate, and election merely as a preliminary to it. It is not surprising, therefore, that eventually the link between the local community and the choice of a minister was considered relatively unimportant and ultimately dispensable. Deacons, and later presbyters, too, were generally not elected at all, but appointed directly by the bishop, acting alone.[8] In some cases, the voice of the local church in the election of its bishop was represented merely by presbyters, without the laity; in others the bishops of the province, or even the secular ruler, controlled the selection. Even in those instances where others retained a part in the process, it was eventually reduced to no more than a nominal act, lacking any real power or influence in the outcome. Yet, in spite of the decline of the electoral process, vestigial traces of the former arrangement can still be detected among the preliminaries of the later ordination rites of both East and West.

Although the *Apostolic Tradition* does not indicate the form by which the congregation's approval of the candidate was expressed, later rites are more explicit. In the *Canons of Hippolytus* (p. 110) in the case of a bishop, and possibly also of presbyters and deacons, the clergy and people say, "We choose him." *Apostolic Constitutions* (p. 113) refers to the approval by the people solely with regard to the episcopate, and no formulary is given for this, but since the questions put to the people ask whether the candidate is worthy of the office, one might presume that their reply would have been the cry, *Axios*, "[he is] worthy," as is the case in some later rites. The principal evidence for this liturgical response occurs in two traditions from very different geographical regions, Armenia and Gaul.

The early Armenian rites (pp. 128 and 130) begin with an announcement of the nomination of the candidate, made by a deacon in the case of an ordination to the diaconate and by a presbyter in the case of an ordination to the presbyterate. The formulary ends with the statement, "in accordance with the testimony of himself and of the congregation: he is worthy." This was doubtless originally intended to be a question, to which a congregational response was expected, as it still is in another manuscript probably dating from no later than the thirteenth century:

"Divine and heavenly grace, that always fulfills the needs of the holy ministry of the apostolic Church. They call N. from the diaconate to the priesthood for the ministration of the holy Church. According to the testimony of himself and of the congregation, is he worthy?

"And the congregation say three times: He is worthy."[9]

In the ancient Gallican tradition in the West, the rites for the episcopate, presbyterate, and diaconate all begin with an address to the people, announcing the nomination of the candidate to the office and inviting them to indicate their acceptance of him by shouting, "He is worthy" (pp. 225, 226, and 228). Interestingly, while the form in the rite for the episcopate continues to imply that the people have an inherent right of election, that for the presbyterate tends to stress the role of counsel and consultation instead, and that for the diaconate makes it clear that their involvement is not absolutely necessary. The much later Mozarabic rites have no equivalent texts: presumably they had disappeared when the people's acclamation ceased to be a reality in that tradition.

At Rome, the approval by the people took a somewhat different form. In the case of candidates for the diaconate and presbyterate, a document known as a *breve advocationis* was read aloud by a lector at the stational services on the Wednesday and Friday prior to the ordination, and apparently by the Pope himself at the beginning of the ordination liturgy. This announced the names of the candidates, the order to which they had been appointed, and the church to which they were assigned; and invited anyone who had any objection to make to any of these men to declare it (p. 239).[10] Thus, here it was silence rather than a vocal acclamation that signified the approbation of the congregation.

In the case of the episcopate, the candidate was elected in his own diocese before being sent to Rome for ordination by the Pope, and hence there was apparently no expression of approval within the rite itself. However, the acclamation *dignus*, "worthy," seems to have been used in ancient times at the election of the bishop of Rome. Eusebius recounts the story of the appointment of Fabian in A.D. 236, when a dove is said to have alighted on his head during the election: this was taken by the people as a sign of the divine choice, and they unanimously cried that he was worthy, and sat him on the episcopal seat.[11] Augustine gives the impression that in fifth-century North Africa a variety of words of acclamation might be used.[12] At the same period, Arnobius the Younger implies that in Rome, *dignus et justus*, "worthy and just," had now become the standard form,[13] possibly as a result of assimilation to the response in the eucharistic dialogue. The same expression is attested for Gaul in the sixth

The Structure of the Rites

century by Gregory of Tours,[14] and is also found in the East Syrian rite for the episcopate, where it now follows immediately after the bidding to pray (p. 163), but in earlier times was probably the response to a formal announcement of the candidate.

The absence of an equivalent liturgical formulary from the beginning of the other rites of the East is probably to be explained by the decline of the people's role in the appointment of ordained ministers. However, it is not always completely absent but instead tends to occur at a different point within the rites. The earliest example of this is in the rite for a bishop in the fifth-century *Testamentum Domini*, where the acclamation "worthy," repeated three times, appears at the end of the ordination prayer (p. 118). It is also found at the end of the Coptic rites for bishops, presbyters, and deacons (pp. 145, 147, and 155); and in the same position both in the Melkite rites for presbyters and deacons (pp. 208 and 205), and in later Byzantine texts, though not in the eighth-century Barberini manuscript, which contains no form of congregational assent. Its absence from this, however, need not necessarily indicate that such a formula was not used at the time, but only that it was not thought necessary to specify it among the sparse rubrics of this version of the rite. Indeed, although the formulary is not mentioned by Pseudo-Dionysius in his description of ordination practice (probably written in Syria *c.* A.D. 500),[15] the fifth-century ecclesiastical historian Philostorgius recounts that, when the Arian Demophilos was appointed as Bishop of Constantinople in A.D. 370, many of the people shouted *anaxios*, "unworthy," instead of *axios*.[16] In the Jacobite rite for the episcopate, the acclamation comes at the very end of the whole proceedings, after the enthronement of the new bishop (p. 185).

It seems likely that its original position in all these rites was at the beginning, and that it was subsequently moved to what was no doubt thought a more logical place for an acclamation—toward the end of the whole proceedings—when the people's former role in the election of the candidate had been forgotten, or was in the process of being discounted. It is also possible that its transfer was encouraged by the coronation rite of the Byzantine emperor, where the same acclamation was located at its conclusion.[17] On the other hand, there is also the interesting fact that in the *Apostolic Tradition* the kiss given to the bishop at the end of the ordination prayer is said to be "because he has been made worthy" (p. 108). If it was already thought that it was God's response to the prayer of the Church that made the candidate truly worthy of the office, rather than any intrinsic merit that he previously possessed, such a notion may have contributed to the subsequent relocation of the acclamation.

PROCLAMATION/BIDDING

In the Byzantine tradition, the rites for the episcopate, presbyterate, and diaconate all include the reading of a scroll containing the formulary beginning, "The divine grace . . ." (pp. 133, 134, and 136). In 1957, Bernard Botte made an important contribution to the study of ordination rites in his analysis of this formulary, which is found in one form or another in all later Eastern rites for the ordination of bishops, presbyters, and deacons, and in some cases has spread to the minor orders as well.[18] From a comparison of the different versions in the various traditions, he concluded that there tended to be greater variety in the formulary's wording in the case of the presbyterate and the diaconate than there was in the case of the episcopate, and that the most primitive form was that found in the Byzantine rite, which was identical in the conferral of all three offices apart from the name of the particular order.[19]

He then went on to point out that this formulary was apparently known to Pseudo-Dionysius, who refers to an *anarresis*, "proclamation," in his description of the rite of ordination: "The bishop makes the proclamation of the ordinations and the ordinands, the mystery signifying that the consecrator, beloved by God, is the interpreter of the divine choice. He does not lead the ordinand to ordination by his own grace, but he is moved by God for all the consecrations."[20] Moreover, there seemed to be allusions to such a proclamation at an even earlier date. John Chrysostom complained that "many of these ordinations happen not by divine grace but by human ambition"[21]; and Gregory of Nazianzus, when speaking of the ordination of his father, noted that "when it was conferred upon him, the grace was glorified as if it were really the grace of God and not that of men," but said of other ordinations, "I am close to believing that the civil authorities are more orderly than ours for which the divine grace is proclaimed."[22] All this suggested that it was already in use in the Antiochene tradition in the fourth century, and subsequently spread from there to the other rites. With this judgment, other scholars have since agreed, and indeed Gy and Lanne have added other possible early allusions to it.[23]

However, Botte then proceeded to draw a more questionable conclusion about the function of the formulary. Morin in his collection of texts had considered it to be simply the charter of the election read prior to the ordination proper, but Botte believed that it was intended to be the sacramental form of ordination itself. He admitted that it was pronounced by a deacon in the later Coptic and Jacobite rites,[24] and so could not have that function there, and was also in a preliminary position in the Byzantine rites for the presbyterate and diaconate in the eighth-century Barberini manuscript. But he judged that the Byzantine rite for the episcopate, together with the East Syrian and Maronite rites, had retained the true primitive usage, confirmed by Pseudo-Dionysius, in which the proclamation was made by the presiding bishop during the imposition of the hand.[25] He explained its absence from the ordination rites of the *Apostolic Constitutions* and the *Testamentum Domini* on the grounds that these were both derivatives of the *Apostolic Tradition* and not authentic Syrian texts. Its apparent relegation to a less central position in the other rites he believed to have been the result of the introduction of secondary elements—a second imposition of the hand in the Jacobite rite and the ordination prayers themselves in the Byzantine tradition: these tended to push the formulary into the shade, in a process analogous to the introduction of the *porrectio instrumentorum*, the bestowal of symbols of office, in Western ordination rites.

Most other scholars have rejected Botte's theory.[26] Gy has pointed out that Pseudo-Dionysius made a clear distinction between the proclamation, which was common to all three orders, and the invocations (*epicleses*), which were proper to each of them and through which the consecrations were effected. He has suggested that, on the contrary, the formulary grew rather than declined in importance in the course of the centuries as the ordination prayers came to be recited in a low voice for reasons of reverence: the second Byzantine prayer was already recited in this way while the litany was still being said in the eighth-century Barberini manuscript (pp. 134, 135, and 137), and later the first prayer too would be performed in a similar manner.[27]

Moreover, to this can be added the fact that in the eleventh-century Grottaferrata manuscript of the Byzantine rite the formulary is read *before* the imposition of the hand in the ordination of a bishop as well as in the rites for the presbyterate and diaconate, and contains an opening phrase that strengthens its association with the electoral process: "By the vote and approval of the most divinely-beloved bishops and the most holy presbyters and deacons. . . ." It seems improbable that this variation would have been a late insertion, especially since the election had in practice been restricted to the episcopal college alone for many centuries, and therefore likely that it is a survival from the more ancient tradition, which had already undergone some modification in the Barberini manuscript.

The formulary thus appears originally to have served as a sort of bridge between the two parts of the ordination process, proclaiming the result of the election and inviting the congregation to pray for the ordinand.[28] It may well have assumed this composite form when the approbation of the candidate by the people ceased to be a feature of this part of the rite and there was no longer a response between the announcement of the election and the bidding. Its wording confirms that the exercise of human choice was thought of as manifesting the divine will; and that the ordination was seen as effected by the grace of the Holy Spirit acting in response to the prayer of the Church.

Although this formulary was eventually adopted in one form or another by all other Eastern rites, our sources reveal that prior to this various traditions had their own equivalents of it. Moreover, in some cases there are signs that may point to the existence of an even more primitive form of the "divine grace" formulary than that found in the Byzantine rite. Thus, while the Coptic rites seem to have inherited the formulary through the Jacobite tradition, the rite for a bishop has an extensive proclamation/bidding of its own (p. 149). The Georgian rite similarly has a rather lengthy formulary of the same kind, pronounced by a deacon, that was used, with appropriate modifications, in appointment to all the orders (p. 166). This may have originated in the Jerusalem tradition, and has no doubt undergone some expansion and elaboration in the course of its history. In the case of ordinations to the episcopate, presbyterate, and diaconate, it is followed by another formulary, said by the bishop, that has some resemblance to the Byzantine one: "The grace of God heals the sick, satisfies them that are in need: hands are laid on this our child."

In the Armenian rites for the diaconate and presbyterate, the call for the assent of the people is followed in each case by another version of the same formulary, which appears to have been conflated with elements of the Byzantine one, and ends with a bidding (pp. 128 and 130). It seems likely that, prior to Byzantine influence, this was a simple bidding to pray for the ordinands. It is interesting to note that the inserted material is remarkably like that found in the Georgian rite, especially in the case of the presbyterate ("Divine and heavenly grace that ever fulfills the needs of the ministry of the holy apostolic Church . . . I lay hands upon him"), and a similar phrase also recurs in the version in the Melkite rite (pp. 206 and 209). This may possibly be a clue to an earlier form of the Byzantine formulary that was originally used at Antioch.

In their present form, the East Syrian rites do not include a proclamation of the election as such, but the archdeacon merely pronounces a bidding that names the candidates and the churches to which they are appointed. Like the others, this tradition also adopted a version of the "divine grace" formulary, but completely transformed it into a preparatory prayer for the presiding bishop himself. Its wording suggests that the form that it received may not have been very different from that underlying the ones in the Armenian and Georgian rites (pp. 156, 158, 160, and 163).

The Melkite rites also have their own equivalents of the Byzantine formulary. Those for deacons and presbyters begin with the presentation to the bishop of a scroll announcing the result of the election of the candidate: for a presbyter it reads, "N. appoints N. from deacons to presbyters," whereas for a deacon it is said to have read, "The divine grace appoints the deacons of this place, now. . . . Amen." Since in this form the latter fails to name the candidate, it would appear to have suffered some corruption. Furthermore, in all of the rites there is a presentation/bidding, said by a presbyter at the ordination of a presbyter, and by the chief deacon at the ordination of a deacon, subdeacon, or reader; and an expanded version of this occurs in the Maronite rites, where it is explicitly addressed to the presiding bishop. In addition, in both traditions a version of the "divine grace" formulary then follows, this being said by the bishop while hands are laid on the ordinand (pp. 188, 189, 191, 194, 197, 201, 203, 206, and 209).

With the exception of the Roman rite for a bishop, the Western traditions do not have a formulary equivalent to the Byzantine, probably because the final stage of the election process, the approbation by the people, managed to retain a vestigial place at the beginning of those rites. Instead, they all have a simple invitation to pray for the ordinands. In the case of the diaconate and presbyterate at Rome, the form appears in the sacramentaries (pp. 216 and 217). Like the Byzantine formulary, it indicates that the selection of the candidates was seen as the act of God, and the version for the presbyterate suggests that what was being sought was an increase in the grace already received by the ordinand.[29] At an ordination to the episcopate at Rome, however, according to the *Ordines*, the Pope used a formulary similar to those of the East, which announced the name of the elect and invited the congregation to pray for him (p. 220). Since the text of this formulary was not included in the sacramentary itself, the Northern recensions provided a simple bidding instead, in order to bring the rite as it was known there into line with those for deacons and presbyters (p. 242). The Gallican rites have a very extensive solemn bidding for the episcopate, and much briefer forms for the presbyterate and diaconate, that also appear in the Mozarabic tradition (pp. 225, 226, 228, 232, and 234).

THE PRAYER OF THE PEOPLE

In the ordination of a bishop in the *Apostolic Tradition* and its derivatives, the whole community prays in silence for the descent of the Holy Spirit before the ordination prayer is said by the presiding minister, and one would therefore naturally expect that the prayers of the people, in one form or another, would follow the biddings found in the later ordination rites. In fact, this is not always the case, and a variety of arrangements can be seen in the different traditions.

In the East Syrian rites, the silent prayer of the community has entirely disappeared, and the ordination prayers follow directly after the biddings (pp. 158, 160, and 163). The Jacobite rites have the normal Eastern prayer response *Kyrie, eleison,* "Lord, have mercy," following the proclamation/bidding, before they move on to a short prayer for the ordinand, said secretly by the presiding bishop, and then to the longer ordination prayer proper (pp. 178, 181, and 183). Once again, the prayer of the people seems to have been compressed and to have all but disappeared. As one might expect, the Coptic and Maronite rites are similar, except that in the case of the episcopate in the former, a full litany with a special suffrage for the ordinand does still intervene after the bidding (pp. 143, 145, 150, 191, 194, and 197).

In the Georgian rite, the deacon who pronounces the bidding is directed to say three times, "Lord, have mercy and make him worthy" (p. 166). This was doubtless originally a congregational response, and may even be a conflation of two responses that were earlier quite separate, an acclamation of the candidate's worthiness in reply to the announcement of his election, and the normal form of supplication. A litany occurs here in the text at the beginning of the whole collection of prayers, but with a rubric that directed that it was to be used at the ordination of bishops, presbyters, and deacons. Presumably, it was intended to be said between the bidding and the ordination prayers.

In the Melkite ritual, a threefold "Lord, have mercy" follows the first bidding, and then comes the Byzantine proclamation/bidding formulary and a litany, except in the rite for the diaconate, where the litany comes in what was very probably its original position, prior to Byzantine influence, directly after the first bidding (p. 206). Like that bidding, the litany is said by a presbyter at the ordination of a presbyter, and by the chief deacon at other ordinations.

In the Barberini manuscript of Byzantine rites, the triple response "Lord, have mercy" is explicitly mentioned as following the proclamation/bidding only in the case of the episcopate (p. 133), but it may also have been practiced in the other rites that employ the same formulary (presbyters, deacons, and deaconesses), even though it is not specified in the rubrics. In every case, however, a litany with appropriate petitions for the ordinands appears, not directly after the bidding, where one would have expected it, but later in the rite, between the two ordination prayers. This unusual arrangement suggests that the first ordination prayer is a later addition to the rites that destroyed the natural liturgical sequence and left the *Kyrie* response high and dry. As we shall see in subsequent chapters, the literary relationship of the prayers lends support to this conclusion.[30] Though such litanies were normally led by a deacon, in the rite for the episcopate a bishop fulfills this function, and in the rite for the presbyterate it is undertaken by a presbyter.

In the ninth-century text of the Armenian rite, the litany similarly intervenes between the first and second ordination prayers for deacons and presbyters (pp. 129 and 131). This arrangement is very probably the result of Byzantine influence on the structure of the services, and not part of the indigenous tradition, and it does not persist in later manuscripts.

In the Western rites, the prayer of the people was obviously intended originally to occur between the biddings and the prayers, as is still the case in Roman *Ordo* XXXIV (pp. 219 and 221). However, in the fusion of Roman and Gallican material in the Gelasian Sacramentary and related sources, the litany was instead placed before all the prayer texts, including the biddings— probably the result of a failure to appreciate the true nature of these texts—and there it remained in the later composite rites of the West (p. 239).

THE SIGN OF THE CROSS

The earliest allusion to the use of the sign of the cross in ordination is found in the *Canons of Hippolytus*, where the prayer for a deacon contains the clause, "make him triumph over all the powers of the Devil by the sign of your cross with which you sign him" (p. 111). Its existence at Antioch is confirmed by John Chrysostom, who speaks of it being used "in the ordinations of the priests" [i.e., bishops].[31] The "cruciform seal" immediately after the initial imposition of the hand is mentioned by Pseudo-Dionysius as being common to all the major orders,[32] and later Eastern rites show this to be the case. The practice appears to have been restricted to the East, however, since there is no sign of it in any of the Western rites. The use of the sign of the cross in early baptismal rituals may have provided the precedent for its adoption in Eastern ordination practice, especially as it is given a similar interpretation: the *Canons of Hippolytus* implies that it was seen as apotropaic, and Pseudo-Dionysius says that it signified "the cessation of all carnal desires and the imitation of the divine life."

THE IMPOSITION OF THE HAND

The imposition of the hand is almost universally attested as the principal ritual gesture of ordination,[33] though there is some variation between the different rites with regard to the particular ministers participating in it, about which more will be said in the later chapters. Much has been written about its origin and significance, but the matter is still far from clear. It has often been thought that primitive Christianity may have adopted the practice from rabbinic ordination in Judaism, but this is very uncertain. Indeed, Lawrence Hoffman has claimed that the term "rabbi" itself did not come into use until after the destruction of the Temple in A.D. 70, and that, although subsequently individual rabbis did appoint their disciples themselves, yet if there ever was any liturgical ceremony associated with this act, we do not know anything about it.[34] In any case, even if it were derived from this source, it may not have been used with the same meaning in early Christianity.

Similarly, 2 Timothy 1:6 speaks of a gift being bestowed through the laying on of hands, but it would be dangerous to conclude from that sole reference that such was its universal interpretation in early ordination practice. In particular, one must not assume that the imposition of hands was thought to transmit grace from ordaining minister to ordinand. Indeed, the ordination prayer for a bishop in the *Apostolic Tradition* implies that the bestowal of the Holy Spirit was effected by a fresh outpouring at each ordination in response to the prayer of the Church (p. 107).

It is interesting that the imposition of hands is only rarely mentioned in the earliest Christian allusions to the process of ministerial appointment. This may indicate that the gesture was not regarded as especially significant at this time, and was perhaps no more than the normal action that accompanied all solemn prayer and indicated its object. Certainly, the more ancient sources all agree that the imposition of hands was originally performed during the time that prayer was being offered for the ordinand. Thus, it was only much later that in the East, its use was extended to biddings or other formularies in the rites. In the West, the gesture became entirely detached from the prayers and took place in silence before they were said. This latter development was a consequence of the fact that the directions concerning the imposition of hands taken from the *Statuta Ecclesiae Antiqua* were placed at the head of the various texts for each order in the later composite rites and not at the point where it was really intended that the action should be done (pp. 239–241).

The increased importance given to the imposition of hands as ordination rites evolved may be due at least in part to the ambivalence of the Greek term *cheirotonia*, "the lifting up of hands." In classical Greek usage, this signified the act of election, but early Christianity extended it to designate not just the first half of the process of ministerial appointment, but the whole ordination—both election and prayer with the laying on of hands. Later the word seems to have been understood as referring primarily to the second action rather than the first—the lifting up/laying on of hands in prayer—and so gave that gesture greater prominence.[35] A similar shift in the meaning of the Latin terms *ordinatio* and *ordinare* can also be seen in the West.[36]

THE ORDINATION PRAYER(S)

The second half of the ordination process, the service of prayer for the ordinand, originally culminated in a solemn oration recited by the presiding minister. In many of the later rites, however, the number has increased, in what was doubtless considered to be a process of enrichment, either by the bringing together of prayers formerly belonging to different traditions, or by the composition of new prayers, often articulating more precisely than the older texts the functions of the particular order of ministry. In some cases, a further stratum expressing the personal devotions of the ordaining minister has grown up around this nucleus. The result of all this has generally been to obscure the structure and dynamic of the rite. The content of the various prayers and their relationship to one another will be considered more fully in the succeeding chapters.

CONCLUDING CEREMONIES

As rites of ordination evolve, concluding ceremonies tend to multiply. Their purpose is not to confer further powers or status upon the newly ordained, but rather to articulate more fully by their symbolism the reality that has taken place in the rite.

(a) *The Kiss.* The only such symbolic ceremony mentioned in the *Apostolic Tradition* is the exchange of a kiss between the assembly

The Structure of the Rites

and the new bishop (p. 108). This does not appear to be merely the kiss of peace that would normally occur within the eucharistic rite, for what evidence there is from the ante-Nicene period suggests that the latter formed the conclusion of the prayers of the faithful rather than the beginning of the eucharistic action.[37] The ordination kiss seems instead to have been intended to express the acceptance by the community of their new relationship with the ordained. This ceremony is repeated in the other church orders derived from the *Apostolic Tradition*, though the *Apostolic Constitutions* describes it as taking place after the new bishop's enthronement (p. 114).

No indication is given by any of the patristic sources as to whether a similar kiss was also exchanged in the case of the presbyterate and diaconate, with the sole exception of the *Testamentum Domini*, which directs that both "priests and people" are to give the kiss of peace to a newly ordained presbyter (p. 119). On the other hand, it is a consistent feature of later Eastern and Western rites. Pseudo-Dionysius, for example, describes it as an element common to all the orders. By then, however, the ritual had apparently been clericalized: the kiss was given to the newly ordained minister by the bishop and all the clergy, and no reference is made to the laity's involvement in the action. Pseudo-Dionysius interprets the kiss as symbolizing "the sacred communion of like minds and their loving joy toward one another."[38]

Although no directions are given about the kiss in the ninth-century Armenian text, the closing prayer in each of the rites does make reference to its existence, and describes it as a welcome that is given by all (pp. 129 and 132). Later manuscripts of the rite for the presbyterate, however, while preserving the prayer in this form, direct that the salutation be done only by the bishop and the other priests.[39] In later Byzantine practice, there was a further development, and participation became restricted to those thought of as effecting the ordination: thus, only the bishops present kiss a newly ordained bishop, and only the presiding bishop kisses a new presbyter or deacon (pp. 134, 136, and 137).[40] On the other hand, in other traditions, the kiss is sometimes described as being given *by* the newly ordained deacon, presbyter, or bishop *to* the other ministers present. This is the case in the East in the Coptic rite for a presbyter (p. 147), and in the West in the Roman *Ordines*, and also in the Mozarabic rite for a deacon, though not that for a presbyter (pp. 219–221, and 234).

(b) *The Bestowal of Symbols of Office.* One of the significant developments in the historical evolution of ordination rites is the process of mutual assimilation that took place between the major and minor orders. Not only do the latter tend gradually to acquire elements that at first had been characteristic of the former, but the ritual bestowal of appropriate symbols of office, which had originally been the principal and distinctive feature of the conferral of the minor orders, was later also appended to the ordination of bishops, presbyters, and deacons. The details of this will be discussed further in the relevant chapters.

(c) *The Declaration of Ordination.* A number of later Eastern rites— the Coptic, East Syrian, Jacobite, Maronite, and Melkite—include within the closing ceremonies a solemn declaration or proclamation that the candidate has been duly ordained to the particular order. Khouri-Sarkis argued that, at least with regard to the Jacobite rite, where it was accompanied by an imposition of the hand (pp. 179, 182, and 184),[41] its purpose was juridical—to bestow on the newly ordained a specific ministerial responsibility in a particular church. Such a distinction, however, between sacramental and juridical effects of ordination, would have been foreign to the thinking of the early Church, and in any case in two of the other traditions, the East Syrian and the Melkite, the formulary makes no reference to the place of ministry. If, therefore, this practice is really as ancient as it appears to be, its original purpose is much more likely to have been symbolic—to express the completion of the ordination process.

3 Bishop

Rites for the episcopate appear to have had a somewhat different history from those for the presbyterate and diaconate. Neither the Melkite ritual nor the ancient Armenian rites, for example, include any form at all for conferring the episcopate. The same is also true of the Mozarabic *Liber Ordinum*. With regard to the Armenian tradition, Conybeare stated that "bishops do not seem to have been separately ordained before the thirteenth century," and referred to a manuscript written in A.D. 1492 as the first extant text to make provision for such an ordination in that tradition.[1] However, elsewhere in his work, Conybeare cited the claim of the historian Stephanos Asolik, writing between A.D. 991 and A.D. 1019, that John Mandakuni, Catholicos during the last decade of the fifth century, "brought to perfection" the rites for deacon, priest, and bishop. There is also a letter of George, Catholicos in the late ninth century, which refers to the imposition of hands on presbyters and bishops.[2]

There is perhaps, therefore, an alternative explanation for the absence from these texts of a rite for the episcopate. Although every individual bishop during his ministry would have needed the liturgical forms for the conferral of the other orders readily to hand, he would not have wanted the rite for the episcopate, which would only have been required after his own decease. Moreover, it is probable that at the ordination of his successor the prayers used would not have been those peculiar to the local diocese, but those of the metropolitan or patriarchal see. Thus, there is no particular reason why every collection of ordination prayers should have included the material for such a rite.

As we shall see later in this chapter (page 50), even where rites for the episcopate do exist in Eastern traditions, their prayers tend to show evidence of a different origin and history from that of the rites for the presbyterate and diaconate. Furthermore, not only because of the importance attached to the episcopal office, but also because they were less frequently used than rites for the other orders, episcopal rites display less diversity between the several traditions and tend to be much more conservative in character, often retaining ancient elements that have apparently dropped out in the other cases and sometimes preserving simpler versions of formularies that are common to all the orders.

THE CONTEXT

In the *Apostolic Tradition*, the ordination of a bishop is immediately followed by the presentation of the bread and wine and the eucharistic prayer. It is often assumed that the liturgy of the word would have preceded the ordination, but this is not explicitly stated, and it may simply have been omitted. In the *Apostolic Constitutions*, however, the ordination precedes the full eucharistic liturgy, presumably in order that the new bishop might preside over the whole of the rite. This custom continued in the later Byzantine and Coptic traditions, as well as in the East Syrian rite, where the bishop was expected to read the gospel, preach, and offer the oblation (pp. 133, 148, and 165).

In the Jacobite and Maronite traditions, the ordination was deferred until the eucharistic consecration had been completed, in order that the consecrated bread and wine might be used in conjunction with the imposition of the hand (pp. 183 and 197). However, at least in the case of the Maronite tradition, the earliest manuscripts suggest that the ordination once followed the liturgy of the word and the dismissal of the catechumens.[3] In the Jacobite rite, the new bishop is then directed to receive communion and assume the presidency of the rite for the remainder of the celebration.

At Rome, on the other hand, the ordination of a bishop, like that of presbyters and deacons, took place immediately after the gradual psalm (p. 220). The sole exception to this was in the case of the ordination of the Pope himself, which took place at the very beginning of the eucharist,[4] a custom perhaps copied from the East. It is difficult to explain why all the other ordinations were performed in the middle of the liturgy of the word. It seems most unlikely that the practice reflects continued adherence to a very primitive stage in the evolution of the eucharistic rite, when there was as yet no gospel reading and hence the ordinations would have occurred at what was then the conclusion of the liturgy of the word. On the other hand, it is not easy to see an alternative explanation.

As we have already indicated,[5] from at least the middle of the third century, if not earlier, a local church had to obtain from neighboring bishops approval of the candidate proposed as their bishop, and this was usually signified by the presence of the bishops at the ordination itself. In the fourth century, the number of bishops requisite for a valid ordination was formalized. Canon 4 of the Council of Nicea ruled that all the bishops of the province should be involved, but if that were not possible, then there should be a minimum of three, with the rest sending their approval in writing. Canon 6 permitted a majority verdict to suffice where unanimity could not be reached. Similar legislation is repeated in later councils, and also occurs in the *Apostolic Constitutions*:

"A bishop is to be ordained by three or two bishops. If anyone is ordained by one bishop, both he and the one who ordained him are to be deprived. But if necessity causes an ordination by one, because more are unable to come together, there being a persecution or other such reason, the vote of approval of more bishops is to be presented."[6]

One of the more obvious effects of the presence of several bishops at an episcopal ordination was that they were generally not content to remain merely as spectators, passively observing the proceedings, but took an increasingly active role. In some cases, they began to share in certain of the actions of the presiding bishop, especially the imposition of hands, and in other cases, they took over what were traditionally diaconal roles in the rite, especially the leading of the prayers of the people and the holding of the gospel book. This development in turn also had an effect on the rite for the presbyterate in some traditions, with presbyters assuming the diaconal functions there.

THE IMPOSITION OF THE GOSPEL BOOK

The *Apostolic Constitutions* gives the instruction that deacons are to hold the book of the gospels open over the head of the ordinand at the point in the service at which one would have expected the imposition of the hand (p. 113). The latter is not explicitly mentioned at all, which raises the possibility that the imposition of the gospel book may here have been intended to replace rather than merely supplement the imposition of the hand. The ceremony of the gospel book was not something invented by the author of the *Apostolic Constitutions*, since there is evidence that it was also practiced at Antioch before the end of the fourth century, being mentioned briefly by Palladius,[7] and more fully by Severian of Gabala, who interpreted it as being a symbol of the descent of the Spirit on the ordinand. Severian believed that the appearance of the Holy Spirit in the form of tongues of fire on the Apostles at Pentecost was the sign of their ordination, and that

"the custom remains even to the present: because the descent of the Holy Spirit is invisible, the Gospel is placed on the head of him who is to be ordained high-priest; and when this is done, one must not see anything other than a tongue of fire resting on his head—a tongue, because of preaching, a tongue of fire, because of the saying, 'I have come to cast fire on the earth.' "[8]

There is also a reference to it in a homily attributed to Chrysostom. Here it is interpreted as being a symbol of the submission of the bishop to the law of God, and the equivalent in the New Covenant of the high-priestly crown of Aaron:

"In the ordinations of priests [i.e., bishops] the gospel of Christ is placed on the head so that the ordinand may learn that he receives the true crown of the gospel, and so that he may learn that even if he is the head of all, yet he acts under these laws, ruling over all and ruled by the law, judging all and being judged by the Word. . . . The fact that the high-priest has the gospel is a sign that he is under authority."[9]

As with many of the homilies included among Chrysostom's works, its authorship has been questioned, and it has on other grounds been ascribed to Severian of Gabala by several scholars.[10] However, the fact that the interpretation given to the ceremony here differs from that in the work of Severian cited earlier may cast some doubt on this attribution.

Pseudo-Dionysius is the first to mention explicitly that the ordination included the imposition of the hand as well as the imposition of the book, which he describes simply as "the Scriptures" rather than the gospels. He believes that the book is laid on the bishop because it symbolizes "all the sacred words and works" given to him, which he transmits proportionally to others.[11]

The imposition of the gospel book is also found in most later Eastern rites, but here it is generally performed by one or more of the bishops themselves rather than by deacons. However, the fact that it was deacons who performed the same ceremony in the West at the ordination of the bishop of Rome[12] seems to confirm that the original custom had been as described in the *Apostolic Constitutions*, and that Eastern practice had subsequently changed in order to give less prominence to the diaconate and to increase episcopal action in the rite.

Although the ceremony is not mentioned in the Georgian text, in the Byzantine rite it precedes the imposition of the hand, and is performed by the archbishop himself, with the other bishops present also touching the book (p. 133). Moreover, the open book is here laid on the head *and neck* of the ordinand. The action was apparently understood as symbolizing "the yoke of the gospel" that the new bishop received, since in the later manuscripts of the rite, though not in the Barberini text, this allusion is incorporated into the first ordination prayer. In the Jacobite and Maronite rites, two bishops hold the book over the head of the ordinand during the imposition of the hand (pp. 183 and 198). In the East Syrian rite the archbishop is directed to place the book on the back of the ordinand in such a way that "it faces the one who is to read from it." A gospel reading follows, after which the book is closed and left on the ordinand's back during the imposition of hands and the prayers (p. 163).

In the Coptic tradition, on the other hand, the ceremony is restricted exclusively to the consecration of the Alexandrian patriarch, and does not appear in the normal rite for the episcopate, despite the fact the Coptic tradition is so heavily dependent on both the *Apostolic Constitutions* and the Jacobite rite. It is true that the imposition of the gospel book is mentioned in connection with the ordination of a bishop in the Arabic *Canons of Basil*, which appear to have circulated in Egypt in the sixth century. It is doubtful, however, how far this work reflects authentic indigenous practice.[13] At Rome, too, the imposition of the book was employed only at the ordination of the bishop of Rome, and, as mentioned earlier, it was here held open by deacons. It would appear that the ceremony was adopted in both these places in imitation of Syrian practice when it was desired in some way to distinguish ordination to the patriarchal see from that of other bishops. Botte thought it had been introduced at Rome prior to the time of Gregory the Great.[14] It must also have been of some antiquity at Alexandria, since it was able to withstand the influence of both the *Apostolic Constitutions* and the Jacobite rite and remain restricted to patriarchal consecration.

The imposition of the gospel book is also found in the Gallican *Statuta Ecclesiae Antiqua*, where it takes place at all episcopal ordinations (p. 222), and from here it eventually spread into all later Western rites for the episcopate, including that of Rome itself. Charles Munier has argued that there is no evidence to support the commonly held view that the author of the *Statuta* derived the ceremony from papal ordination practice. Moreover, it seems unlikely that the author would have dared to extend to all bishops something he knew was reserved in the West to the bishop of Rome alone. Munier suggests, therefore, that the source was the *Apostolic Constitutions* itself.[15] In contrast to both the *Apostolic Constitutions* and Roman practice, however, two bishops and not two deacons were to hold the book, and no mention is made of it being open: consequently in later Western rites the ceremony was always performed with the book closed, except in the case of papal ordination.[16]

What then was the original meaning and purpose of the imposition of the book? As we have seen, Severian understood it to symbolize the descent of the Holy Spirit on the ordinand; (Pseudo-)Chrysostom, the submission of the bishop to the law of God; Pseudo-Dionysius, the words and works given to the bishop; and the Byzantine rite, the yoke of the gospel, and the East Syrian treated it as the use of the ordinand as a human lectern. The diversity of these interpretations gives the impression that they are attempts to find a meaning for a ceremony the earlier sense of which had been forgotten. This is especially so in the case of the Byzantine and East Syrian rites, where its form appears to have been deliberately altered in order to make it more intelligible (the book being placed on the head and neck in the former, and on the back in the latter).

Botte suggested that the original meaning of the ceremony had been that the power of the gospel should fill the ordinand, which is what he understood Severian to be saying,[17] but there seems no particular reason why this interpretation is to be preferred above the others. E. C. Ratcliff, on the other hand, conjectured that it may possibly have been the vestigial remains of an ancient practice of attempting to discern the divine choice of candidate by reference to the passage at which the book fell open, a version of the casting of lots used at the appointment of Matthias in Acts 1:26.[18] This theory has been criticized by O. Bârlea, who denies that there is any real evidence for it.[19] Moreover, in every case, the ceremony seems firmly associated with prayer for the ordinand rather than with the remains of the electoral process in the rite.

Its real origin, therefore, still remains a mystery. The evidence suggests that the custom was originally peculiar to Syria, and the fact that its meaning was in doubt by the end of the fourth century implies that it was no recent innovation there, but already of some antiquity. It is conceivable that it may have been adopted when a separate episcopal office first emerged from the corporate presbyterate, and it was thought inappropriate for presbyters to lay hands on a bishop as they had presumably done up till then when ordaining new presbyters. Alternatively, the ceremony may have been introduced when neighboring bishops began to attend those episcopal ordinations and challenge the right of the local presbyterate to conduct the proceedings. Rather than deciding whether presbyters or bishops should perform the imposition of hands on the ordinand, the dilemma may perhaps have been resolved by the adoption instead of the imposition of the book of the gospels by deacons, the gospel of Christ symbolizing the action of Christ himself ordaining a new member of the apostolic college.

If this conjecture is correct, then only later would the imposition of the book have become a supplement to the imposition of the hand, as the Syrian tradition accommodated itself to ordination practice elsewhere. It is therefore possible that in the case both of the *Apostolic Constitutions* and of papal ordination at Rome, the absence of any explicit reference to an imposition of the hand really does mean that the gesture was not used, and the same may also have been true of earlier practice with regard to the ordination of the Alexandrian patriarch. It is easy to see how the adoption of the imposition of the gospel book in place of the imposition of hands by other bishops would have been attractive at both Alexandria and Rome, since it would have avoided the implication that the higher office of patriarch could somehow be conferred by those in the lower rank of the episcopate. On the other hand, not too much significance can be given to the absence of any direct reference to the imposition of hands in the case of papal ordination, since the early *Ordines* do not always mention it in the case of the conferral of all the other orders, where presumably it was in fact employed.

THE IMPOSITION OF THE HAND

According to the text of the *Apostolic Tradition*, all the bishops present take part in an imposition of hands on a candidate for the episcopate, and this direction is repeated in the *Testamentum Domini* (pp. 107 and 117).[20] In the *Canons of Hippolytus*, however, only the minister who says the ordination prayer[21] lays his hand on the ordinand (p. 110), and this continues to be the custom in most of the later traditions. The Georgian rite has only a general direction at the beginning that hands are to be laid on candidates for the diaconate, presbyterate, and episcopate, and no explicit rubric in conjunction with the prayers for a bishop (p. 167), but in the Byzantine rite, the archbishop alone is directed to lay his hand on the ordinand (which hand is not specified), and the other bishops merely touch the gospel book (p. 133). Similarly, in the Jacobite and Maronite rites, though other bishops hold the gospel book, only the patriarch lays his right hand on the ordinand (pp. 183 and 198). In the East Syrian rite, too, the presiding bishop alone lays his right hand on the ordinand, and the other bishops simply place their right hands on the ordinand's sides (p. 163).

Thus, it would appear in these cases that, though the involvement of other bishops had in the course of time grown from their passive witness and approbation of the proceedings to more active participation, it had not extended as far as sharing in the imposition of hands in exactly the same manner as the presiding bishop. It might of course be objected that a collegial imposition of hands on the ordinand's head did once exist but has subsequently disappeared as a result of the introduction of the imposition of the gospel book, which would have covered the ordinand in such a way as to prevent the other bishops from touching his head. However, in the Coptic rite, where there was no imposition of the gospel book, the bishops still only lay their hands on the ordinand's arms and not on his head (p. 152). Furthermore at Rome, where again the imposition of the gospel book was not originally employed, the Pope alone laid his hand on the head of a candidate for the episcopate (p. 221).[22]

The only exception to this rule is the Gallican *Statuta Ecclesiae Antiqua*, which directs that the rest of the bishops are to touch the head of the ordinand while the ordination prayer is said (p. 222). However, it has already been observed that this document appears in part to derive its prescriptions from the *Apostolic Tradition*.[23] It would seem, therefore, that just as in the case of the imposition of the gospel book, the author is here introducing a new custom that he has read about, rather than reflecting the traditional indigenous practice of his region. Through the influence subsequently exercised by his composition, however, it was destined to become the standard practice of the later Western rites.

This evidence thus suggests that the arrangement proposed by the *Apostolic Tradition* may well have been unique among ancient rites, and indeed it is even conceivable that it was never actually practiced in its present form either in the third century or later, but that it represents a textual emendation of an original direction that the local presbyters themselves should preside over the rite and lay their hands on the candidate chosen to be their bishop, as they would have done at the ordination of a fellow presbyter. Clearly, such a statement would have seemed impossible when read by fourth-century eyes accustomed by then to a bishop alone performing this function, and so might have led to the substitution of the collective imposition of hands of the bishops for that of the presbyters, in order to make it more acceptable to contemporary orthopraxis.[24]

As indicated before, both the Jacobite and Maronite rites display a unique feature in relation to the imposition of the hand: the patriarch first extends his hands over the consecrated bread and wine three times before proceeding to lay his right hand on the ordinand (pp. 183 and 197). This ceremony seems to have been introduced in order to express the idea that it was not the presiding bishop himself but Christ who ordained his ministers, and it was his spiritual power that was bestowed upon them.

Although none of the older sources make any reference at all to the posture to be adopted by the ordinand during the ordination prayer and imposition of the hand, Pseudo-Dionysius states that he was to kneel on both knees,[25] and this is supported by the more extensive rubrics found in some of the later texts.

THE ORDINATION PRAYERS (PATRISTIC)

Three of the patristic texts have a literary dependency on the *Apostolic Tradition*, merely modifying its ordination prayer either by addition or by deletion, and thus only the *Sacramentary of Sarapion* represents a truly independent euchological tradition. Before undertaking a comparison of these texts, however, it is necessary to give some consideration to the questions of the original form and possible sources of the prayer in the *Apostolic Tradition* (p. 107). Although the present version is commonly regarded as being substantially what the author wrote, Ratcliff claimed that it had "undergone considerable revision so as to be conformed to the standards and usage of the fourth century."[26] Eric Segelberg has attempted to discern an original text beneath what he regards as later strata, though admitting that one of these other layers might well be the redaction by the author himself of older liturgical material and not necessarily a subsequent interpolation.[27] Moreover, several scholars have drawn attention to apparent parallels between a number of phrases in the prayer and expressions that occur in 1 Clement (*c.* A.D. 96),[28] and this has led Georg Kretschmar to conclude that it "clearly draws from the First Epistle of Clement in several places."[29]

However, this alleged literary dependency on 1 Clement is scarcely certain. The passages in question are not very numerous, and the close verbal similarities amount to little more than the fact that both use such words as "high-priest" and "blamelessly." At best, all that can be claimed is that the two documents derive from the same world of ideas, which is not surprising if the *Apostolic Tradition* is indeed of Roman provenance. Nor is Segelberg's reconstruction entirely convincing. Whilst there may be some merit to the main criteria that he uses in his analysis, that the earliest liturgical texts tend to have biblical allusions rather than direct quotations, and that Old Testament allusions are likely to be more primitive than New Testament ones, these are not immutable laws, and it is difficult to share his conclusions without reservation.

Nevertheless, both in Segelberg's reconstructed version and in the received text, the main themes of the prayer are the same. It begins by recalling God's activity among the people of the old covenant and especially his raising up of both princes and priests. Such Old Testament imagery, both here and in other ordination prayers, is not merely incidental: it witnesses to a belief in the fundamental continuity of God's work throughout history, the promise of the new covenant in the old, and the fulfillment of the old covenant in the new. Thus, the mention of princes and priests is an indication of the dual nature of the office to which the bishop was seen as succeeding, and this is confirmed by the second half of the prayer, where, on the one hand, it is the power of the *princely* Spirit that God is asked to pour forth so that the bishop may be a *shepherd* to his people, and on the other hand, it is also said to be in order that he may exercise the *high-priesthood*, and various liturgical functions are then enumerated in the remainder of the text.

Several other points can also be noted about the prayer. Firstly, it is interesting that in neither half is there any reference to the prophetic/teaching ministry: this suggests that such a ministry was not seen as fundamental to the episcopal office in the tradition in which the prayer arose. Secondly, it contains a clear affirmation that the choice of the candidate was seen as the work of God ("whom you have chosen for the episcopate") and not just that of the congregation. Thirdly, the relationship of the bishop's ministry to that of Christ and the apostles is given only a very subordinate expression: they are merely said to have received the same spirit of leadership that is being sought for the ordinand. Even this meager reference is deleted in Segelberg's putative original version.

The *Canons of Hippolytus* adopts the substance of the prayer from the *Apostolic Tradition* (p. 110), a sharp contrast with its normal practice, which is to omit or modify extensively the prayers found in that source, presumably because they did not conform to the euchology of the author's own tradition. Does the adoption of this oration imply, therefore, that there was no firm indigenous tradition for the form of the prayer to be recited at the ordination of a bishop, perhaps because of the extreme rarity of its use?

On the other hand, although the prayer is heavily dependent on the equivalent text in the *Apostolic Tradition*, yet some significant changes have been made in it. In particular, all the Old Testament typology for the episcopal order is omitted: the sentence "you appointed princes and priests, and did not leave your sanctuary without a ministry" finds no place in this version; and "to exercise the high-priesthood before you," "to propitiate your countenance unceasingly," and "the spirit of high-priesthood" are not included among the gifts sought for the new bishop. Even "to confer orders" does not appear in this list of episcopal functions, but "to cure the sick and crush Satan under his feet swiftly" (cf. Rom 16:20) is added instead,[30] and more is said about the moral qualities required for the effective exercise of his office—a theme that recurs frequently elsewhere in the document. This suggests a somewhat different concept of the episcopate, for which the cultic language of the Old Testament was not thought appropriate, and in which the ministry of healing played a more prominent part. As we shall see, both of these are also characteristic of other Eastern ordination prayers, whereas the West tended to follow the path established by the *Apostolic Tradition*.

The *Apostolic Constitutions*, as is the case with all its euchology, expands considerably the text of the prayer from the *Apostolic Tradition* (p. 113). In addition to piling up attributes of God the Father, this version gives a more prominent place to Christ: it was through his incarnate mission that structures of the Church were established; it is through his mediation that God is now asked to pour forth the power of the Spirit; and it was through him that the eucharist that the new bishop will offer was instituted. Additional references are also made to the Spirit: the structures of the Church were established "by the witness of the Paraclete;" and among the gifts sought for the new bishop is "the fellowship of the Holy Spirit." Perhaps not surprisingly, the Old Testament typology too is expanded, with the priestly theme being given some precedence over that of leadership. Although acknowledgment is made here that Samuel was both priest and prophet, this latter image is not taken up in the rest of the prayer, which adheres closely to the list of episcopal functions enumerated in the *Apostolic Tradition*, merely adding that the bishop is to "gather the number of those being saved," and making a more explicit reference to the celebration of the eucharist. In this process, it defines the "sweet-smelling savor" more narrowly than in the *Apostolic Tradition*, as referring to this liturgical act rather than to the offering of the bishop's whole life. Finally, we can note that the episcopal college itself is also given greater prominence in the prayer: the "bishops present" are closely associated with the apostles, and they are also designated as the agents through whom God is asked to pour forth his Spirit on the ordinand.

The version of the prayer in the *Testamentum Domini* is even more expanded (p. 117). Once again, in addition to an increase in the attributes of God the Father, Christ is given a prominent place in the early part of the prayer, this time through references to his salvific mission and the illumination that he brought to the Church. The Holy Spirit too features strongly, being invoked on the ordinand three times in the course of the prayer. On the other hand, the Old Testament typology is not as extensive as in the *Apostolic Constitutions*, the figure of Enoch alone being added to that of Abraham. The reason for this choice is to be found in a major new theme that the author has woven into the prayer— the correlation between heavenly and earthly sanctuaries—since Enoch was said to have been assumed into heaven (Gn 5:21–24; Heb 11:5). The pattern for the ministry of the Church is not now primarily that of the Old Testament, but the unseen ministry above. In contrast to the prayer in the *Apostolic Constitutions*, the episcopal college is not mentioned and the apostolate receives only a brief reference. What is sought for the bishop in the prayer is chiefly the gift of the personal qualities requisite for the effective exercise of his priestly and princely office rather than the power to perform specific functions. In this, there is an emphasis on an intercessory role on behalf of his people, and some hint of a teaching ministry, which is made more explicit in the preceding preparatory prayer.

By comparison with all these prayers, that in the *Sacramentary of Sarapion* is extremely simple (p. 122). It differs, however, not merely in its form, but in its theological ideas. In contrast to the prayer in the *Apostolic Tradition*, but in line with the modifications we have observed in its later derivatives, this prayer begins, not with Old Testament typology, but with God's sending of Christ to the world, and it continues with references to his sending of the apostles and his ordination of bishops. In this way it not only emphasizes that ordination is the action of God, but sets the episcopal office in line of succession to the apostolate, a concept that also recurs later in the prayer, when God is asked to make this ordinand "a holy bishop of the succession of the holy apostles." When this theme is coupled with the fact that God is here addressed as the "God of *truth*," and is asked to bestow the same Spirit as was bestowed on his *own/genuine* servants, prophets, and patriarchs, it suggests an origin in a community that was troubled by heresy and hence saw the bishop primarily as the guardian of true apostolic tradition, a development we have not previously encountered in ordination euchology. There is also a complete absence of Old Testament cultic imagery, as was the case in the *Canons of Hippolytus*, which is similarly thought to have originated in Egypt, nor is there any reference to the liturgical dimension of the office, the images used all being of teaching/leadership—prophets, patriarchs, shepherd.

THE ORDINATION PRAYERS (EASTERN)

As we indicated before, the ordination prayers for the episcopate in the East reveal evidence of a different origin and history from those of the rites for the presbyterate and diaconate. In particular, as the synopsis in Appendix B illustrates, there seems to be a literary connection between some of the principal prayers in five of the six traditions having rites for the episcopate in their oldest manuscripts, something that is not found in the prayers for the other orders.

The very close parallels between the East Syrian ordination prayers and certain of those in the Georgian rites for bishops, presbyters, and deacons have already been mentioned in Chapter 1, and no attempt has been made to demonstrate the full extent of this resemblance in the synopsis: only those passages that one or both of these versions have in common with at least one other prayer have been listed. There is, however, a difference between the Georgian rite for a bishop and those for the presbyterate and diaconate. In the case of the latter, the first prayer for each order closely resembles the second prayer of the Melkite rites (which has led to the suggestion that it derives from Jerusalem), and the prayer from the *Testamentum Domini* and that parallel to the East Syrian one come in second and third places, respectively. However, this is not so in the case of the episcopate, where the prayer from the *Testamentum Domini* and that resembling the East Syrian one assume the first and second places, respectively, instead. This change of sequence implies that the text of the Jerusalem tradition known to the compiler did not include a prayer for the episcopate, and that the third prayer here was a later addition to the rite, made in order to conform its structure to that of the other two (p. 172).[31] The presence of a special rubric before it seems to lend support to this suggestion. It is a short prayer of unknown origin, and may even have been specially composed for the purpose.

There is also a difference between the Byzantine rite for the episcopate and those for the presbyterate and diaconate. As the synopsis shows, in the case of the episcopate, there is no obvious resemblance between the second Byzantine prayer and Jacobite ordination prayer, as there is in the case of the other two orders, but there are some similarities to the Georgian/East Syrian prayer (pp. 134, 164, and 171). Although these are not extensive, they are sufficiently marked for it to be impossible to dismiss them as merely coincidental: both refer near the beginning to God establishing teachers in the Church; both later speak of Christ the true shepherd laying down his life for the sheep as the model for the episcopate;[32] both then quote from Romans 2:19–20—verses that it is unlikely would have been a natural choice for two compilers working independently of one another; and both end with allusions to those entrusted to the bishop's care, to his confident stand before the judgment-seat, and to the reward prepared for him. Thus all three prayers appear to share a common origin.

Gy arrived at a similar conclusion with regard to these texts, but he went further still: building upon a hypothesis put forward by Botte with regard to the Byzantine prayers for the presbyterate,[33] he proposed that a single original prayer for a bishop in the Byzantine rite had become divided into two,[34] a development that he later explained as the result of "a liturgical phenomenon that is well known in the history of the eucharistic prayer, namely the silent recital of prayers."[35] He consequently regarded as part of the common source the reference to apostles, prophets, and teachers, as well as the invocation of the Holy Spirit on the ordinand, both of which are found in the first Byzantine prayer.

Attractive though this suggestion may seem, it is not without its difficulties. The reference to apostles, prophets, and teachers only appears in the first Byzantine prayer and in the East Syrian text: it is absent from the Georgian version, which, like the second Byzantine prayer, speaks simply of teachers. One would, therefore, have to assume that the other words had been removed from this text, either accidentally or deliberately, and the second alternative is certainly not very likely because, as Gy himself admitted, liturgical texts tend to move in the direction of increasing conformity to biblical parallels rather than away from them. To this must be added the consideration that there are also two prayers in the rite for the presbyterate—where Gy's theory has less to support it—and in the rite for the diaconate, where it seems to be positively excluded and where even Gy himself admitted that things were less clear than in the other two cases.[36]

Moreover, although the practice of saying the second half of a prayer in a low voice could have given rise to the notion that it was a quite separate formulary and led to the sort of development Gy outlines, that does not appear to be how silent recitation was in fact done. Instead, the whole prayer (at least as far as the beginning of the doxology) was said secretly. Such a method seems more likely to have given rise to a custom of beginning the prayer while the preceding litany was still being chanted, and to the later insertion of another complete prayer in close association with the only remaining audible formulary in the rite, the proclamation/bidding. Thus, as we have commented earlier,[37] the structure of the rites seems rather to favor the idea that the second prayer is the older of the two and the first a considerably later development. It was perhaps not added until at least the sixth century, when the silent recitation of prayers seems to have begun in Eastern liturgical practice.

All the other elements of the first prayer certainly appear to be less primitive than those of the second prayer, as Gy himself observed[38]; and as a whole, it seems to have a less profound and homogeneous sense. The institution of the ministry is primarily "for the service of your venerable and pure mysteries at your holy altar." The reference to "undertaking" the gospel and the high-priestly dignity seems to be an attempt to give some interpretation to the practice of the imposition of the gospel book.[39] The importance attached to the agency of the bishop who recites the prayer and his colleagues belongs to a later way of thinking about ordination, first encountered in ordination euchology in the *Apostolic Constitutions*. Moreover, the typology of prophets, kings, and high priests has been imported from the blessing of the oil in the rite of Christian initiation, and sits uneasily with the earlier allusions to apostles, prophets, and teachers.

Since the second Byzantine prayer is considerably shorter than the Georgian/East Syrian version, one might expect it to be closer to the original form. However, there are at least two peculiarities about it that cast doubts on this and suggest that this prayer too has undergone some modification. Firstly, it is addressed, not to God the Father, but to Christ ("you, the true shepherd").[40] Secondly, its description of teachers as those "who approach your throne to offer sacrifice and oblation" is a strange mixture of images, and appears to be a secondary adaptation made in order to incorporate a cultic dimension rather than a part of the primary stratum of the prayer. On the other hand, the absence of a direct invocation of the Holy Spirit, let alone an explicit reference anywhere to the third person of the Trinity, in contrast to the other versions, may accurately reflect the earliest form of the prayer, since there seems to be no reason why such a feature would have been excised from the text. The invocation may well have been added to the other prayers at a later date when it was thought necessary that ordination prayers should include this element.

Although the principal ordination prayer for a bishop in the Coptic tradition (p. 152) begins by following quite closely the text of the prayer for a bishop from the *Apostolic Constitutions*, the second half is without parallel in that document, but contains nearly all the elements common to the Byzantine and Georgian/East Syrian prayers, although the allusion to the true shepherd and the quotation from Romans 2:19–20 appear in reverse order. Moreover, the prayer shares two other features with the Byzantine version, neither of which occurs in the Georgian/East Syrian form: it prefixes the phrase "guide of the blind" to the Romans quotation and ends with a reference to those preaching the gospel. Unfortunately, because it has been grafted on to the preceding prayer, it has no introductory section of its own, and so cannot assist in determining what the original form of that might have been. Once again, this arrangement represents a significant difference from the rites for presbyters and deacons, where the prayers from the *Apostolic Constitutions* suffer only minor alterations and any secondary prayers are derived from the Jacobite tradition.

On the other hand, while the Jacobite prayer has virtually nothing in common with the Byzantine/Coptic "branch" of the text in this case, it does have some similarity to the Georgian/East Syrian version (p. 184). In its present form, it displays evidence of considerable expansion, especially in its detailed listing of episcopal functions, not generally a feature of more ancient prayers. If, however, one excises the section beginning "may ordain priests" as being a later development, what remains parallels quite closely the general outline of that prayer (even if it lacks many of the details found in the other versions) and so implies that it too shares a common origin.

The presence of such similar euchological material in very diverse milieu suggests, therefore, that the nucleus of this prayer is as old as some of the patristic sources and was in established use before the divisions that took place in the Eastern churches during the fifth century. It seems to have been ancient enough to have developed in at least two distinct forms prior to that time, as evidenced by the Coptic/Byzantine version on the one hand[41] and the Georgian/East Syrian(?/Jacobite) version on the other. The latter strengthened the Christological dimension of the prayer (a development that we have already observed in the case of some of the patristic texts) and, like the prayer in the *Canons of Hippolytus*, added a more extensive reference to the healing ministry of the bishop.

The two images of the episcopal office that seemingly constitute part of the original nucleus of the prayer are those of shepherd (as in the patristic sources, but here brought into explicit association with Christ the true shepherd), and teacher/guardian of the truth (a contrast with most of the patristic texts). Cultic/liturgical imagery seems to have had no place at all in the earliest stratum, but to have been gradually introduced at a later stage in the various traditions. In some cases, a clumsy fusion of ideas took place, as with the teaching and priestly themes in the opening of the Byzantine prayer, or the notion of the "perfect priest after the example of the true shepherd" in the Georgian version. In other cases, a simple addition was made, such as the insertion of "priests" after the Pauline "apostles, prophets, and teachers" in the East Syrian prayer. In the Jacobite prayer, there was direct substitution, with, for example, "every priestly order" replacing "teachers," which resulted in an all but total obliteration of the earlier themes.

The "odd one out" in these rites for the episcopate is the Maronite. The central prayers here apparently have no literary connection with those of any other rite, not even the Jacobite (p. 197). Furthermore, the basic theme of what appears to be the main ordination prayer, the long oration beginning, "God of Gods and Lord of Lords," is quite distinct from those found in all the other rites, with the sole exception of the *Testamentum Domini*: for here the primary pattern for the episcopal office is not sought in Old or New Testaments, but in the conformity of the earthly ministry to the heavenly archetype. Moreover, the Maronite prayer does not ask God to ordain the candidate or bestow the Holy Spirit on him, but rather to accept, through the intercession of Mary, the mother of God (which is the sole allusion to Christ in the whole prayer), the ordination that is being performed by unworthy bishops. The only functions explicitly mentioned as belonging to the bishop are those of governor and protector from evil powers. All this would seem to suggest that, at least in its present form, this prayer belongs to a somewhat later stage of evolution than that evidenced by the ordination prayers of the other Eastern traditions.

THE ORDINATION PRAYERS (WESTERN)

In marked contrast to the authentically Eastern prayers, but in line with the *Apostolic Tradition* and its subsequent development in the *Apostolic Constitutions*, the Roman ordination prayer for a bishop is centered primarily around Old Testament cultic imagery, specifically that of the two ceremonies that constituted the ordination of the high priest, the vesting and anointing (p. 215). The episcopate, however, is not portrayed as the direct descendant of this office, but rather as its spiritual counterpart. After a brief allusion to heavenly worship, Moses appears not as a pattern for the leadership role of the bishop, but as the communicator of the divine injunctions concerning liturgical vestments, and Aaron as the type of the high priest who wore the priestly robe. This vestment is understood as symbolic of the adornment of mind and spirit required of a Christian bishop, and God is asked to bestow on the ordinand the personal qualities that correspond to the richness of that outward dress, and in addition to sanctify him with a spiritual unction corresponding to the oil that was poured on the head of Aaron and flowed over all his body. Gy has suggested that, in the light of a homily of St. Leo (*Serm.* 48.1) and of patristic exegesis in general, this last image was understood allegorically as expressing the benefit that flowed from episcopal ordination over the whole body of the Church.[42] There is no Christological reference anywhere in the prayer; the Holy Spirit receives only a relatively incidental mention; and the only explicit designation of a specific episcopal function is the petition that God would grant the ordinand a chair (*cathedra*) to rule the Church.

The Gallican interpolation in the Roman prayer, on the other hand, is almost entirely a pastiche of biblical quotations and allusions, mostly from the New Testament,[43] which speak instead of a ministry of preaching, teaching, reconciliation, and the exercise of discipline, although the preceding allocution also describes the office as that of shepherd, teacher, and priest (p. 228). The bidding uses the term "high-priest" (thus suggesting perhaps that this formulary belongs to a later stage in the evolution of episcopal typology than the allocution), and also stresses the role of ruler and leader. In this material, as in the Roman texts, references to Christ and the Holy Spirit occupy a very subordinate place.

The only other extant Western ordination prayer is that which is found in several English medieval pontificals and that exhibits some striking parallelism of thought with the prayer in the *Apostolic Tradition* (p. 236). It begins with a brief Christological reference and moves on, through the promise made to Abraham, to the founding of the Church. The primary images for the episcopal office are those of the high priest and shepherd, and God is asked to let the Holy Spirit be with the ordinand so that he may exhibit the qualities requisite for the discharge of his office, in which teaching and the ministering of discipline seem to be major features.

CONCLUDING CEREMONIES

At the end of the ordination prayer in the *Apostolic Tradition*, the bishop exchanges a kiss with the community and then proceeds immediately to preside at the eucharist (p. 108). No other concluding ceremonies are mentioned. The *Canons of Hippolytus*, however, in its comments on the ordination of a presbyter, refers to a ritual seating of a new bishop, and this also appears in the *Apostolic Constitutions* (pp. 111 and 114). This development is hardly surprising since the bishop's chair was an important symbol of his presidential role in the community.[44] The other concluding ceremony in this latter document, the placing of the "offering" on the hands of the newly ordained bishop, is possibly an imitation of the consecration of the Jewish high priest (see Lv 8:27). As nothing like this is mentioned in any other sources, it may well be an invention by the author.

Of the older Eastern texts, the Georgian makes no mention of any concluding ceremonies, and the prescriptions of the eighth-century Barberini manuscript of the Byzantine rite are scarcely more elaborate than those of the patristic sources: the bestowal of the *omophorion* (the Eastern equivalent of the Western pallium), the exchange of the kiss, and the seating (p. 134). Early Western practice seems to have been somewhat similar, except that at Rome the ordinand was vested in the robes of his new office immediately before the ordination prayers and not afterward (p. 220): this is probably a remnant from the older practice that saw ordination as a twofold process—the election as the means by which the candidate was actually appointed to the office, with the prayers then being made for his successful fulfillment of that into which he had already entered. The later rites of both East and West increase the number of vestments and insignia that are to be bestowed on the new bishop and elaborate the enthronement ritual.

4 Presbyter

No indication is given in any of the patristic texts concerning the relationship between the ordination of a presbyter and the celebration of the eucharist, though it seems extremely probable that, as in the case of the episcopate, the rite took place within the context of the community's Sunday eucharist. With the sole exception of the East Syrian tradition, which permits presbyteral ordination to take place at any time, all later sources consistently locate the rite within a eucharistic celebration, though they differ with regard to the precise point within the service at which it is to take place.

The oldest manuscript of the Armenian rite gives no explicit direction concerning the eucharist, but the fact that a full ministry of the word appears toward the end of it suggests that the ordination may have taken place at the very beginning of the celebration (p. 132), and this impression receives some confirmation from later manuscripts, where the rite similarly includes the ministry of the word and concludes with the direction that the bishop is to offer the sacrifice.[1] In the Byzantine tradition, on the other hand, a presbyter is ordained later in the eucharistic rite, immediately after the entrance of the gifts, so that he may then fulfill his new liturgical role by participating in the eucharistic action (p. 134). The Coptic tradition follows the same pattern.

In the Jacobite and Maronite rites, as in the case of the episcopate, the ordination came to be deferred until the eucharistic consecration had been completed, in order that the consecrated bread and wine might be used in conjunction with the imposition of hands (pp. 181 and 195). The Melkite rite seems to have followed a similar practice, since toward the end of his ordination the new presbyter was given the consecrated bread, and proclaimed the invitation to communion, "Holy things for holy people" (p. 211). In the case of the Maronite tradition, however, the earliest manuscripts once again suggest that the ordination formerly took place at an earlier point, this time at the very beginning of the eucharist prior to the ministry of the word.[2]

At Rome, the ordination of a presbyter, like that of bishops and deacons, took place immediately after the gradual psalm (p. 220). As has already been observed, it is difficult to see the reason for this particular location.[3]

THE IMPOSITION OF HANDS

In the *Apostolic Tradition* the bishop is directed to lay his hand on the ordinand's head, and the presbyters also are to touch him, an arrangement that is followed in the *Testamentum Domini* (pp. 108 and 119). The corporate involvement of the presbyterate in the imposition of hands probably antedates the emergence of a separate episcopal order, the development of which must inevitably have raised questions about it. Hence, it is not surprising that the *Apostolic Tradition* takes pains to explain that the presbyters' touching of the ordinand does not mean that they are doing what the bishop does: "for a presbyter has authority only to receive; he has not authority to give." Instead, the *Apostolic Tradition* interprets the action as "sealing," and says that it is done "because of the common and like spirit of their order." The very fact that it was thought necessary to include this explanation suggests that at least some persons were interpreting the gesture in a different way, though whether this section was part of the original composition or a subsequent addition is a matter for debate.[4]

Other traditions, including later Roman practice itself, generally seem to have avoided this difficulty by prescribing that the bishop alone should lay his hand—usually specified as the right hand—on a candidate for the presbyterate. There seem to have been only two exceptions to this rule. One is the Armenian rite, where the rubric directs that after the ordinand kneels down, "the priests lay their hands upon his," but where the hands are to be placed is unclear. A parallel rubric in the rite for the diaconate specifies "his hands," perhaps with the intention of differentiating the priests' action from that of the bishop (pp. 128 and 130). Later manuscripts of the presbyteral rite, however, while exhibiting some further confusion over the rubric, seem to agree that it is the ordinand's shoulders on which the other priests are to lay a hand.[5]

The second exception is the Gallican tradition. Here the *Statuta Ecclesiae Antiqua* prescribes that the presbyters are to hold their hands on the candidate's head beside that of the bishop during the prayer, and this instruction was subsequently incorporated in the later composite rites of the West (pp. 222 and 240). Since, however, we have already concluded that the directions given by the *Statuta* concerning the ordination of a bishop appear to have been derived from literary sources rather than the indigenous practice of the region,[6] this too may well be an innovation made by the compiler on the basis of the *Apostolic Tradition*.

As in the case of the episcopate, the older texts of presbyteral ordination rites make no reference at all to the posture to be adopted by the ordinand during the imposition of hands and the prayers, but once again Pseudo-Dionysius states that he was to kneel on both knees,[7] a directive supported by the more extensive rubrics in the eleventh-century Grottaferrata manuscript of the Byzantine rite and in other later Eastern texts. The Mozarabic rite in the West, however, directed that a candidate for the presbyterate should kneel only on one knee—perhaps in order to distinguish this ordination from that of a bishop, who presumably knelt on both knees (p. 234).

THE ORDINATION PRAYERS (PATRISTIC)

The *Apostolic Tradition* appears to require the same prayer to be used for a presbyter as for a bishop, but then quite contrarily goes on to provide the text of a different one (p. 108). Early this century, C. H. Turner advanced the suggestion that what had really been intended was that the first part of the prayer for a bishop should also be used for a presbyter, but that when the petitions specific to the episcopate were reached, the prayer for a presbyter should be substituted[8]; and this resolution of the problem was subsequently adopted by W. H. Frere,[9] by Gregory Dix,[10] and by Douglas Powell.[11] On the other hand, it was rejected by Botte,[12] by Ratcliff,[13] and by A. F. Walls, who pointed out that Turner's suggestion, "though apparently simple, involves no small subtlety of thought in the users of Hippolytus's manual"[14]; but none of these offered an alternative solution to the apparent contradiction.

One possibility would seem to be, however, that the text of the direction underwent some emendation after it left the author's hands. We have already suggested earlier that the original form of the rite for the episcopate in the *Apostolic Tradition* may have directed that the presbyters rather than the bishops of neighboring churches should perform the imposition of hands on the candidate.[15] If this were so, then is it possible that the words "and he shall say" were absent from the original Greek of the rubric in the rite for the presbyterate? Thus, what was being enjoined was that the imposition of hands on a candidate for the presbyterate should follow the same pattern as for a candidate for the episcopate—all the presbyters touching him. When the practice of presbyters laying hands on a candidate for the episcopate ceased, the interpretation of this rubric would have become problematic. Hence, it may then have been understood as referring in some way to the prayer, and this was eventually clarified by the insertion of *et dicat* into the Latin translation of the document and by the recasting of the entire end of the sentence in the Oriental versions so that it read: "and let him pray over him according to the manner which we said before about the bishops."

The author of the *Canons of Hippolytus* was apparently somewhat confused by the enigmatic nature of the direction, since he interpreted it to mean that everything in the rite for the episcopate was also to be done in the case of a presbyter, including the same prayer, except that the term "presbyter" be used instead of "bishop," and, consequently, he simply omitted the entire text of the presbyteral prayer (p. 111).

There is also one somewhat strange feature about the text of the prayer itself: its final petition asks for "the Spirit of your grace" to be preserved not in the ordinand but "in *us*, and make *us* worthy. . . ." Segelberg argued that the change to the first person plural here was an indication that this section of the prayer was not part of the original, although he allowed that it might already have been incorporated in it by the time of Hippolytus.[16] The later derivatives—the *Apostolic Constitutions* and the *Testamentum Domini* (pp. 115 and 119)—both convert it to differing extents into a petition for the ordinand, and on this basis, Dix was of the opinion that a similar clause had formerly stood in the *Apostolic Tradition* and had subsequently fallen out in the Latin translation.[17] It seems more likely, however, that the later versions have tried to improve upon the original.

As was the case in the prayer for the episcopate, the office to which the candidate is being admitted is defined by use of Old Testament typology, this time that of the seventy elders appointed by Moses to govern the people (Nm 11:16f.). Some scholars have seen this allusion as intended to express the subordinate nature of the presbyterate, deriving from and participating in the ministry of the episcopate, just as the elders received the Spirit that had originally been given to Moses.[18] However, as David Power has argued,[19] the parallel between Moses and the bishop is nowhere made explicit, and there is no good reason to believe that it is implied. The parallel is between the elders and the Christian presbyterate, and the "counsel" and "help" that the presbyter is said to give appear to be directed toward the people and not the bishop, who is not mentioned at all in the prayer. Indeed, Dix was of the opinion that the substance of the prayer might be older than the monarchical episcopate and go back to the earliest Jewish-Christian synagogues governed by a college of presbyters, or even to pre-Christian Jewish practice.[20] In support of Dix's opinion can be cited the fact that the text has only the briefest reference to Christ at the beginning and a total absence of any clear New Testament allusions. What is certain is that the prayer viewed the presbyterate as a corporate body that existed primarily for the leadership of the Christian community and not simply for the exercise of specific liturgical functions within it.

The version of the prayer in the *Apostolic Constitutions* is, not surprisingly, considerably expanded (p. 115). It strengthens the Christological dimension somewhat with an opening reference to God's activity through Christ in both creation and preservation, and it then asks for the increase of the Church and of the number of those who preside in it—thus maintaining the concept of the presbyterate as the collegial leadership of the Church found in the *Apostolic Tradition*. To this vision, however, the prayer adds references to a ministry of the word and of healing to be exercised by the new presbyter ("labor in word and deed"; "filled with works of healing and the word of teaching, he may in meekness instruct your people"), and employs the sacerdotal term *hierourgias*, "holy services," to denote these presbyteral functions. These additions, as we shall see later, reflect the role which is assigned to the presbyterate in other Eastern ordination prayers.

The *Testamentum Domini* also expands the prayer, amplifying both the description of the spirit being invoked on the ordinand and also the qualities that are expected of him (p. 119). On the other hand, these developments do not really offer any clearer picture of the nature and function of the office being conferred. The presbyter is expected to display such virtues as "holiness," "cheerfulness and patience," to offer praise day and night, and to bear the cross of Christ, but it is not obvious in what way his role was thought to differ from that of any other Christian, especially as the spirit that is sought for him is said to be that which was given to the disciples of Jesus "and to all those who through them truly believed in you." "Help and govern" do remain from the original version, but as we have seen at other points, the author of the *Testamentum Domini* is capable of maintaining fidelity to his source even when it differs from the practice known to have been current in his own locality. The fact that the prayer twice asks for wisdom for the ordinand may be a hint of a teaching ministry, and there is the interesting petition that he may be worthy "to shepherd your people," which is normally used in reference to the episcopate rather than the presbyterate. Its appearance here may imply that the presbyter was now seen as sharing to some extent in a ministry formerly exercised by the bishop. Perhaps surprisingly, in a prayer of this date, there is a complete absence of sacerdotal language, even though in the rubrics concerning ordination "priest" is generally used in place of "presbyter."

The much shorter prayer in the *Sacramentary of Sarapion* describes the office of a presbyter as that of "a steward of your people and an ambassador of your divine oracles," to reconcile the people to God (p. 122). It also asks for the spirit of truth, for wisdom, for knowledge (twice), and for right faith. All this suggests that, unlike the *Apostolic Tradition*, it was composed in a situation where the primary, if not exclusive, focus was on a teaching ministry, and there was no sense of the presbyterate acting as a collegial governing body. According to the fifth-century Church historian Socrates,[21] preaching by presbyters at Alexandria was prohibited after the time of Arius (*c.* 250–*c.* 336), for fear of the spread of further heresies, and hence this prayer must have originated before that step was taken, or alternatively the situation must have been different at Thmuis or wherever it was composed.

It is true that the ministry of reconciliation may have been understood to involve more than the preaching of the good news, but this is not made explicit, and although the prayer does contain the same allusion to the appointment of elders by Moses as mentioned in the *Apostolic Tradition*, it is employed in a very different way. God is not asked to make the ordinand a presbyter like those whom Moses appointed to govern the people, but to give him a share of the spirit of Christ just as God once gave a share of the spirit of Moses to others. Thus, the parallel is drawn not between the two offices, but between God's action in sharing the Spirit both then and now; and the emphasis does not fall on the ordinand's reception of the spirit of the corporate presbyterate (indeed the word presbyter does not appear anywhere in the prayer at all), but on his individual participation in the spirit of Christ. The presence of this typology does not necessarily mean that it must have been copied directly from the *Apostolic Tradition*, especially as there is no sign of any awareness of that document elsewhere in the sacramentary, and it is quite possible that the author has reworked what was a common image for the presbyterate in early times. As we shall see later, it also occurs in the fourth ordination prayer of the Melkite rite.

THE ORDINATION PRAYERS (EASTERN)

In contrast to the episcopate, where a common nucleus seems to underlie most of the Eastern ordination prayers, the prayers for the presbyterate appear to stem from several quite distinct euchological traditions, no doubt reflecting the considerable local diversity in early ordination practice.

Bernard Botte at one time thought that the second ordination prayer of the Byzantine rite was less ancient than the first,[22] but he subsequently revised his opinion and suggested that the common source of both these prayers and also of the longer prayer parallel to them in the Jacobite rite was the first prayer of the Melkite rite (pp. 134, 181, and 209).[23] Gy later concurred with the suggestion that the two Byzantine prayers had been formed by the division of an originally single prayer, and, as we have already seen, extended the argument to the prayers for the episcopate as well.[24] In an earlier study, however, he was less positive about the theory with regard to the presbyterate, and admitted that, apart from the single phrase "of irreproachable conduct and steadfast faith," and possibly the request "make your servant perfect," all the parallel elements were to be found in the second Byzantine prayer and not the first.[25]

This second prayer displays such strong similarities with the Jacobite and Melkite texts in its beginning, middle, and ending that it is difficult to imagine how it could possibly be only the second half of an originally unified Byzantine prayer, especially as those phrases in the first prayer that have parallels in the prayers of the other two rites do not appear in the same sequence there as they do in those texts. Thus, the true explanation of the evolution of these ordination prayers seems to be that the second Byzantine prayer, the first Melkite prayer, and the Jacobite prayer all share a common origin, but that the first Byzantine prayer is a later addition to the rite, as we also concluded in the case of the episcopate.[26] This common source appears (*pace* Botte) to have been closer to the Byzantine version than to either of the others, which seem to have expanded their source partly with elements that both have in common and partly with developments peculiar to each.

The first Byzantine prayer certainly has the appearance of a later composition, and says nothing particularly profound. Although Tchékan claimed that its opening was intended to present God himself as a "type" of the presbyter,[27] it looks more like a superficial play on words than a serious piece of typology. The explicit reference to the agency of the bishop in the appointment of the candidate and the unequivocal designation of the presbyterate as "the priesthood" both belong to a later way of thinking than is evidenced by the second prayer. The remainder of the prayer appears to be partly a pastiche of recycled phrases borrowed from other sources, the allusion to Romans 15:16 being also found in the second prayer in the rite, and "make your servant perfect" in the first prayer in the rite for the diaconate. Thus, it seems probable that the expression "in irreproachable conduct and steadfast faith should receive this great grace of your Holy Spirit" was also appropriated from a different version of the second Byzantine prayer, one that was closer in form to that underlying the Jacobite and Melkite texts.

Unlike the patristic texts, the second Byzantine prayer does not define the presbyterate by means of biblical typology, probably because nothing could be found that was appropriate to the nature that the office was thought to have. In the context in which the prayer was composed, the presbyterate was apparently no longer seen as part of a collegial governing body. Instead, the prayer employs strictly functional language, asking that the ordinand may be worthy (a) to stand at the altar, (b) to proclaim the gospel and exercise the sacred ministry of the word, (c) to offer gifts and spiritual sacrifices, and (d) to renew the people by the bath of regeneration. The use of the expression "exercise the sacred ministry" (*ierourgein*) strongly suggests that the priestly dimension of the office was seen as finding its fulfillment at least as much in the preaching of the word as in sacramental functions, and this corresponds to what we know of the nature of the ordained ministry at Antioch in the fourth century, where presbyters took a prominent part in preaching, but eucharistic presidency seems still to have been normally an episcopal prerogative.[28] Moreover, Gy has noted the similarity of language to that of John Chrysostom, who in his homily on the day of his presbyteral ordination says that he has been placed among the priests and that the word is his sacrifice.[29]

The other versions of this prayer modify the references to proclaiming the gospel and exercising the ministry of the word, since this later ceased to a function normally exercised by presbyters, and introduce the terms "priest" or "priesthood" instead, since these began to be used unequivocally to denote the presbyterate rather than the episcopate in the East in the fifth century.

The ministry of the word is also given the pride of place in a number of other Eastern ordination prayers. The first Georgian prayer, which parallels the second Melkite prayer and so it is thought may be of Jerusalem origin, begins by linking the earthly ministry to the ministry of heaven, much as was also done in the prayers for a bishop in the *Testamentum Domini* and the Maronite rite, but mentions only the function of true teaching in its petition for the ordinand. The same is true of the third Melkite prayer: while it refers in a general way to the discharging of services (*leitourgias*) on behalf of the Church and to beseeching God's propitiation for all, the only function explicitly specified is the teaching of God's commandments (pp. 170 and 210).

The third prayer in the Georgian rite, which occurs in a somewhat longer and apparently later form in the East Syrian rite, begins by setting the presbyteral order within the context of God's work in creation, of the establishing of the Church, and of the ministries of apostles and prophets, in an allusion to Ephesians 4:11 (pp. 160 and 171). It is possible, therefore, that presbyters were here seen as corresponding to the evangelists mentioned in that text. The prayer then asks God to send the Holy Spirit on the ordinand that he may have "the word of teaching, for the opening of his mouth," before going on to mention the ministry of healing and the celebration of the eucharist. The East Syrian version adds to this the administration of baptism. A similar list of functions also occurs in the fourth Melkite prayer—offering gifts and sacrifices, "utterance in the opening of his mouth," praying for the sick, the administration of baptism, and care of the needy. Because this last prayer opens in the manner of Jewish prayers, with a *berakah* ("Blessed are you, the God who . . ."), and then, like the patristic prayers, refers to the calling of the seventy in the Old Covenant, its roots may be very ancient, even if it has undergone some later expansion (p. 211).

Two of the Armenian prayers for a presbyter, like the first Georgian/second Melkite prayer, also begin with a comparison of the heavenly and earthly ministries (p. 130). The first of these goes on to speak of priests as being "shepherds and leaders" of the congregation, images that elsewhere are used of the episcopal rather than presbyteral order, before specifying the functions of "the word of preaching," the work of healing, the bestowal of the Spirit in baptism, and the celebration of the eucharist. The second prayer merely asks for the bestowal of the sevenfold gifts of the Spirit so that the ordinand may teach and shepherd the people. The third prayer, which is probably a later addition to the rite since it is separated from the rest by the ministry of the word, begins with references to saints, prophets, priests, and apostles, but mentions no particular functions of the order.

The Maronite rite appears to have accumulated four ordination prayers (p. 195). The first two are different versions of the Jacobite ordination prayer. The third prayer, which has some slight similarity to the first Georgian/second Melkite prayer, compares the heavenly and earthly ministries and refers to priestly, teaching, and governing/shepherding functions. The fourth prayer, which has no known parallels, contains similar themes, though chiefly emphasizing the priestly ministry, using language that suggests that at least in its present form it belongs to a later stage in the evolution of ordination euchology than many of the other Eastern prayers.

Finally, the Coptic ordination prayer is a version of the presbyteral prayer found in the *Apostolic Constitutions*. Although it omits some phrases which occur in that prayer, the same functions are specified, with the further addition of a reference to the administration of baptism (p. 146).

THE ORDINATION PRAYERS (WESTERN)

The Roman ordination prayer for a presbyter (p. 218) begins by citing a series of biblical examples in which God instituted subordinate ministries to assist the principal figures in his service— "men of a lesser order and secondary dignity" in relation to the high-priests; the seventy elders in relation to Moses; the two sons of Aaron in relation to their father; and finally, from the New Testament, teachers in relation to the apostles. It then goes on to ask God to grant also to the ordinands "the office of second dignity" so that they may be assistants to the ordaining bishop; and ends with the petition already encountered in Eastern prayers, that they may ultimately render a good account of their stewardship and obtain their due reward.

Three things are remarkable about this oration. Firstly, unlike the majority of other prayers we have studied so far, it is not an expression of the community's aspirations and desires for the ordinands' future ministry to them, spoken on their behalf by the bishop, but rather the articulation of the bishop's own view of their relationship to him, in spite of its being cast in the first person plural: they are to be "assistants to our weakness" and "virtuous colleagues of our order." Secondly, its principal focus is quite obviously on the subordinate nature of the presbyteral role to that of the bishop, almost to the exclusion of all else, which seems to imply that it was composed in a situation in which there was some dispute as to the relationship between the two orders, such as we find in the late fourth century.[30] Thirdly, while the typology of the seventy elders and the teaching function of the presbyterate have already been prominent in other rites, the dominant use here of cultic imagery to define the presbyteral order is something new, but it is in line with the episcopal prayer of the Roman tradition that defined that office in a similar way.

Although the Roman prayer refers briefly to the Holy Spirit— "Renew in their inward parts the Spirit of holiness" —neither the Gallican nor Mozarabic prayer has an explicit epiclesis. (In all three cases, however, the other formularies of the rite, which may be less ancient, do mention the gift of the Spirit.) The Gallican prayer asks that the ordinand may be an "elder," and refers both to a teaching ministry and also to his consecration of the body and blood of Christ (p. 227). The Mozarabic prayer similarly views presbyters as the successors of the Old Testament elders, whom it believes were constituted for a ministry in the temple rather than for community leadership (p. 234). This is the only allusion to the sacramental ministry of the presbyterate, however, since the remainder of the prayer stresses instead the teaching ministry. Both themes recur in the declaration that concludes the rite. It should also be noted that the ordination prayer is addressed, not to God the Father, but to Christ: we have already observed a similar tendency in the Byzantine ordination prayers.[31]

CONCLUDING CEREMONIES

No special concluding ceremonies are mentioned by the patristic sources in the case of the presbyterate, with the sole exception of the *Testamentum Domini*, which explicitly directs that the newly ordained is to receive the kiss of peace from both "priests and people" (p. 119). In the Byzantine rite, the bishop vests the newly ordained presbyter with the robes of his office, gives him a kiss, and seats him with his fellow presbyters (p. 136). Similar ceremonies conclude the other Eastern rites, though there are some unique features: the East Syrian rite includes the presentation of the book of the gospels to the new presbyter (p. 161); in the Maronite rite, he performs several actions that symbolize the liturgical duties of his office—incensing, and carrying the gospel book and then the paten in procession (p. 196); and, as we have mentioned at the beginning of the chapter, in the Melkite rite, which took place immediately before the distribution of communion, the new presbyter was given the consecrated bread and proclaimed the invitation to communion, "Holy things for holy people" (p. 211). The Byzantine rite itself also gives a distinctive function to the new presbyter in the eucharistic consecration that follows the ordination: he holds one of the pieces of bread in his hands throughout the prayer, bowing over the holy table. Like the Melkite custom, this is obviously intended to give symbolic expression to his new role as a participant in the eucharistic presidency.[32]

At Rome, just as in the case of the episcopate, the ordinand is vested in the robes of his new office before, and not after, the ordination prayers (p. 220).[33] In the Mozarabic rite, the new presbyter receives a manual as the symbol of his office—perhaps the closest parallel that could be found for the deacon's reception of the gospel book—and this is accompanied by an exhortation in which the bishop welcomes him "as a colleague of our order for teaching the mysteries of Christ" as well as admonishing him to dispense the sacraments rightly (p. 235). Finally, the Gallican rite includes the anointing of the new presbyter's hands, apparently an eighth-century innovation, since there is no trace of it in older sources from this region (p. 227).[34]

5 Deacon

THE CONTEXT

As in the case of the presbyterate, no indication is given in any of the patristic texts concerning the relationship between the ordination of a deacon and the celebration of the eucharist, though one may reasonably suppose that it took place within the context of the community's Sunday eucharist. Later sources generally place the ordination within a eucharistic celebration, though, as we have indicated earlier, in the Byzantine and Melkite traditions, the diaconate can also be conferred during the Liturgy of the Presanctified, since the diaconal function can equally be exercised there, and in the East Syrian tradition, it can take place entirely outside a eucharistic context.

As in the case of the presbyterate, the various traditions differ with regard to the point in the eucharist at which the ordination takes place. When a deacon is ordained during the celebration of the eucharist in the Byzantine tradition, the rite occurs at the end of the eucharistic prayer, so that he can then fulfill the diaconal function of assisting in the distribution of the consecrated elements to the communicants (p. 136). The same position is adopted in the Jacobite and Maronite traditions, but for a different reason: as in the case of the episcopate and presbyterate, the consecrated elements are used in conjunction with the imposition of hands (pp. 178 and 191). In the Coptic tradition, however, the deacon is ordained at the same point in the rite as the presbyter, after the kiss of peace and before the Anaphora.

At Rome, the ordination of a deacon took place immediately after the gradual psalm (p. 219). It might seem that this was done in order to allow the new deacon to fulfill one of the liturgical functions of his office, the reading of the gospel, but since the ordination of bishops and presbyters also took place after the gradual, it appears unlikely that this was the real reason for it.

In the *Apostolic Tradition*, the bishop alone lays his hands on the ordinand, and the presbyters take no part in the action (p. 108). It is explained that this is because the deacon "is not being ordained to the priesthood, but to the service of the bishop, to do what is ordered by him," nor does he "share in the counsel of the clergy" or "receive the common spirit of seniority in which the presbyters share." This lengthy justification of the practice suggests that it was a matter of some contention in the community from which the document came, or through which it passed in the course of its transmission.[1] Nevertheless, virtually all later traditions follow the same pattern.

The sole exception seems to have been the Armenian rite (p. 128), where it is directed that the other deacons should "lay their hands upon his hands" [sic]: this is probably a deliberate imitation of the practice adopted by the presbyters in the ordination of a presbyter in this tradition, which we have discussed before.[2] On the other hand, mention should perhaps also be made of a phrase, occurring in both the Jacobite and Maronite ordination prayers, that speaks of "the imposition of the hands of us sinners," even though the rubrics themselves refer only to the bishop laying his right hand on the ordinand (pp. 178 and 192). Is this just an interpretation of the bishop's action as being representative of the whole community, or does it indeed reflect an earlier practice in some places of a corporate imposition of hands?

Just as in the cases of the episcopate and presbyterate, the older sources make no reference at all to the posture to be adopted by the candidate during the imposition of hands and the prayers. Pseudo-Dionysius, however, states that the ordinand was to kneel on his right knee,[3] and this posture is mentioned in the more extensive rubrics in the eleventh-century Grottaferrata manuscript of the Byzantine rite and in other later Eastern texts, except for the Armenian, which speaks instead of the left knee (p. 128). This kneeling on one knee was presumably done in order to distinguish diaconal ordination from that of the bishop and presbyter, who knelt on both knees. By contrast, the Mozarabic tradition in the West directed the deacon to stand, since here the presbyter was to kneel on one knee in order that his ordination should be distinguished from that of the bishop (p. 232).

THE ORDINATION PRAYERS (PATRISTIC)

The prayer for a deacon in the *Apostolic Tradition* (p. 108) is incomplete in the Latin version of the text, and the contents of its latter half are only attested by the Ethiopic version and by the use made of it in the *Testamentum Domini*, since both the *Canons of Hippolytus* and the *Apostolic Constitutions* seem not to have employed this source for the compilation of their prayers. One can, therefore, only speak with some caution of what the prayer in the *Apostolic Tradition* originally contained. For example, in the Ethiopic version, the prayer ends by asking that the deacon "may attain the rank of a higher order." However, in the light of the fact that offices were originally conferred for life in the early Church and, hence, there was normally no movement from one order to another, it seems probable that this phrase is a later adaptation of the text, made when the situation had changed, and that originally the reading was an allusion to 1 Timothy 3:13, "may attain a good standing," to which the *Testamentum Domini* bears witness.

The principal theme of the prayer is that of service, and the model for the deacon's ministry is the service of Christ himself, as is also the case in the writings of Ignatius of Antioch early in the second century.[4] What form this service was to take, however, is not clearly revealed. The rubrics that precede the ordination prayer define the deacon's office in terms that suggest that it was primarily an administrative role exercised under the close direction of the bishop. The deacon is ordained "to the service of the bishop, to do what is ordered by him," and he "administers and informs the bishop of what is fitting." None of this, however, appears in the prayer itself, which may belong to an older stratum of material. "Caring" is mentioned in the prayer, and so the service might well have been directed toward the needy, though this is not made explicit. There also seems to have been some reference to a liturgical ministry of assistance to the bishop in his eucharistic offering, unless this feature was added independently by the compilers of the Ethiopic version and the *Testamentum Domini*, though this seems unlikely, especially as the presenting of the offering to the bishop is also designated as a diaconal function in the section of the *Apostolic Tradition* that deals with the eucharist.

The *Testamentum Domini* expands the prayer, partly by the addition of further appellatives of God and Christ, and partly by extending the petitions for the ordinand (p. 120). Although the spirit of caring is no longer mentioned, God is asked to make him love orphans and widows, and to give him the qualities of diligence, serenity, strength, and power. If this corresponds in any way with the realities of the historical situation and is not merely a flight of fantasy by the compiler, it suggests that concern for the needy had here become a major feature of the deacon's office, even if it were not so in the world in which the *Apostolic Tradition* originated.

As was indicated before, the prayers in the *Canons of Hippolytus* and the *Apostolic Constitutions* have little resemblance to that in the *Apostolic Tradition* (pp. 111 and 115). Both of them reject the servanthood of Christ as the model for the diaconate, and instead refer to Stephen as the first deacon, an identification that is first found in the late second century in the writings of Irenaeus,[5] and, as we shall see, is picked up in some other ordination prayers. However, while both prayers ask for the same gifts of spirit and power as Stephen possessed (Acts 6:8,10), they appear to be quite independent of one another, and differ in the form of their reference to him: the *Canons of Hippolytus* speaks of both Stephen "and his companions," but the *Apostolic Constitutions* only mentions Stephen himself and describes him as "the protomartyr and imitator of the sufferings of your Christ." This change of emphasis, which can also be observed in other diaconal ordination prayers, appears to be the result of the emergence of the cult of Stephen. Although this only began to flourish widely after the discovery of his supposed relics in A.D. 415, it must have already taken root in the late fourth century, since Stephen features prominently as a martyr elsewhere in the *Apostolic Constitutions*, which provides the oldest evidence for the existence of a feast in his honor.[6]

A further difference between the prayer in the *Canons of Hippolytus* and that in the *Apostolic Tradition* is the lack of any explicit reference to the liturgical functions of the diaconate. Although the *Canons of Hippolytus* in its rubrics clarifies and extends the role of the deacon by affirming that he is to serve not only the bishop but also the presbyters, both in the liturgy and in the care of the sick and needy, the prayer itself does not mention any of these aspects, but refers simply to the quality of the minister's life: it asks that he may triumph over all the powers of the devil, be without sin, set an example to others, and "save a multitude in the holy Church." The prayer in the *Apostolic Constitutions*, on the other hand, does speak in general terms of the exercise of a sacred ministry, and of eventual promotion to a higher order.

The *Sacramentary of Sarapion* appears to some extent to combine the diaconal models of Christ and of Stephen and his companions encountered in the other patristic prayers (p. 122). The ordination prayer sets the institution of the diaconate within the context of God's sending of Christ, and refers unequivocally to "the seven deacons," who, it says, were chosen "through your only-begotten." It is no more explicit than the other sources, however, with regard to the nature of the office to which the deacon is ordained: all that is sought for him is the "spirit of knowledge and discernment" so that he may serve in his *leitourgia* "in the midst of the holy people."

THE ORDINATION PRAYERS (EASTERN)

The Eastern prayers display both the same variation with regard to the use of the typology of Stephen as was evidenced in the patristic prayers and also a similar tendency to reticence with regard to the actual functions of the diaconate. Where any details of the ministry are mentioned, they almost always relate to the celebration of the eucharist rather than to any wider pastoral responsibility.

We have attempted in earlier chapters to demonstrate the weaknesses of the theory propounded by Botte and Gy that the two Byzantine ordination prayers are the result of the division of an originally single prayer.[7] With regard to the prayers for the diaconate, this theory seems to be positively excluded, and even Gy himself admitted that things were less clear here than in the case of the other orders.[8] In the diaconal rite, the relationship between the Byzantine, Jacobite, and Melkite prayers is quite different from that of the prayers for the presbyterate (pp. 136, 178, and 207). While the second Byzantine prayer has affinities with the principal prayer of the Jacobite rite, as it does in the case of both the other two orders, it has no resemblance to any of the prayers in the Melkite rite. On the other hand, the first Byzantine prayer is almost exactly parallel to the third prayer of the Melkite rite, but has no similarity to the Jacobite prayer, apart from a common reference to Stephen. Not only, therefore, is there a total absence of any evidence for an earlier composite version of the Byzantine texts, but it seems certain that both prayers must at one time have circulated entirely independently of one another for them to have found their way separately into the other traditions.

The first prayer asks for the bestowal of the same grace that was given to Stephen, but has no explicit invocation of the Holy Spirit on the candidate. On the other hand, it does refer at the beginning to God in his *fore*knowledge sending down the Holy Spirit on those *destined* to be ministers: Is this perhaps a reflection of Acts 6:3, where the assembly is directed to choose men already "full of the Spirit" to be appointed to office? It gives little indication of the nature of the ministry for which the deacon is being ordained, except that it is related to the eucharist. It speaks of "those destined . . . to serve at your immaculate mysteries," and cites 1 Timothy 3:9, "holding the mystery of faith in a pure conscience," which some commentators have thought may be intended here, though not in its original context, as a reference to the deacon's function of holding the chalice for the distribution of communion.[9] It ends with the quotation from 1 Timothy 3:13—"for those serving well will gain for themselves a good rank" —which we have already encountered in the deacon's prayer in the *Apostolic Tradition*, and here again the reference is not to ecclesiastical preferment, but to the deacon's standing on the day of judgment.

The second prayer, like the second prayer for a bishop, is addressed to Christ rather than to God the Father, but this appears to be a secondary development,[10] since the Jacobite version begins in a completely different manner. It is difficult to believe that either tradition would have substituted an entirely new beginning for one that was already there, and this suggests that in its original form, the prayer began very simply, perhaps with no more than the word "Lord." The Byzantine form does not use the typology of Stephen, but in its extended introduction links the diaconate to Christ, not claiming that it was directly instituted by him as the *Sacramentary of Sarapion* tried to do, but interpreting his saying in Matthew 20:27 as a prophetic word concerning it. The prayer then goes on to ask for the bestowal of appropriate gifts of the Holy Spirit, these being personal qualities rather than the powers to fulfill any specific functions.

The prayer includes an insistent aside that ordination is indeed effected by the descent of the Spirit and not by the action of the bishop. This has the appearance of a later addition to the original text, though it is ancient enough to have also been included in the Jacobite version (but there strangely in the plural—"the imposition of the hands of us sinners" —to which we have referred earlier[11]). The inclusion of such a strongly defensive doctrinal statement in the prayer suggests that there was some controversy over the issue, and it may have been added in the late fourth century, since John Chrysostom makes a similar statement in one of his writings: "For this is ordination: the man's hand is imposed, but God does all and it is his hand which touches the ordinand's head when he is rightly ordained "[12] Moreover, Chrysostom also implies that the Antiochene baptismal formula was changed from the active to the passive form at this time in order to make a similar point:

"The bishop is not the only one who touches your head; Christ also touches it with his right hand. This is shown by the actual words of the bishop. He does not say, 'I baptize N.,' but rather, 'N. is baptized.' This shows that he is only the minister of the grace and merely lends his hand. . . . "[13]

In the rites for the episcopate and presbyterate, we suggested that the original prayer was the second one, to which the first was subsequently added, and this was probably also the case here. The reference to the bishop's agency in the appointment of the candidate and the description of Stephen as protomartyr in the first prayer imply a less ancient point of origin. But whereas the first prayer for the other two orders gives the impression of having been specially composed for the purpose, in this instance, its presence in the Melkite rite seems to rule out that possibility, since that tradition is hardly likely to have copied the first prayer without the second from the completed Byzantine rite. Instead, it would appear that the first prayer already existed in the Antiochene tradition as a variant form of the diaconal ordination prayer (and, in this way, entered the Melkite rite along with the prayers for presbyter and bishop), and was combined with the second prayer in the Byzantine rite at a later time. Possibly, this was done in order to make the shape of the rite correspond to what had already happened in the case of the other two orders, or, possibly, it was this attempt to incorporate both prayers in the one rite that started the whole process and gave rise to the necessity for the composition of equivalent first prayers for the presbyter and bishop.

The Jacobite ordination prayer modifies the Byzantine version in several ways: it supplies an introduction that sets the ordination of the deacon within an ecclesial framework; it introduces a reference to Stephen, though without the designation "protomartyr"; and it expands the second half of the prayer with petitions for right judgment on the part of those responsible for choosing ordinands. Some of these petitions also occur in the preliminary prayer, "Lord God of hosts . . . ," used in all Jacobite ordinations from subdeacon upward. The Jacobite version also appears to constitute the principal ordination prayer of the Maronite tradition (p. 191), though this rite also includes versions of the first and second Byzantine prayers, as well as the first Melkite prayer.

The first ordination prayer for a deacon in the Georgian rite (here described as an archdeacon) parallels the second prayer in the Melkite rite (pp. 169 and 207), as was also the case in the rite for the presbyterate, and so again is thought to be of Jerusalem origin. It defines the diaconate neither in relation to Christ, who is only mentioned briefly toward the end of the prayer, nor by the typology of Stephen, but simply as one of a list of diverse ministries bestowed by God on the Church—teachers, deacons, presbyters, and ministers. This is an unusual combination of offices: it omits any explicit reference to bishops and does not follow an hierarchical order, nor is it an allusion to any New Testament listing. The Melkite tradition also seems to have found it difficult to comprehend, and has tried to make some sense out of it by arranging the titles in pairs, altering "presbyters" to "priests" in the process. Is it possible, however, that it is a very ancient text, which has preserved a reference to a primitive pattern of ministry, antedating the adoption of the monarchical episcopate? The prayer has no explicit epiclesis, which may be a sign of its antiquity, but on the other hand, at least in its present form, it makes service at the altar the central purpose of the diaconal order and speaks of the ordinand's ultimate promotion to a higher rank, elements that do not seem to belong to the earliest concept of the office.

The third Georgian prayer parallels the East Syrian ordination prayer, once again following the structure of the rite for the presbyterate (pp. 158 and 170). This sets the creation of the diaconate in the context of the mission of Christ and of the apostles (the latter reference being expanded in the East Syrian prayer to prophets, apostles, priests, and teachers, apparently under the influence of Eph 4:11–12), and cites the example of Stephen and his companions. As in the first Georgian prayer, service at the altar is stated to be the principal function of the office, a point that is further strengthened in the East Syrian version by two additional references to the sacraments. There is, on the other hand, no mention of the ordinand's eventual promotion to a higher rank, but merely the petition for a favorable verdict on the day of judgment.

Of the remaining prayers of the Melkite rite, the first (p. 206) has the appearance of being a late composition, since extensive biblical quotation is not a characteristic of more ancient prayers, and it is very much built around Acts 6:5. However, as well as mentioning service of the altar, where it is the only prayer to refer explicitly to the diaconal function of giving communion to the people from the chalice, it also speaks of a ministry to widows and orphans. The position of the fourth prayer, after the bestowal of the symbols of office, suggests that it, too, is a late addition to the rite, even if it is not itself a late composition. It speaks simply of faithful service at the liturgy and of progress to a higher rank, though whether this is ecclesiastical or eschatological is not entirely clear.

The first of the two Armenian prayers for the diaconate, like two of those in the rite for the presbyterate, uses the comparison of the heavenly and earthly ministries (p. 128). It goes on to set the diaconal office within an ecclesial context, and then prays for the gift of appropriate personal qualities for the ordinand. Service at the altar is again designated as the principal function of the order, and the example of Stephen is invoked: he is here described not only as the first martyr and first deacon and minister of God's worship, but also as an apostle! There is no explicit epiclesis, though it is prayed that the ordinand "filled with the Holy Spirit, may stand fast . . . ," and may eventually be worthy of promotion to the priesthood. The second prayer is much shorter and does contain a petition for the gift of the Holy Spirit. Once again, ministry at the holy table is described as the chief function of the office, and the remainder of the prayer seeks God's protection for the new minister. Like the first Armenian prayer, those prayers in the Maronite rite that are without parallel in other traditions also employ the comparison of heavenly and earthly ministries (p. 192).

Finally, the Coptic ordination prayer for a deacon, like that for a presbyter, is a version of the ordination prayer from the *Apostolic Constitutions* (p. 143). It adds to that text a reference to the electoral process, identical to that in the presbyteral prayer: the ordinand is appointed "by a vote and judgment of those who have brought him into the midst." There follows a more explicit description of the ministry as being related to the altar, as well as some further elements from the Jacobite rite.

THE ORDINATION PRAYERS (WESTERN)

Since the Roman prayers for bishop and presbyter were built around Old Testament cultic imagery, it is hardly surprising to find that the same is true of the diaconal prayer (p. 216). After setting the ordained ministry in a Christological and ecclesiological context, it defines the diaconate by the typology of the Levites who constituted the third order of ministry in the Old Testament, and asks God to bestow on the ordinands the sevenfold grace of the Holy Spirit, an allusion to Isaiah 11:2 doubtless occasioned by numerical association with the seven "deacons" of Acts 6, even though the latter are not explicitly mentioned in the prayer. The specific functions that the deacons are to exercise are not further explained, and the rest of the prayer merely defines the personal qualities that are required of them, and refers to their eventual promotion to "higher things." As Gy has suggested,[14] the petitions for "discrete authority, unfailing modesty" may be in part a veiled warning to deacons not to attempt to make too much of their power, as is known sometimes to have happened at Rome.

The Gallican prayer, on the other hand, uses the typology of Stephen and his companions to define the diaconal office, though the preceding bidding does also make reference to the "levitical blessing" (p. 225). The apostles are spoken of as having acted under the direction of the Holy Spirit in appointing the seven, but there is no direct invocation of the Holy Spirit on the ordinands themselves, nor is the order set within a Christological or ecclesiological context, but there is simply an implicit parallel between the diaconate and the ministry of angels. Ministry at the altar is the only function to receive a mention.

The prayer that follows the bidding in the Mozarabic rite is to a large extent an adaptation of the Roman prayer for a deacon, deriving from the Northern recension of that material (p. 232). It omits nearly all of the opening of the Roman version, including the Levitical typology, but inserts a reference to the choosing of the seven by the apostles to be what it describes as "messengers of peace and ministry." The prayer then goes on to define the office still further by use of the images of Joshua attending Moses and of the young Samuel ministering in the temple, thus retaining service at the altar as its principal focus. Although some of these clauses may be of Spanish origin, the prayer as a whole is not the indigenous ordination prayer of this tradition, which Boone Porter suggested was the oration that now follows it[15] (though Gy inclined to the less probable view that it has been preserved instead within the rite for an archdeacon[16]). This shorter second prayer uses the typology of both Levi and Stephen, the latter providing a model for the deacon's obligation to teach the Catholic faith and overcome its enemies—a reflection of the long struggle with Arianism with which the Spanish Church was greatly preoccupied.

CONCLUDING CEREMONIES

As in the case of the presbyterate, the patristic sources make no mention of any concluding ceremonies in the ordination of a deacon, but later rites describe not only a kiss, but also the ceremonial bestowal of various symbols of his office. Although the Armenian and Georgian rites do not refer to any concluding ceremonies, the other Eastern rites consistently speak of the new deacon being vested in the diaconal stole, but differ with regard to the bestowal of other symbols. All that the Coptic rite has is an exhortation that reminds the deacon of his ministry toward the needy and alludes to his function of giving communion from the chalice (p. 144). In the Byzantine rite, however, he is given the fan with which to perform his duty of fanning the eucharistic elements on the altar, and after receiving communion himself, he is given the chalice and assists in giving communion to the people (p. 137). In the Melkite rite, he is given the book of the gospels and reads a short passage from it, before receiving the eucharistic vessels and the fan (p. 208). In the East Syrian rite, he is given the book of the epistles (p. 159), the presbyter being given the book of the gospels, apparently in order to express the superiority of his order over that of the deacon. In the Jacobite rite, he is given the thurible to swing (p. 180). The Maronite rite, not surprisingly, has a very elaborate ending that includes a ceremonial vesting, the reading of a passage from the epistles by the new deacon, and his performance of other actions that symbolize the liturgical duties of his office—incensing, carrying the epistle book in procession, and waving the chalice veil (p. 194).

The early Roman rite was much more simple, and involved only a vesting in stole and dalmatic in addition to the kiss (p. 219). We have no details of what early Gallican practice might have been, but the Mozarabic rite ended with the handing over of the gospel book to the deacon, accompanied by an exhortation that not only referred to his functions of reading the liturgical gospel and ministering at the altar, but also stressed the subordination of his office to both the presbyter and the bishop (p. 233). In contrast to the rite for the presbyterate in this tradition, however, the final rubric speaks of him kissing the bishop rather than of the bishop giving him a kiss. Was this also intended as an expression of his subservience to the bishop?

6 Deaconess

Deaconesses appear to have been virtually unknown both in the ancient churches of the West and also in Egypt. Only in Gaul are any traces found of the existence of female deacons, and this institution was condemned by a succession of councils, Nimes (A.D. 396), Orange (441), Epaone (517), and Orleans (533).[1] It is true that from the seventh century onward, the term "deaconess" appears in Italian sources, but here it apparently designates a category of women religious rather than an ecclesiastical ministry proper.[2] Hence, the *Apostolic Tradition* of Hippolytus speaks only of an order of widows who, it insists, are not ordained and do not receive an imposition of hands. It seems, however, to have to protest rather too much against such an idea, if it were uncontroversial at the time, and the reasons given are not altogether logical: if "ordination is for the clergy, on account of their liturgical duties," why are subdeacons and readers not ordained, according to this document, since they also have liturgical duties? It gives the impression that the author, or perhaps a later redactor, was anxiously seeking some rational grounds to defend a distinction that he believed to be right. Widows were instead to be appointed "by word only." This expression could mean that there was simply to be some formula declaring them to be admitted to the order, or, alternatively, it could mean that there was to be prayer for them, but no imposition of hands. Although most modern scholars have understood it to mean the former,[3] both the *Canons of Hippolytus* and the *Testamentum Domini*, as we shall see, apparently interpreted in the latter sense.

This Church order appears to have wanted to make an even clearer distinction between widows and the liturgical ministers, and so transferred the instructions about them from the position they seem to have occupied in the *Apostolic Tradition*, after the ordination of bishops, presbyters, and deacons, and before the directions concerning readers and subdeacons, to the very end of that section of the document, and insisted that "ordination is for men." It directs that widows are to be prayed over at their appointment, but does not provide any form to be used for this purpose

DIDASCALIA APOSTOLORUM

In Syria, things seem to have been somewhat different, and this third-century text refers both to widows, who seem to have occupied a similar position to those in the West, and also to female deacons, who are assigned the diaconal duties that propriety prevented a male deacon from performing—visiting women in their homes and anointing the bodies of female baptismal candidates. No clear indication is given whether the form of their appointment was parallel to that for male deacons or significantly different from it.[4]

APOSTOLIC CONSTITUTIONS (p. 116)

This is the first source to include a rite for the institution of deaconesses, which is placed immediately after that for deacons and closely resembles it. Just as the ordination of a deacon was to be conducted in the presence of the presbytery and the deacons, so the rite for the deaconess was to take place in the presence of the presbytery, the deacons, and the deaconesses. As in the case of all the other orders, it consisted of a prayer invoking the Holy Spirit and accompanied by the imposition of hands. Nevertheless, it should be noted that the word "ordination" does not appear at the beginning of the instruction concerning deaconesses nor in that for readers, whereas it does in the case of the deacon, and also of the subdeacon. This omission may be intended to indicate a subtle distinction in status between the various offices: the deacon is ordained in public; the deaconess is instituted in public; the subdeacon is ordained, but not in public; the reader is instituted, but not in public. In the light of this, the debate between A.-G. Martimort and Roger Gryson as to whether deaconesses were here thought of as receiving a sacramental ordination and as being part of the clergy may not only be anachronistic but also oversimplistic: the categorization of the liturgical ministries of the early Church cannot be reduced to a simple division between clergy and laity.[5]

Is the status here granted to the deaconess, however, simply a product of the imagination of the compiler of the *Apostolic Constitutions*, or does it have some real foundation in the ecclesiastical tradition from which he came? This question obviously cannot be answered with total certainty, but since the Byzantine rite also closely assimilates the rite for a deaconess to that for a deacon, and yet maintains some distinctions between the two, it suggests that this trend was already evident in fourth-century Syria. The alternative possibility—that the provisions of the Byzantine rite were directly influenced by the contents of the *Apostolic Constitutions*—seems improbable, although it is suggested by Martimort.[6]

The prayer itself offers three biblical precedents to justify the office of deaconess—women in the Old Testament who were endowed with prophetic spirit; the birth of Christ from a woman; and the somewhat shadowy female figures who are said to have ministered at the entrance of the tent of the testimony (adding the gratuitous assumption that they also continued to exercise this ministry in the later temple). Images similar to the first two of these also occur at the beginning of the first prayer in the Byzantine rite, albeit in the reverse order, and this suggests that they may already have been traditional in the euchology of fourth-century Syria. The third, on the other hand, is not otherwise found in prayers for deaconesses, and may, therefore, be an attempt by the compiler to find a biblical foundation for what was apparently the principal function of deaconesses, mentioned elsewhere in the document,[7] the supervision of the admission and seating of women in the liturgical assembly.

The fact that women endowed with the spirit of prophecy are mentioned may seem to suggest that deaconesses, too, had some sort of prophetic or teaching ministry, but this need not necessarily follow. As we shall see in the next chapter, the prayer for a reader in the *Apostolic Constitutions* also makes much of that office, asking for the gift of the prophetic spirit and even compares the reader's role to that of Ezra! But there is no other evidence that would support the notion that readers did have so important a standing in Christian worship at this period. Thus, both cases may owe more to the compiler's enthusiasm to find some Old Testament typology for the office than to a reflection of the true status of the order in the Church. The parallel image in the Byzantine prayer speaks merely of God giving the Holy Spirit "not to men alone but also to women." The compiler, therefore, may have developed that idea, interpreting endowment with the Spirit as referring to its extraordinary manifestation in the Old Testament and not to the baptismal gift in the New Testament (which seems to be the sense of the Byzantine text[8]). He thus naturally places it before, instead of after, the allusion to Christ's birth from a woman.

Although earlier in the *Apostolic Constitutions*, in the material derived from the *Didascalia*, the deaconess had continued to be expected to visit women in their homes and anoint female baptismal candidates,[9] no reference to these functions appears in the prayer for her institution. Instead, as we have mentioned already, it merely alludes to the deaconess's role of supervising the admission and seating of women in the liturgical assembly. This has led Martimort to propose that the compiler derived it from a different tradition from that represented by the *Didascalia* and analogous to that found in the later *Testamentum Domini*, in which the deaconess was only assigned this more limited and lowly ministry.[10] This argument from silence, however, is at best an uncertain one: as we have already seen, prayers for deacons in all traditions also tend not to make explicit mention of assistance with the administration of baptism or the reading of the gospel, though it is known from other sources that these were functions exercised by this order. Thus, we cannot really tell from the prayer what were envisaged as the limits of the ministry of the deaconess.

Finally, the prayer contains a hint that the liturgical ministry of women may not have been too readily accepted in the milieu in which it was composed: the inclusion of the petition to cleanse the candidate from all filthiness of flesh and spirit, echoing 2 Corinthians 7:1, seems to imply the existence of some doubt as to whether they were sufficiently holy for such a task, especially as the quotation has no special reference to women in its original context. Such a view would hardly be surprising in the light of common attitudes toward the ritual impurity of women in the early Church,[11] but as in the case of the other elements of this rite discussed above, it is difficult to distinguish clearly between the personal views of the compiler and the actual attitudes and practices of the ecclesiastical community of which he was a part.

This Church order paints a rather curious picture. Here the order of widows is retained from the *Apostolic Tradition*, and appears to be accorded considerable importance. Thus, for example, during the eucharistic oblation the widows are directed to stand behind the presbyters, on the left side, opposite the deacons on the right, and they are to receive communion after the deacons, and before the subdeacons and readers.[12] The form of institution of a widow also has some features in common with the higher orders: the same Syriac word is used to denote the process as is employed for those orders, and it takes place after she has been "chosen" and includes an appropriate prayer. Martimort denies that this is significant, and points out that the word is quite neutral and can simply mean "designation" or "election" rather than "ordination."[13] Nevertheless, it is true that appointment to the minor orders is described somewhat differently: although the same word is also used in the rite for a subdeacon, a different term is employed for the reader, and neither of them is said to have been "chosen," nor does a form of prayer seem to have been prescribed for them.[14] But even this distinction does not warrant the conclusion drawn by Gryson that widows were here "undeniably . . . considered a part of the clergy,"[15] especially as they do not appear to receive an imposition of hands.

Although the prayer to be said over widows is of a very general nature and includes no biblical typology or petitions for grace and power to fulfill any specific ministerial functions, elsewhere in the document widows are assigned duties that are very similar to those of the female deacons in the *Didascalia*—the anointing of female baptismal candidates, and the pastoral care of the women members of the congregation.[16] Yet this cannot simply be dismissed as a case of the substitution of the nomenclature of its literary source, since the *Testamentum* also mentions the existence of deaconesses. They are accorded a role greatly subordinate to that of the widows, who apparently are to supervise them.[17] Nothing at all is said about their appointment, and they are directed to receive communion with the laity and not with the other ministerial orders, as the widows were.[18] They were to remain near the door of the church,[19] which might seem to imply that their principal duty was to supervise the arrival and seating of women in the liturgical assembly, but elsewhere it is said that a deacon controlled the entrance of both men and women, and that the deacons—assisted by readers and subdeacons—kept order among women in the church.[20] The only function that the deaconesses are described as performing is the taking of communion to any pregnant women unable to attend the Easter eucharist.[21] They are thus something of an enigma.

THE BYZANTINE RITE (p. 137–139)

Here the institution of a deaconess is not only described as an ordination, but is still more closely assimilated to that for a deacon than was the case with the *Apostolic Constitutions*, even to the extent of her also being given a chalice. Some differences between the two rites, however, still remain. Whereas the deacon kneels to receive the imposition of hands, this was considered an improper posture for a woman, and hence the deaconess remains standing and merely bows her head. Propriety also apparently prevents the bishop from giving her a kiss at the conclusion of the rite. Similarly, though she does receive the diaconal *orarion*, she does not wear it in the same way as the deacon, but with the two ends brought out in front; and she is not given the fan, as the deacon was, since fanning the altar is not one of her duties. Moreover, whereas the deacon proceeds to give communion to the people from the chalice he has received, this is not part of the deaconess's functions and so she merely places it on the altar.

The prayers themselves, however, which are probably considerably older than the rubrics of the rite, are not merely adaptations of those for deacons, but independent compositions, though they are no more explicit about what it is that deaconesses do than the prayers for a deacon are about the functions of deacons. The first justifies the ministry of women on two grounds—the fact that Christ was born of a woman, and the fact that women as well as men had been given the Holy Spirit, themes to which we have already referred in discussing the prayer in the *Apostolic Constitutions*. The second prayer opens with no such apology, but uses the typology of Phoebe (Rom. 16:1–2) in order to provide an equivalent for that of Stephen in the second prayer for a deacon. It also reveals an interesting difference between the understanding of the offices of deacon and deaconess. Although, like the first prayer, it explicitly asks for the bestowal of the Holy

Spirit—in contrast to the prayers for subdeacon and reader, which do not—it does not claim that the candidate has already been chosen by God, as do the prayers for a deacon. On the contrary, it implies that this ministry is something that the candidate has volunteered to undertake: it speaks of "women offering themselves and wishing to minister" and asks God to give the Holy Spirit to "your servant who wishes to offer herself to you."

Which of the two prayers is the more ancient? We have suggested in earlier chapters that the second prayer in the Byzantine rites for bishops, presbyters, and deacons is the older of the two, and the first a later addition. This, however, does not seem to be true here. Not only does something similar to the first prayer appear to have been known to the compiler of the *Apostolic Constitutions*, but, as we shall see later, it also has parallels with other Eastern prayers for deaconesses, which suggests that it originated quite early in the Church's history. The language of the second prayer, on the other hand, implies a somewhat later period when the ordination of a deaconess was beginning to be seen more in terms of consecration to the religious life,[22] and thus it seems to have been composed at a time when the rite for a deacon already had two prayers and a conscious attempt was being made to harmonize the two rites by providing an equivalent formulary to its second prayer.

OTHER EASTERN RITES

Formularies for deaconesses are not found in extant collections of Jacobite, Maronite, and Melkite rites, but they do appear in the Armenian, East Syrian, and Georgian traditions. Since the Georgian rite has little by way of rubrics (p. 168), it is difficult to know how far ordination of a deaconess here was assimilated to that of the deacon: the proclamation/bidding formula makes no reference to her office, and nothing is explicitly said about the use of the litany or the imposition of hands in her case. On the other hand, three prayers are provided for her, as for the bishop, presbyter, and deacon. We have already seen that the first of the three prayers in the rites for presbyter and deacon is thought to have originated in Jerusalem, the second is derived from the *Testamentum Domini*, and the third is related to the equivalent East Syrian prayer. Since the *Testamentum Domini* had no rite for the appointment of deaconesses, one would not expect to see its influence in the case of this order, but it is hardly surprising to find that, while the first and the third prayers have no known antecedents, the second does indeed have some resemblance to the East Syrian prayer for a deaconess.[23]

Neither the first nor the third prayer includes an explicit invocation of the Holy Spirit on the candidate. The third prayer may well have been specially composed in order to bring the total number up to that of the other orders, especially since it is extremely brief and very general in its petitions, and, like the second Byzantine prayer, seems to belong to a time when deaconesses were seen more as a part of the religious life than as a strictly ministerial office (note particularly "accept her vow for good"). On the other hand, the fact that the prayer paralleled in the East Syrian rite comes second rather than first in the sequence may be an indication that the first prayer too was not a new creation, but derived from some other tradition. Could it perhaps have been Jerusalem, as was suggested in the case of the rites for the presbyterate and diaconate? It is true that deaconesses are not explicitly mentioned in the fourth-century descriptions of liturgical practice at Jerusalem by Cyril and Egeria, but there is a funeral inscription, from perhaps the fifth or sixth century, of "Sophia the deacon," which describes her as "the second Phoebe."[24] It may, of course, be just a coincidence that this same New Testament allusion also appears in the Georgian prayer, though one should note that it was not widely used as a type of the deaconess in the early Church and is not otherwise found in an ordination prayer, with the exception of the first Byzantine prayer described earlier. Whatever its origin, it is the only prayer to designate clearly that the functions to be exercised by the deaconess included a baptismal ministry as well as teaching.

The East Syrian rite in its extant form shows signs of an ambivalence of attitude toward the status of deaconesses: it is not placed next to the rite for deacons in the various manuscripts, and tends to be described as a blessing rather than an ordination (p. 162). Although the prayers include an invocation of the Holy Spirit, other features of the rite for deacons are not found—the archdeacon's bidding, the sign of the cross,[25] the vesting with the *orarion*, and the concluding declaration—and the rite takes place in the sacristy rather than in the church. The central prayer does not follow the Georgian version quite as closely in this rite as was the case with those for bishops, presbyters, and deacons, and, in particular, it omits the reference to the equality of the sexes brought about by Christ's incarnation from a woman: this may well be deliberate excision, a further indication of a reluctance to grant the deaconess too high a status. On the other hand, it does add an explicit reference to at least part of her functions: she was to give instruction to women. As in the Byzantine rite, the deaconess remains standing during the prayers (though bowing low), since kneeling before the bishop was thought improper.

An even closer parallel to the second Georgian prayer than the East Syrian one is provided by the Armenian tradition. Although the oldest extant collection of Armenian ordination rites does not include a form for deaconesses, one does occur both in a manuscript that dates from 1216 and also in one from the seventeenth century, which is supposed to have been copied from a ninth-century original. It consists of this single prayer, and no mention is made of an imposition of hands or any other ceremony in connection with it:

"Gracious and most merciful Lord, you who created all things with a word of command, and by the incarnation of your only-begotten Son made equal in holiness both male and female— since it has seemed good to you to grant not only to men but also to women the grace of the Holy Spirit: choose now in the same way your servants to perform the work of service as needed by your holy Church and give them the grace of your Holy Spirit; may he keep her in the pure justice, mercy, and compassion of your Christ, to whom with you, almighty Father, and the life-giving and liberating Holy Spirit, is given all glory, power, and honor now and for ever. . . . "[26]

Although the very close similarity between this and the Georgian version is in marked contrast to the prayers for presbyter and deacon, where the Armenian texts seem entirely independent, it is also repeated in the case of the prayer for a reader.[27] Why these rites should be different from the others is not easy to see. Did these two offices perhaps fall into disuse at an early date and their prayers ossify in a primitive form, while those for the other orders continued to develop? Or, alternatively, were prayers for these orders unknown in early Armenian practice and merely "borrowed" from Georgia or elsewhere at a somewhat later period? What does seem clear, when the Armenian/second Georgian/East Syrian prayers for a deaconess are compared with the first prayer in the Byzantine rite, is that a common root underlies them all. The Byzantine text seems closest to the earliest form, with the Armenian/Georgian version representing one line of development, and the East Syrian another.

7 Minor Orders

In addition to the orders of bishop, presbyter, and deacon, which are found universally from the second century onward, the early Church also knew of other permanently appointed officials designated to exercise certain liturgical functions—what later centuries would come to call the minor orders. The most ancient of these offices seem to have been those of reader and subdeacon, which are the only ones to appear consistently in the later rites of the East. The first source explicitly to mention both offices together is the *Apostolic Tradition* of Hippolytus (p. 109), but they may well have existed for some considerable time before this. It is possible that the fact that the reader is listed before the subdeacon in this document may be a sign that it was considered the superior office of the two at this period, and not the inferior, as in later thought, but it seems more probable that it merely indicates the chronological order in which the two offices emerged.[1] This sequence was retained in the *Canons of Hippolytus*, where the reader is required to have "the virtues of the deacon," which suggests that his was by no means considered an inferior rank, but was reversed in the *Apostolic Constitutions* and in the *Testamentum Domini* (pp. 111–112, 116, and 121).

A clear distinction in status between these offices and those of bishop, presbyter, and deacon is indicated by the different procedure adopted for their appointment in the *Apostolic Tradition*. Firstly, the candidates do not seem to have been elected by the community, but were apparently chosen by the bishop alone.[2] Secondly, they do not seem to have required the prayer of the community. Indeed, a reader was appointed simply by the bishop giving him the book from which he would read. The ruler of the Jewish synagogue had used the same gesture when inviting someone to read the Scriptures at a service,[3] and this may be the source of the Christian practice. A subdeacon was merely nominated to his office. In the *Canons of Hippolytus*, it was "the gospel" that the reader was given at his appointment, which suggests that its reading was not yet restricted to the diaconate, as it was in the fifth century at Alexandria.[4] In this document, the term "ordained" seems to have been used with regard to the subdiaconate, but there is no indication whether his institution included any of the customary ritual elements of ordination.

In the *Apostolic Constitutions,* on the other hand, a substantial prayer invoking the Holy Spirit and accompanied by the imposition of hands was prescribed in the case of both subdeacon and reader. This elaboration of the appointment procedure might seem to betoken an increase in the value attached to these orders. Such a conclusion, however, does not necessarily follow. It is all too easy to cite instances where extensive rituals surround offices that lack any real significance in the life of the community in which they are found. Indeed, it frequently seems to be the case that such rituals tend to grow in complexity as the actual importance of the office declines. In the absence of any corroborating evidence for an increase in the status of these orders in the fourth century, therefore, it seems more likely that it is the desire for some measure of symmetry between all the ecclesiastical offices that has brought about this assimilation to the rites for bishops, presbyters, and deacons.

Nevertheless, the assimilation is not total: the rite for the subdeacon is still distinguished to some extent from those for the bishop, presbyter, deacon, and deaconess, and the rite for the reader in turn from that of the subdeacon. It is directed that bishops should be ordained in the presence of other bishops, the presbytery, and the people; presbyters and deacons in the presence of the presbytery and deacons; and deaconesses in the presence of the presbytery, deacons, and deaconesses; but no such prescription is included for subdeacons or readers: here the bishop apparently still acted alone. Moreover, whereas the term "ordain" is extended to the subdeacon, it is not applied to the reader. It is not clear whether there is any significance in the fact that the plural "hands" is mentioned with regard to the subdeacon, but only the singular with regard to the reader.

Just as in the case of the deaconess,[5] we have to ask whether both the assimilation to the higher orders and the subtle distinctions retained between subdeacons and readers are a product of the imagination of the compiler, or whether they have some real foundation in the ecclesiastical tradition from which he came. Once again, the fact that we shall find similar features in other

Eastern traditions seems to confirm that the latter is more likely the case.

Following the model of other ordination prayers, the prayers for both subdeacon and reader employ Old Testament typology to define the offices being bestowed. The prayer for a subdeacon looks to the gate-keepers of the tent of the testimony, who are ranked immediately below priests and Levites in 1 Chronicles 9, and focuses on the responsibility for the liturgical vessels as his principal function. The prayer for a reader asks for the bestowal of the spirit of prophecy on the candidate, and compares his role to that of Ezra, who read God's laws to the people! While the typology of the subdeacon's prayer appears to be a perfectly natural development, the features of the reader's prayer seem somewhat excessive, since, as we have already remarked in the preceding chapter,[6] there is no other evidence to support the notion that readers really did have such a prominent place in Christian worship at this period. Hence, the typology of this prayer looks more like a product of the compiler's own desire to find some Old Testament precedent for the office than a reflection of a genuinely exalted status enjoyed by readers in the Church, especially as the prayer ends by seeking the candidate's ultimate promotion to a higher order.

In contrast to the *Apostolic Constitutions*, the *Testamentum Domini* retains the more primitive practice for the institution of a reader: neither prayer nor the imposition of hands is used, but he is simply given the book of readings accompanied by an exhortation or charge from the bishop. The situation with regard to the subdeacon is less clear. A different word is used to describe his institution than is employed in the case of the reader, but as this same word is also used for the institution of widows[7] as well as for the higher orders, it is difficult to determine whether this is significant. It is also said that the bishop is to pray over the subdeacon, but the text that follows is a similar exhortation or charge to that for the reader. Is the word "pray" simply being used loosely here or was it expected that a form of prayer, perhaps accompanied by the imposition of hands, would precede this charge? Whatever distinction may have been intended between the two offices, in both cases, the instructions prescribe that the appointment is to take place on a Sunday—the first source explicitly to state this—and the exhortation expects there to be eventual promotion to a higher rank.

Although the *Sacramentary of Sarapion* does mention the existence of subdeacons, readers, and interpreters,[8] it does not include any prayers for use at their appointment, which suggests that such had not yet developed in that tradition.

EASTERN RITES

As we have already remarked, a process of assimilation similar to that observed in the *Apostolic Constitutions* can also be seen in the later traditions of the East, though to different degrees. In some cases, the rites for both subdeacons and readers are closely conformed to those for the higher orders; in others, only the subdiaconate is treated in this way, since it is regarded as a lower degree of the diaconate, and the rite for a reader retains a distinctive shape; and in other traditions, there are signs of unwillingness to go too far in modifying the traditional distinction for either the subdeacon or the reader.

Thus, the Armenian tradition extends appointment by prayer and the imposition of hands to both readers and subdeacons, but there is only a single oration in each case and not the multiplicity of prayers or the proclamation/bidding and litany found in the rites for deacons and presbyters (p. 127). Similarly, in the Georgian tradition (p. 167), whereas the proclamation/bidding is used for subdeacons and readers, the "divine grace" formula and litany are not, and whereas the other orders are given three ordination prayers each, the subdeacon has only two and the reader one (though in the text as it now stands, the bishop's charge to the ordinand is also counted as a prayer in the rite for the reader, but not in that for the subdeacon). The East Syrian rites too are very simple: although the bishop says the "divine grace" formulary as a preparatory prayer for all the orders, the rites for readers and subdeacons do not include the bidding, final declaration, or other preparatory prayers found in the case of the higher orders, but only a single prayer accompanied by the imposition of hands. Distinctions in status are also expressed by the reader being ordained on the lowest step of the bema, the subdeacon on the middle step, and the higher orders on the bema itself (pp. 156–157).

In the Jacobite tradition, on the other hand, whereas the rite for a reader has a distinctive shape of its own, consisting of a series of three prayers, that for a subdeacon is closely conformed to the structure of the others orders, including the use of the consecrated elements in the ordination (pp. 174–177). Even so, the version of the thanksgiving prayer in this rite remains shorter than those in the other rites, and speaks only of a blessing having been performed through God's kindness instead of an ordination through the advent of the Holy Spirit. Moreover, in the case of both reader and subdeacon, there are signs of some unease about extending the imposition of hands to these lesser offices, and apparently as a compromise, the bishop merely touches the ordinand's temples. The Coptic tradition was heavily influenced by the Jacobite and so displays the same characteristics: in the case of the reader, merely adding a version of the prayer from the *Apostolic Constitutions* to the three Jacobite orations, and in the case of the subdeacon, combining the prayer for a subdeacon from the same source with that from the Jacobite rite (pp. 140–143).

The Melkite tradition, however, preserves no such distinctions. here the institution of both reader and subdeacon is assimilated to the rites for the other orders, including the imposition of hands (pp. 201–205). The sole remaining differences are that only two ordination prayers are provided for a reader, three for a subdeacon, and four for deacons and presbyters; and whereas a presbyter kneels on both knees and a deacon on the right knee, the subdeacon kneels on the left knee, and the reader seems to remain standing. Apparently as a parallel to the reception of the book of readings by the reader, the subdeacon is given the vessels for the *lavabo* at the conclusion of his ordination. The Maronite rites represent a mixture of the Jacobite and Melkite practices: because most of the prayers are similar to those of the Jacobite tradition, some variation in structure between the rites for readers and subdeacons still remains, and the rubrics speak of touching the temples of the ordinands; but many of the features of ordination to the higher orders have also been introduced (pp. 188–191).

In the Byzantine tradition, though both subdeacon and reader receive an imposition of hands with prayer, the eighth-century Barberini manuscript continues to maintain the distinction between the two orders found in the *Apostolic Constitutions* (p. 139): the rite for subdeacon is called an ordination, whereas that for a reader is merely an "appointment." (Later manuscripts, however, cease to distinguish between them in this way and use the term "ordination" for the reader as well.) Moreover, in contrast to the other orders, these two offices are now conferred in private, apparently in the *diaconicon* (sacristy) and outside the context of a celebration of the eucharist. In spite of this, however, they still conclude with the symbolic exercise of the principal liturgical functions of the order conferred. As in the *Apostolic Tradition* of Hippolytus, the reader is given the book of the readings,[9] and he then proceeds to read a short passage from this. The subdeacon says three times, "Those who are faithful," and then assists the bishop in performing the *lavabo*. The subdeacon's announcement constitutes the beginning of the prayers of the faithful, and is said immediately after the dismissal of the catechumens in the Byzantine eucharist. In all existing texts of that rite it is said by a deacon, but may originally have belonged to the subdeacon as part of his responsibility for guarding the doors of the church. Later manuscripts of the ordination rite also prescribe the delivery to the subdeacon of the ewer, basin, and towel for the *lavabo*, as was also done in the Melkite rite. Though it is not specified in the rubrically sparse text of the older manuscripts, this ceremony may well have been practiced from earlier times, especially as it also turns up in the fifth-century Gallican *Statuta Ecclesiae Antiqua*, which seems to have been subject to some Eastern influence.

EASTERN PRAYERS (SUBDEACON)

Not unexpectedly, some similarities can be seen between the Byzantine, Jacobite, and second Melkite prayers (pp. 139, 176, and 204). However, there are also marked differences between them. The resemblance is greatest in the petitions in the second half of the prayers, whereas in the first half, the Jacobite and Melkite texts are similar to one another, but the Byzantine has a quite different beginning that exhibits some parallels with the first prayer for the diaconate. This suggests that the original from which these are descended had no extensive introduction and that the Byzantine and Jacobite/Melkite versions have each created their own, the former being influenced by the diaconal prayer, the latter merely utilizing the stock imagery of prophet, priest, and king, which has no particular relevance to this order. The second half of the prayer describes the subdeacon's functions as ministry at the doors of the church and the lighting of its lamps (and in the Jacobite rite, he even receives the oil for the lamps rather than the vessels for the *lavabo* as the symbol of his office). This section is also to be found appended to the prayer for a subdeacon from the *Apostolic Constitutions* in the Coptic rite (p. 141).

In the Georgian rite, there is an admonition to the candidate, obviously based on that in the *Testamentum Domini*, followed by two prayers (p. 167). As in the rites for the presbyterate and diaconate, the first of these is parallel to one of the prayers in the Melkite rite (in this case the first: p. 204) and so probably derives from Jerusalem. The Georgian version is the shorter, and so probably closer to the original, and refers only to service at the door of the church and ultimate advance to some greater honor—whether ecclesiastical or eschatological is unclear— whereas the expanded version in the Melkite rite includes phrases reminiscent of the Byzantine/Jacobite/second Melkite prayer. The second Georgian prayer, on the other hand, has no obvious similarities to any other tradition, and says virtually nothing about the office being conferred: it may therefore have been specially composed in order that this rite should have one more prayer than that for a reader, and one less than that for a deacon. The same would also appear to be true of the third prayer in the Melkite rite, which similarly says very little and exhibits no parallels with any other tradition, especially as it follows the vesting of the ordinand and his performance of the *lavabo*, which one might have expected to conclude the rite.

As in the case of the higher orders, the Armenian prayer for a subdeacon seems entirely independent of the other traditions, and it does not define any of the functions of the office, but merely speaks of it in very general terms (p. 127). In surprising contrast to the higher orders, however, there is no close similarity between the Georgian and East Syrian prayers for either the subdeacon or the reader. It is of course possible that the East Syrian prayers may have changed so much in subsequent centuries that they lost all resemblance to their earlier forms, but if this were the case for these relatively insignificant offices, why did it not happen also in the prayers for the higher orders? Thus, it seems more likely that orations for these orders were simply not included in the early collection of East Syrian ordination prayers known to the Georgian compiler. Indeed, perhaps prayer was not used in the appointment to these particular offices in the early period of that particular tradition, as it was not in the milieu from which the *Apostolic Tradition* came, and so was only added to it later. As with the Armenian prayer, the East Syrian speaks only in very general terms about the ministry of the subdeacon (p. 157).

EASTERN PRAYERS (READER)

It is noteworthy that, with the exception of the Jacobite rite, none of the Eastern prayers for a subdeacon contains an explicit petition for the gift of the Holy Spirit on the candidate, and the same is true of the prayers for a reader. Even the Coptic prayers which are derived from the *Apostolic Constitutions* do not adhere to its text exactly, but merely ask for "holy spirit" and "a spirit of prophecy" respectively (pp. 140 and 141). Moreover, in the case of the reader, there seems to be some literary connection between nearly all the traditions, since similar phrases are to be found in many of the prayers. Of course, one might naturally expect there to be some resemblance between the prayers of the different churches for the conferral of this office, since there are certain very obvious things that anyone would want to include in such an oration, but the similarities go beyond this and suggest a common source.

The closest parallels are between the Armenian and Georgian versions (pp. 127 and 167)—the only case, apart from that of the deaconess,[10] where the Armenian euchology appears to have any connection with another tradition. It is interesting to recall that it was the rite for the reader that Armenian tradition credited to Gregory the Illuminator, and not to the liturgical work of Sahak.[11] Although this attribution may well be inaccurate, it does imply that the rite was thought to be very ancient, or at least had a different origin from the others. The Georgian prayer is preceded by an admonition that seems to be an expanded version of that in the *Testamentum Domini*, and also has some parallels with those in the Coptic and Melkite rites.

The Byzantine and second Jacobite prayers seem to constitute another line of development from the same nucleus (pp. 139 and 174), and between these two groups stands the second prayer of the Melkite rite, which has some similarity to both, but lacks the distinctive features of either, and contains its own peculiar characteristics (p. 202). The first prayer of the Melkite rite and the first and third prayers of the Jacobite rite, although expressing sentiments similar to this common prayer, appear to be independent compositions, as is the East Syrian prayer (p. 156). The three Jacobite prayers also recur in the Coptic and Maronite rites, though the latter also has an additional prayer without direct parallel in other rites (pp. 140 and 188).

THE WEST

Although the *Apostolic Tradition* spoke only of readers and subdeacons, a letter written by Pope Cornelius reveals the presence at Rome by the middle of the third century of subdeacons, acolytes, exorcists, readers, and doorkeepers.[12] The same offices, listed in exactly the same sequence, also occur in the third of the Good Friday *Orationes solemnes*, which represent the ancient prayers of the faithful of the Roman rite.[13] Thus, whatever may have been the situation underlying the *Apostolic Tradition*, here the reader has been relegated to a very subordinate position. On the other hand, there is no trace of the existence of any liturgical rite in connection with appointment to the orders of exorcist and doorkeeper. *Ordo* XXXIV, the oldest extant account of Roman ordination practice, dating from the middle of the eighth century, makes provision solely for acolytes and subdeacons, perhaps because they were the only ones directly associated with ministry at the altar (p. 218). Both orders could be conferred just before the distribution of holy communion during any eucharistic celebration, and the rite was extremely simple. It consisted essentially of the delivery of an appropriate symbol of the office accompanied by a short blessing: the acolyte was given the linen bag to hold the bread for the eucharist, and the subdeacon received the chalice. This custom goes back at least as far as the sixth century, for it is also described by John the Deacon.[14]

Ordo XXXV, originating in France, c. A.D. 1000, describes a Roman rite for the order of reader, but it appears that by this time, the office was usually conferred on adolescents whose parents wished them to embark upon an ecclesiastical career rather than upon those intended primarily to exercise the liturgical function. Its form is similar to that for the other minor orders in the earlier *Ordo*, consisting of the testing of the boy's ability to read, followed by a simple blessing by the Pope.

We have already suggested that the prescriptions for the ordination of bishops and presbyters in the *Statuta Ecclesiae Antiqua* seem to be an imagined ideal influenced by literary sources rather than a faithful reflection of actual Gallican practice of the period.[15] The same also appears to be true of its directions for the minor orders, which speak of six offices—subdeacon, acolyte, exorcist, reader, doorkeeper, and psalmist or cantor (p. 222). Other early Gallican evidence reveals no trace of the existence of the offices of acolyte or psalmist in this region, apart from a single inscription concerning an acolyte at Lyon in A.D. 517.[16] Institution to each of the orders is effected by the delivery of an appropriate symbol of office, except in the case of the psalmist, who can be appointed merely by the command of a presbyter, without reference to the bishop.

It prescribes a twofold delivery of the symbols of office for both the subdeacon and the acolyte: the subdeacon is to receive the paten and chalice from the bishop, and the ewer, basin, and towel from the archdeacon; the acolyte receives a candle and candlestick from the archdeacon, and also an empty wine cruet (from whom is not specified). This unusual arrangement suggests an attempt to combine two separate traditions. In the case of the subdeacon, since the delivery of the chalice is also found in the Roman tradition and the delivery of the paten and chalice in later Gallican and Spanish practice, this may well represent an indigenous custom, whereas the delivery of the ewer, basin, and towel appears to have been imported from the East.[17] With regard to the acolyte, the ceremonies have no known parallel: the delivery of the candle and candlestick may have been influenced by the Eastern custom of making the subdeacon responsible for lighting the lamps, and the wine cruet may have been an adaptation of the Roman practice of delivering to the acolyte the linen bag for the consecrated bread, since the latter practice was unknown in the Gallican tradition.

The later Gallican texts provide for the appointment of five minor orders—subdeacons, exorcists, readers, acolytes, and doorkeepers, though the order of precedence varies (pp. 223–225 and 237–239). A specific prayer is prescribed for each one, and in nearly all instances, a preceding bidding as well, though what is described as a bidding in the case of the reader looks more like an older formulary for admission to the office, which refers to an election by the other readers—an unusual practice. The prayer for the acolyte is the only one to lack a bidding, and in the short version of the *Missale Francorum*, speaks merely of the duty of lighting the lamps. In the much longer version of the Gelasian Sacramentary and its derivatives, however, reference is also made to the presenting of wine and water at the eucharist: perhaps these texts, therefore, were composed under the influence of the *Statuta*, and were not a part of the more ancient tradition. In the *Missale Francorum*, a delivery of symbols of office is mentioned only in the case of the subdeacon, and here it is the chalice and paten alone that are given and not the vessels for the *lavabo* as well. The other texts, however, incorporate in full the rubrical directions of the *Statuta* for all the orders. Interestingly, the prayer for the subdeacon is the only one in the whole Gallican tradition explicitly to ask for the bestowal of the Holy Spirit, and what is sought are the sevenfold gifts of Isaiah 11:2. Since this text is not particularly relevant to the office, it may well have been influenced by the Roman prayer for a deacon, where the same request is made, apparently because of the numerical association with the seven "deacons" of Acts 6.

If ritual forms of appointment for all the minor orders ever existed in the Mozarabic tradition—which is certainly questionable —they have been lost, for the only text to have been preserved is that for a subdeacon (p. 231). Here there is both a substantial ordination prayer, which includes an invocation of the Holy Spirit, and also an elaborate delivery of symbols of office, not just the chalice and paten mentioned in Canon 28 of the fourth Council of Toledo (633), but the vessels for the *lavabo* referred to in the *Statuta Ecclesiae Antiqua* (from whence the practice is probably derived) and also the book of the epistles, which it is here part of the subdeacon's liturgical duties to read. All of this suggests that in its present form, the rite is of a relatively late date.

PART II
PATRISTIC TEXTS

Apostolic Tradition of Hippolytus[1]

2. OF BISHOPS

Let him be ordained bishop who has been chosen by[2] all the people, and when he has been named and accepted by all, let the people assemble, together with the presbytery and those bishops who are present, on the Lord's day. When all give consent, they shall lay hands on him, and the presbytery shall stand by and be still. And all shall keep silence, praying in their hearts for the descent of the Spirit; after which one of the bishops present, being asked by all, shall lay his hand on him who is being ordained bishop, and pray, saying thus:

3. PRAYER FOR THE ORDINATION OF A BISHOP

God and Father of our Lord Jesus Christ, Father of mercies and God of all comfort,[3] you dwell on high and look on that which is lowly[4]; you know all things before they come to pass[5]; you gave ordinances in the Church through the word of your grace[6]; you foreordained from the beginning a race of righteous men from Abraham; you appointed princes and priests, and did not leave your sanctuary without a ministry. From the beginning of the age it was your good pleasure to be glorified in those whom you have chosen: now pour forth that power which is from you, of the princely Spirit[7] which you granted through your beloved Son Jesus Christ to your holy apostles[8] who established the Church in every place as your sanctuary, to the unceasing glory and praise of your name.

You who know the hearts of all,[9] bestow[10] upon this your servant, whom you have chosen for the episcopate, to feed your holy flock and to exercise the high-priesthood before you blamelessly, serving night and day; to propitiate your countenance unceasingly, and to offer to you the gifts of your holy Church; and by the spirit of high-priesthood to have the power to forgive sins according to your command,[11] to confer orders according to your bidding,[12] to loose every bond according to the power which you gave to the apostles,[13] to please you in gentleness and a pure heart, offering to you a sweet-smelling savor[14]; through your child Jesus Christ our Lord, with whom be glory and power and honor to you, with the holy Spirit, both now and to the ages of ages. Amen.

4. And when he has been made bishop, all shall offer the kiss of peace, greeting him because he has been made worthy. . . .

7. OF PRESBYTERS

And when a presbyter is ordained, the bishop shall lay his hand on his head, the presbyters also touching him; and he shall say according to what was said above, as we said before about the bishop, praying and saying:

God and Father of our Lord Jesus Christ, look upon this your servant, and impart the Spirit of grace and counsel of the presbyterate, that he may help and govern[15] your people with a pure heart; just as you looked upon your chosen people, and commanded Moses to choose presbyters whom you filled with your Spirit which you granted to your servant.[16] And now, Lord, grant the Spirit of your grace to be preserved unfailingly in us, and make us worthy to minister to you in faith and in simplicity of heart, praising you through your child Jesus; through whom be glory and power to you with the holy Spirit, in the holy Church, both now and to the ages of ages. Amen.

8. OF DEACONS

And when a deacon is ordained, let him be chosen according to what was said above, the bishop alone laying on hands, in the same way as we also directed above. In the ordination of a deacon, the bishop alone shall lay on hands, because he is not being ordained to the priesthood, but to the service of the bishop, to do what is ordered by him. For he does not share in the counsel of the clergy, but administers and informs the bishop of what is fitting; he does not receive the common spirit of seniority in which the presbyters share, but that which is entrusted to him under the bishop's authority. For this reason the bishop alone shall ordain a deacon; but on a presbyter the presbyters alone shall lay hands, because of the common and like spirit of their order. For a presbyter has authority only to receive; he has not authority to give. For this reason he does not ordain the clergy, but at the ordination of a presbyter he seals, while the bishop ordains.

Over a deacon, then, [the bishop] shall say thus:

God, who created all things and ordered them by your Word, Father of our Lord Jesus Christ, whom you sent to serve your will and make known to us your desire, give the holy Spirit of grace and caring and diligence to this your servant whom you

have chosen to serve your Church and to present[17] in your holy
of holies that which is offered to you by your appointed high-
priest to the glory of your name; that, serving blamelessly and
purely, he may attain the rank of a higher order,[18] and praise
and glorify you through your Son Jesus Christ our Lord; through
whom be glory and power and praise to you, with the holy
Spirit, now and always and to the ages of ages. Amen.

[Section 9, of confessors, then follows.]

10. OF WIDOWS

*When a widow is appointed, she is not ordained, but is chosen by name.
If her husband has been dead a long time, let her not be taken on trust;
even if she is old, let her be tested for a long time, for often the passions
grow old with him who makes a place for them in himself. A widow
shall be appointed by word only, and shall join the rest. But hands shall
not be laid on her, because she does not offer the offering, nor has she a
liturgical duty. Ordination is for the clergy, on account of their liturgical duties; but a widow is appointed for prayer, which belongs to all.*

11. OF A READER

*A reader is appointed by the bishop giving him the book, for he does not
have hands laid on him.*

12. OF A VIRGIN

Hands shall not be laid on a virgin: her choice alone makes her a virgin.

13. OF A SUBDEACON

*Hands shall not be laid on a subdeacon, but he shall be named in order
that he may follow the deacons.*

14. OF GIFTS OF HEALING

If anyone says, I have received a gift of healing by a revelation,
*hands shall not be laid on him, for the facts themselves will show
whether he has spoken the truth.*

Canons of Hippolytus[1]

CANON 2. OF BISHOPS

Let the bishop be chosen by all the people, and let him be without re-
proach, as it is written concerning him in the Apostle.[2] The week[3] when
he is ordained, all the clergy and the people say, We choose him.
There shall be silence in all the flock after the approbation, and they are
all to pray for him and say, O God, behold him whom you have
prepared for us. They are to choose one of the bishops and presbyters;
he lays his hand on the head and prays, saying:

CANON 3. PRAYER OVER HIM WHO BECOMES BISHOP,
AND ORDER OF THE LITURGY

O God, Father of our Lord Jesus Christ, Father of mercies and
God of all comfort,[4] dwelling on high and looking upon the
lowly,[5] knowing everything before it comes to pass,[6] you who
have fixed the boundaries of the Church, who have decreed
from Adam[7] that there should exist a righteous race—by the in-
termediary of this bishop—that is [the race] of great Abraham,
who have established authorities and powers, look upon N. with
your power and mighty spirit, which you have given to the holy
apostles by our Lord Jesus Christ, your only Son, those who
have founded the Church in every place, for the honor and glory
of your holy name. Since you know the heart of everyone,[8]
make him shepherd your people blamelessly, so that he may be
worthy of tending your great and holy flock; make his life higher
than [that] of all his people, without dispute; make him envied
by reason of his virtue by everyone; accept his prayers and his
offerings which he will offer you day and night; and let them be
for you a sweet-smelling savor.[9] Give him, Lord, the episcopate,
a merciful spirit, and the authority to forgive sins; give him
power to loosen every bond of the oppression of demons, to
cure the sick and crush Satan under his feet swiftly; through our
Lord Jesus Christ, through whom be glory to you, with him and
the Holy Spirit, to the ages of ages. Amen.

And all the people say, Amen.

After that they are all to turn toward him and give him the kiss of
peace, because he is worthy of it. . . .

CANON 4. CONCERNING THE ORDINATION OF PRESBYTERS

When a presbyter is ordained, one is to do for him everything which one does for the bishop, except the sitting on the seat. One is to pray over him all the prayer of the bishop, except the name of the bishop only. The presbyter is equal to the bishop in everything except the seat and ordination, because to him is not given the power to ordain.

CANON 5. CONCERNING THE ORDINATION OF DEACONS

When a deacon is ordained, one is to do for him according to the same rules, and one is to say this prayer over him. He is not appointed for the presbyterate, but for the diaconate, as a servant of God. He serves the bishop and the presbyters[10] in everything, not only at the time of the liturgy, but he serves also the sick of the people, those who have nobody, and he informs the bishop so that he may pray over them or give to them what they need, or also to people whose poverty is not apparent but who are in need. They are to serve also those who have the alms of the bishops, and they are able to give to widows, to orphans, and to the poor. He is to perform all the services. So this in truth is the deacon of whom Christ has said, "He who serves me, my Father will honor him."[11] The bishop lays his hand on the deacon and says this prayer over him, saying:

O God, Father of our Lord Jesus Christ, we beseech you, pour out your Holy Spirit on N.; count him among those who serve you according to all your will like Stephen and his companions; fill him with power and wisdom like Stephen[12]; make him triumph over all the powers of the Devil by the sign of your cross with which you sign him; make his life without sin before all men and an example for many, so that he may save a multitude in the holy Church without shame; and accept all his service; through our Lord Jesus Christ, through whom be glory to you, with him and the Holy Spirit, to the ages of ages. Amen.

[Canon 6 concerns confessors.]

CANON 7. CONCERNING THE CHOICE OF READER AND OF SUBDEACON

When one chooses a reader, he is to have the virtues of the deacon. One is not to lay the hand on him before, but the bishop is to give him the Gospel.

The subdeacon [is to be appointed] according to this arrangement: he is not to be ordained still celibate and if he has not married, unless his neighbors bear witness for him and testify that he has kept himself away from women during the time of his maturity.

One is not to lay the hand on someone in the state of celibacy, unless he has reached his maturity or is entering into mature age and is thought [worthy], when one bears witness for him.

The subdeacon and the reader, when they pray alone, are to keep themselves behind, and the subdeacon is to serve behind the deacon.

CANON 8. CONCERNING THE GIFTS OF HEALING

If someone asks for his ordination, saying, I have received the gift of healing, *he is to be ordained only when the thing is manifest and if the healing done by him comes from God.*

A presbyter, when his wife has given birth, is not to be excluded.

CANON 9. CONCERNING THE PRESBYTER WHO LIVES IN A FOREIGN PLACE, AND OF THE FUNCTION OF WIDOWS

If a presbyter goes to live in a foreign place and the clergy of that place accept him, the bishop of his see is to be questioned, for fear that he is fleeing for some reason. If his town is distant, let one examine first if he is instructed—that is the sign of presbyters—and after that, he is to be accepted and given a double honor.[13]

Then, one is not to ordain the widows who are appointed—there are in effect for them the precepts of the Apostle.[14] *They are not to be ordained, but one is to pray over them, because ordination is for men. The function of widows is important by reason of all that is incumbent upon them: frequent prayer, the ministry of the sick, and frequent fasting.*

Canons of Hippolytus

Apostolic Constitutions[1]

8.4.2. First, therefore, I Peter say that, as we have all together ap-
pointed above, a bishop to be ordained is to be blameless in all things,[2]
chosen by all the people. When he has been nominated and approved, the
people are to assemble, together with the presbytery and the bishops who
are present, on the Lord's Day, and the principal of the others is to ask
the presbytery and the people whether he is the one whom they want as
their leader. And if they assent, he is to ask further whether he has
testimony from all that he is worthy of this great and illustrious leader-
ship, whether what pertains to his piety toward God is right, whether
just dealing with human beings has been preserved, whether his domes-
tic affairs have been well regulated,[3] whether the conduct of his life has
been irreproachable.[4] And if all together testify according to truth and
not according to prejudice that he is such a person, as before the tribu-
nal of God and Christ, the Holy Spirit also being present, and all the
holy ministering spirits, again for a third time they are to be asked
whether he is truly worthy of the ministry, so that out of the mouths of
two or three witnesses every word may be established,[5] and if they agree
the third time that he is worthy, they are all to be asked for their con-
sent, and are to be heard giving it eagerly. And when there is silence,
one of the leading bishops together with two others is to stand near
the altar and, the rest of the bishops and presbyters praying in silence,
and the deacons holding the divine Gospels open on the head of the
ordinand, he is to say to God:

8.5. Great being,[6] sovereign Lord, almighty God, alone unbegotten and ruled over by none; who always are and existed before the ages; who lack nothing and are above all cause and beginning; alone true, alone wise, who alone are most high, invisible by nature, whose knowledge is infinite, alone good and incomparable, who know all things before they happen, and are
cognizant of hidden things,[7] inaccessible and without superior;
the God and Father of your only-begotten Son, our God and
Savior; the creator of all through him; the provider; the protector; the Father of mercies and God of all comfort,[8] who dwell on
high and look on that which is lowly,[9] you who gave the rules of
the Church through the coming of your Christ in the flesh, by
the witness of the Paraclete, through your apostles and us teachers,[10] the bishops present by your grace; who foreordained from

the beginning priests for the government of your people, Abel first, Seth and Enos and Enoch and Noah and Melchizedek and Job; who called Abraham and the rest of the patriarchs with your faithful servants Moses and Aaron and Eleazar and Phineas; who appointed from them rulers and priests in the tent of the testimony; who chose Samuel as priest and prophet; who did not leave your sanctuary without a ministry; who delighted in those in whom you wished to be glorified.

Now through the mediation of your Christ pour forth through us the power of your princely Spirit which was at the service of your beloved child Jesus Christ, which was given by your will to the holy apostles of you, the eternal God. Grant in your name, God who know the heart,[11] to this your servant, whom you have chosen as bishop, to feed your holy flock and to exercise the high-priesthood for you, blamelessly serving night and day and propitiating your countenance; to gather the number of those being saved, and to offer to you the gifts of your holy Church. Grant to him, almighty Lord, through your Christ the fellowship of the Holy Spirit,[12] so that he may have power to forgive sins according to your command,[13] to give lots according to your bidding,[14] to loose every bond according to the power which you gave to the apostles,[15] to please you in gentleness and a pure heart, steadfastly, blamelessly, and irreproachably offering to you a pure and bloodless sacrifice which you instituted through Christ, the mystery of the new covenant, for a sweet-smelling savor[16]; through your holy child Jesus Christ, our God and Savior, through whom [be] glory, honor, and worship to you in the Holy Spirit, now and always and to the ages of ages.

And after he has prayed this, the other priests respond, Amen, *and with them the whole people.*

And after the prayer, one of the bishops is to place the offering on the hands of the newly-ordained. And in the morning he is to be enthroned in the place reserved for him by the rest of the bishops, all giving him the kiss in the Lord. . . .

8.16. *Concerning the ordination of presbyters, I the beloved by the Lord make this constitution for you bishops: when you ordain a presbyter, O bishop, lay your hand on his head, the presbytery and the deacons standing around you, and pray and say:*

Apostolic Constitutions

Almighty Lord, our king, who have created all things through Christ, having brought him into existence before all and through him providing appropriately for all—for he who has the power to make varied creatures also has the power to provide variously: for through him, O God, you provide for the immortal by care alone, but for the mortal by succession, for the soul by provision of laws, for the body by supplying its needs—therefore now look upon your holy Church and increase it, and multiply those who preside in it and give them strength that they may labor in word[17] and deed for the building up of your people. Look now also upon this your servant who has been admitted into the presbytery by the vote and judgment of the whole clergy, and fill him with the spirit of grace and counsel to help and govern[18] your people with a pure heart, just as you looked on your chosen people and commanded Moses to choose presbyters whom you filled with spirit.[19] And now, Lord, preserving unfailingly in us the spirit of your grace, grant that, filled with works of healing and the word of teaching, he may in meekness instruct your people and serve you sincerely with a pure mind and a willing soul, and may blamelessly fulfill the holy services for your people through your Christ, through whom [be] glory, honor, and worship to you in the Holy Spirit for ever. Amen.

8.17. *Concerning the ordination of deacons, I Philip make this constitution: you shall appoint a deacon, O bishop, laying hands on him, all the presbytery and the deacons standing around you, and you shall pray and say:*

8.18. Almighty God, true and faithful, bestowing riches on all who call upon you[20] in truth, fearful in counsels, wise in understanding, powerful and great, hear our prayer, Lord, and give ear to our supplication,[21] and let your face shine on this your servant[22] who is appointed to you for ministry, and fill him with spirit and power, as you filled Stephen the protomartyr and imitator of the sufferings of your Christ.[23] And grant that he, acceptably performing the sacred ministry entrusted to him, steadfastly, blamelessly, and irreproachably, may be worthy of a higher rank[24] through the mediation of your Christ, your only-begotten Son, through whom [be] glory, honor, and worship to you in the Holy Spirit for ever. Amen.

8.19. Concerning a deaconess, I Bartholomew make this constitution: O bishop, you shall lay hands on her in the presence of the presbytery and of the deacons and deaconesses, and say:

8.20. Eternal God, Father of our Lord Jesus Christ,[25] creator of man and woman, who filled with the Spirit Miriam[26] and Deborah[27] and Anna[28] and Huldah[29]; who did not disdain that your only-begotten Son should be born of a woman; who also in the tent of the testimony and in the temple appointed women to be guardians of your holy gates[30]: now look upon this your servant who is being appointed for ministry, and give her the Holy Spirit and cleanse her from every defilement of body and spirit[31] so that she may worthily complete the work committed to her, to your glory and the praise of your Christ, through whom [be] glory and worship to you in the Holy Spirit for ever. Amen.

8.21. Concerning subdeacons, I Thomas make this constitution for you bishops: when you ordain a subdeacon, O bishop, you shall lay hands on him and say:

Sovereign God, creator of heaven and earth and all in them, who also in the tent of the testimony made temple-keepers guardians of your holy vessels;[32] now look upon this your servant appointed subdeacon, and give him the Holy Spirit that he may worthily handle your liturgical vessels and do your will always through your Christ, through whom [be] glory, honor, and worship to you in the Holy Spirit for ever. Amen.

8.22. Concerning readers, I Matthew, also Levi, once a tax-collector, make a constitution: appoint a reader by laying your hand on him, and, praying to God, say:

Eternal God, great in mercy and compassion, who have revealed the ordering of the world by your operations,[33] and preserve the number of your elect in the whole world; now look upon this your servant who is being entrusted with the reading of your holy Scriptures to your people, and give him the Holy Spirit, the prophetic Spirit. You who instructed Esdras your minister to read your laws to your people,[34] now in answer to our prayers instruct your servant, and grant that, having blamelessly completed the work entrusted to him, he may be shown worthy of a higher rank, through Christ, through whom [be] glory and worship to you in the Holy Spirit for ever. Amen.

Testamentum Domini[1]

I.21. *Let him who is of this sort receive laying on of hands on the first day of the week, all consenting to his appointment and bearing witness to him, with all the neighboring presbyters and bishops. Let those bishops lay hands on him, first having washed their hands. But let the presbyters stand near them quietly, with awe, lifting up their hearts in silence. Next, the bishops lay hands on him, saying:*

We lay hands on this servant of God who has been chosen by the Spirit for the firm and pious appointment of the monarchic and indissoluble Church of the invisible and Living God, and for the preservation of true judgment and divine and holy revelations, and of divine gifts and trustworthy doctrines of the Trinity; through the cross, through the resurrection, through incorruptibility, in the holy Church of God

After this, let one of the bishops charged by the other bishops lay hands on him, saying the invocation of the ordination thus:

PRAYER OF THE ORDINATION[2] OF A BISHOP

O God, you who have made and fixed all things in power, and have founded the inhabited world in thought, you who have adorned the crown of all these things made by you, who have granted these to keep your commandments in fear; you who have bestowed understanding of truth upon us, and have made us to know your good Spirit; you who sent your beloved Son, the only begotten Savior, without stain, for our salvation; O God and Father of our Lord Jesus Christ, Father of mercies and God of all comfort,[3] who everlastingly dwell in the pure heights, who are exalted, glorious, revered, great, and all-seeing, who know all things before they are,[4] with whom all things were before they came into existence[5]; you who gave enlightenment to the Church through the grace of your only begotten Son; you who predetermined from the beginning [for] those who take pleasure in just things and do those things which are holy to dwell in your mansions; you who chose Abraham who pleased you through his faith,[6] and who translated holy Enoch to the treasury of life[7]; who ordered princes and priests for your high sanctuary, Lord, who called [them] to praise and glorify your name and [the name] of your only-begotten in the place of your glory; Lord God, you who did not leave your high sanctuary without a ministry before the foundations of the world, and even before the foundations of the world you adorned and beautified your sanctuaries with faithful princes and priests in a type of your heaven; you, Lord, even now have been pleased to be praised, and have deigned that there be leaders for your people.

Make shine and pour out understanding and grace from your princely Spirit[8] which you delivered to your beloved Son Jesus Christ; give, O God, wisdom, reasoning, strength, power, unity of spirit to do all things by your operation. Give your Spirit, O holy God, who was given to your Holy One; send [him] to your holy and pure Church and to every place which has been consecrated to you; and grant, O Lord, that this your servant may be pleasing to you for doxology and unceasing praise, O God; for fitting hymns, suitable times, acceptable prayers, faithful petitions, correct doctrine, a humble heart, conduct of life,[9] and humility and truth, for the knowledge of uprightness.

O Father who knows hearts,[10] [grant][11] to this servant whom you have chosen for the episcopate to feed your holy flock, and to stand in the high-priesthood without blame, serving you day and night. Grant that your countenance may appear to him; make him worthy, O Lord, to offer you the offerings of your holy Church circumspectly, with all awe. Grant him to have your powerful Spirit to loose all bonds, just as you granted to your Apostles.[12] In order to please you in humility, fill him with love, knowledge, understanding, discipline, maturity, strength, and a pure heart, as he prays for the people and while he mourns for those who act foolishly[13] and draws them toward relief, while he offers you praise and thanksgiving and prayers for a sweet savor[14]; through your beloved Son our Lord Jesus Christ, through whom to you be praise and honor and might, with the Holy Spirit, both before the worlds, and now and always and to the generation of generations and to worlds without end of worlds. Amen.

Let the people say, Amen.

Then let them cry out, He is worthy, he is worthy, he is worthy.

After he is [ordained], let the people keep feast for three days as a sign of him who rose from the dead in three days. Then let everyone give him the Peace.

I.30. *Then let the ordination of a presbyter be thus: after all the priestly college have brought him, while the bishop lays his hand on his head and the presbyters are touching him and holding him, let the bishop begin, saying thus:*

PRAYER OF THE ORDINATION[15] OF A PRESBYTER

O God, Father of our Lord Jesus Christ, the Ineffable, the Luminary, who has neither beginning nor end, Lord, you who have ordered all things, and set [them] in a limit, and in thought have determined the order for all things you have created; hear us, and turn toward this your servant, and make [him] a partaker and grant him the spirit of grace and of reason and of strength, [the] spirit of the presbyterate which does not age indissoluble, homogeneous, loving the faithful, admonishing, to help and govern your people in labor, in fear, with a pure heart, in holiness, and in excellency, and in wisdom, and by the operation of your Holy Spirit through your care, Lord. In like manner as when you attended to your chosen people you commanded Moses to ask for the elders, when you filled [them with] Holy Spirit you bestowed your minister[16]; and now, O Lord, bestow your unfailing Spirit upon him, which you gave to those who became disciples through you, and to all those who through them truly believed in you; and make him worthy, being filled with your wisdom and with your hidden mysteries, to shepherd your people in the holiness of a pure and true heart, praising, blessing, lauding, acknowledging, always offering a doxology, day and night, to your holy and glorious name, laboring in cheerfulness and patience, so that he might be an instrument of your Holy Spirit, always having and bearing the cross of your only-begotten Son, our Lord Jesus Christ, through whom to you be glory and might, with the Holy Spirit, to all the ages of ages.

Let the people say, Amen.

Let them give him the Peace, both priests and people, with a holy kiss.

I.38. *Then let the ordination of a deacon be thus: let the bishop alone lay his hand on him, because he is not ordained to the priesthood but to the ministry of attending to the bishop and the Church. Therefore, let the bishop say thus over the deacon:*

PRAYER OF THE ORDINATION[17] OF A DEACON

O God, you who created all things, and who adorned [them] by the Word, you who rest in the pure ages, you who ministered eternal life to us through your prophets, you who have enlightened us with the light of your knowledge; O God who does great things, the maker of all glory, the Father of our Lord Jesus Christ whom you sent to minister to your will so that all the human race might be saved; you made known to us and revealed your Thought, your Wisdom, your Action, your beloved Son Jesus Christ, the Lord of light, the Prince of princes, and God of gods; bestow the spirit of grace and diligence upon this your servant, so that there might be given to him diligence, serenity, strength, power to please you; grant him, O Lord, to be a lawful laborer without shame, kind, a lover of orphans, a lover of pious things, a lover of widows, fervent in spirit, a lover of good things; enlighten, Lord, the one you have loved and have appointed to minister to your Church to offer in holiness to your sanctuary those things offered to you from the inheritance of your high-priesthood, so that he may minister without blame and in purity and holiness and with a pure conscience may be proved worthy of this high and exalted rank through your will, praising you continuously through your only-begotten Son Jesus Christ our Lord, through whom be praise and might to you for ever and ever. *The people:* Amen.

[CONCERNING WIDOWS]

I.41. *Let her ordination be thus: while she is praying at the entrance of the altar and looking down, let the bishop say in a low voice so that [only] the priests can hear:*

PRAYER OF INSTITUTION OF WIDOWS WHO SIT IN FRONT

O God, holy one and exalted one, who sees humble women, who has chosen the weak and the mighty, O honored one, who has created[18] even those things which are despised; bestow, O Lord, a spirit of power upon this your handmaid, and

strengthen her with your truth, that, keeping your command-
ment and laboring in your sanctuary, she may become an honored vessel for you and may praise on the day on which you
will praise your poor ones, O Lord; and grant her the power
gladly to practice these your teachings which you fixed as a rule
for your handmaid; give her, O Lord, a spirit of humility and of
power and patience and of kindness, that, bearing your burden
with ineffable joy, she may endure labors; yea, O Lord God, you
who know our weakness, perfect your handmaid for the praise
of your house; strengthen her for edification and a good example; sanctify, grant wisdom, encourage [her], O God, because
your kingdom is blessed and glorious, O God [and] Father; and
to you be praise and to your only-begotten Son our Lord Jesus
Christ and to the Holy Spirit honorable and worshiped and life-
giving and consubstantial with you, now and before all worlds
and to the generation of generations and to the ages of ages. *The
people:* Amen.

I.44. CONCERNING SUBDEACONS
*Likewise let the subdeacon be ordained; let him bow while the bishop
prays over him. On Sunday let the bishop say over him, all the people
listening:*

N., serve and obey the gospel in the fear of God. In holiness
cultivate self-knowledge; observe purity; practice the ascetic life;
regard and obey and listen in humility; do not neglect prayers
and fasts, that the Lord may grant you rest and deem you worthy of a greater rank.

And let all the priests say, So be it, so be it, so be it.

I.45. CONCERNING THE READER
The reader is constituted[19] *pure, gentle, humble, well-tested, skilled and
learned, mindful, vigilant, that he may be suitable for a higher rank.
First let the book be given to him while the people look on, on the first
day of the week. A hand is not laid upon him, but he hears from the
bishop:*

N., Christ has called you to be a minister of his words; take care
and strive, that you may appear approved both in this rule and
in a higher rank, even to Jesus Christ, that he may reward you
for these things with a good wage in his eternal mansions.

And let the priests say, So be it, so be it, so be it.

Sacramentary of Sarapion[1]

IMPOSITION OF HANDS OF THE APPOINTMENT OF DEACONS

Father of the only-begotten, who sent your Son[2] and ordered the things on the earth and gave rules to the Church and orders for the help and salvation of the flocks, who chose bishops and presbyters and deacons for the sacred ministry[3] of your catholic Church, who chose through your only-begotten the seven deacons and bestowed on them holy Spirit: make this man also a deacon of your catholic Church and give in him a spirit of knowledge and discernment,[4] so that he may be able in the midst of the holy people purely and blamelessly to serve in this sacred ministry; through your only-begotten Jesus Christ, through whom to you [be] glory and power in holy Spirit both now and to all the ages of ages. Amen.

IMPOSITION OF HANDS OF THE APPOINTMENT OF PRESBYTERS

We stretch forth the hand, sovereign God of the heavens,[5] Father of your only-begotten, on this person and we ask that the Spirit of truth[6] may dwell on him. Bestow on him prudence and knowledge and a good heart.[7] May a divine spirit be in him to enable him to be a steward of your people and an ambassador of your divine oracles and to reconcile[8] your people to you the uncreated God. You who bestowed holy Spirit from the spirit of Moses on your chosen ones,[9] apportion also to this man holy Spirit from the Spirit of the only-begotten for the grace of wisdom and knowledge and right faith,[10] so that he may be able to minister to you with a clear conscience;[11] through your only-begotten Jesus Christ, through whom to you [be] glory and power in holy Spirit both now and to all the ages of ages. Amen.

IMPOSITION OF HANDS OF THE APPOINTMENT OF A BISHOP

You who sent the Lord Jesus for the benefit of the whole world,[12] you who through him chose the apostles,[13] you who from generation to generation[14] ordain holy bishops: make, God of truth,[15] this man also a living bishop, a holy bishop of the succession of the holy apostles, and give him grace and divine Spirit, which you bestowed on all your genuine[16] servants and prophets and patriarchs; make him be worthy to shepherd your flock[17]; and also let him continue blamelessly and without offense in the episcopate; through your only-begotten Jesus Christ, through whom to you [be] glory and power in holy Spirit both now and to all the ages of ages. Amen.

PART III
EASTERN TEXTS

Armenian[1]

CANON OF LAYING HANDS ON *ANAGANOS*, WHO ARE READERS

Psalm 119: Blessed are the spotless.

And the priest says this prayer: Lord God, establisher and maker of all things, fashioner of humanity, who are glorified by the all-holy watchers[2] in your unspeakable and incomprehensible nature, Father and Son and Spirit of your holiness: regard our supplications, and sanctify this your servant N.; Lord that are strong and God of all, elect him, you who are holy and glorious. Make him worthy, through all wisdom and understanding, to perform the readings of your divine Scriptures. Preserve him free from all blemish, and through your mercy make us also together with him worthy to glorify Father, Son, and Holy Spirit, now and ever and to eternity.

CANON OF LAYING HANDS ON SUBDEACONS

Psalm 122: I was glad when they said to me, let us go into the house.

The deacon proclaims: Let us ask in faith and concord.

The bishop lays his right hand and says the following prayer: God of all and Lord of hosts, and orderer of all things that exist, who welcomes the praise-givings of those who truly glorify you. Lord, show your goodness to this your servant N., who alone are almighty Lord, through the Word begotten of the Father and by your Holy Spirit. And elect him among the godly, according to your great mercy. And render him worthy without shame to fulfill his ministration, with all readiness of will and meekness, through the compassion and mercy of your Christ; with whom to you, Father almighty, together with the Holy Spirit who gives us life and liberates, are due glory, dominion, and honor.

CANON OF THE LAYING OF HANDS ON DEACONS

Psalm 15: Lord, who shall abide in your tabernacle?

The bishop makes the sign of the cross on the head, and they cut the hair as far as the bishop's hand reaches.

Again they say Psalm 25: To you, O Lord, have I lifted up my soul.

The deacon calls upon the bema three times, turning him toward the east: They call N. from being a clerk to the diaconate of the Lord, to the service of holy Church, to its ministration, in accordance with the testimony of himself and of the congregation: he is worthy.

And then he kneels on the left [knee], and the deacons lay their hands upon his hands. The bishop lays his right hand on his head, and says the following prayer: The divine and heavenly grace, which ever and always fulfills the needs of the holy ministration of the catholic Church, calls N. from being a clerk to the diaconate unto the Lord's service and the ministry of holy Church; according to the testimony of himself and of all the congregation I lay hands upon him. Do you all offer up your prayers that he be worthy to serve in the rank of the diaconate before God, and the holy altar, all the days of his life.

Lord God, mighty and glorified by all, to your great and awful will and holy powers all creatures are ministering, on earth as in heaven, with unflagging obedience. More especially the rational and intelligent ones, appointed of their free will to wait upon you, accomplish your commands with great joy. We thank you, who in all things are mighty and lack nothing; but because of your love for humanity looked upon humanity, and chose for yourself a Church from among us, a temple of dwelling for your all-holy and glorious Trinity. And you have appointed in it deacons to minister to your holy Church. We pray you, Lord, and entreat of your beneficence, look with favoring eye from your dwelling-place which you have prepared upon this your servant, who has now had hands laid on him, for the serving of the holy altar. Uphold him secure in the calling to which he has been called. Set him far from all things evil, and strengthen him in good works. Increase in him love and faith. Give him the strength and grace of Stephen the apostle and first martyr, and first deacon and minister of your worship. To the end that, filled with the Holy Spirit, he may stand fast in the service of your holy altar, perfuming your Church with the incense of a sweet-smelling life[3] and with exemplary good works. May he cause himself and all your servants, near and far, to rejoice. And may he become worthy in due season to attain to the high rank of the priesthood; through the grace and love of our Lord Jesus Christ, with whom to you, Father almighty, are due dominion and power and glory, together with your holy and life-giving Spirit, now and ever and to eternity.

And the deacon proclaims: Let us all in concord supplicate with faith loving God on behalf of our bishop N. To the end that he may graciously vouchsafe him to his Church for a long time, with right teaching and exemplary works to shepherd with wisdom the Lord's people, conferring imposition of hands on those who are worthy, to meet the needs of the holy altar. May he live with innocent mind, and with spotless conduct abide before the Lord all the days of his life.

Let us make entreaty for N., his diaconate, that holily and irreproachably he may prosper in the work of the ministry of this holy altar, and receive lot and heritage together with all the saints in the kingdom of heaven.

And again for our blessed bishop N., for faith, for life and salvation of us all, let us ask of the Lord.

Make us to live and have mercy.

Thrice: Lord, have mercy.

The bishop says the following prayer: Receive the supplications of us all, and fill with your Holy Spirit this your servant whom you have chosen and called to the ministry of your holy table. Prosper him in all works of virtue, becoming his helper and protector in every season. Under the shelter of your all-powerful arm guard him fearless from the seen and unseen enemies of the truth, that he may walk without spot or blemish according to your will in all the ways of righteousness, and become deserving of eternal life together with all your saints; and with a spiritual and holy kiss may we all welcome him now as always. And may we in this present thankfully glorify Father, Son, and Holy Spirit, now and ever and to eternity.

CANON OF THE LAYING ON HANDS OF PRIESTHOOD

Psalm 132: Remember, Lord, David, and all his affliction.

The priest calls upon the bema, having turned him to the west, as the deacon. But they only change the name, "... this man from the office of deacon to that of priest. ...."

Then the candidate shall kneel down before the holy table, and the priests lay their hands upon his. The bishop lays his right hand upon him, and says the following prayer: Divine and heavenly grace that ever fulfills the needs of the ministry of the holy apostolic Church. They call N. from the diaconate to the priesthood, according to the testimony of himself and of all the congregation, I lay hands on him. Offer your prayers, all of you, that he may become worthy to serve in the rank of priesthood, without blemish before the Lord all the days of his life.

Lord God, almighty, all-merciful, all-provident, maker of all creatures visible and invisible, dwelling in light unapproachable and passing understanding, and the abysses of the deeps are manifest to your all-seeing eyes, around you stand the heavenly hosts, angels and archangels, principalities and powers, seraphim and cherubim, and all the fleshless armies, victorious, for ever thankfully praise and glorify you. You, Lord of all hosts, strong in everything and lacking nothing, of your benevolent goodwill had compassion on the lowliness of humanity; and separated from among all people a congregation of your own, holy Church; and named it your own body and member. You instituted therein priests, shepherds and leaders of your congregation: hear, Lord, now also the voice of our supplications; and preserve this man whom you have chosen and accepted as your servant for the priesthood, who now has hands laid on him; guard him unshaken in the priesthood to which he has been called. Graciously endue him with a sober mind, that he may vigilantly and cautiously keep your commandments, and love you with all his heart and all his strength, and with his entire understanding[4]; to the end that he may walk truthfully in the paths of righteousness, with a holy heart, with unfeigned faith, and abound in good works agreeable to your benevolent will; that he may stand firm and without blemish in the priesthood before you in the catholic Church, built and established on the rock of faith; without shame, to epitomize rightly the word of the preaching, to sow abroad the quickening and orthodox faith of the apostolic Church in all places to them that listen. Give him apostolic grace to expel and drive away the diseases of sufferings and all foul spirits from humanity; by laying his hands

Armenian

on them and calling on your all-powerful name, let him bestow in grace assistance and healing on the afflicted.[5] May he be worthy and meet to call down your Holy Spirit from heaven for the spiritual quickening of those who are born over again in the luminous font, whereby they attain to the mighty grace of your adoption and the inheriting of the kingdom of heaven. May he with faith order the dread and heavenly mystery of the body and blood of our Lord Jesus Christ, for the remission of the sins of those who worthily partake thereof. But may he also with due excellence accomplish all the offices of the priesthood. May he become a magnifier of the holy Trinity, and in recompense receive together with the blessed apostles eternal life, worthy of twofold honor[6]; through the grace and loving-kindness of our Lord and Savior Jesus Christ, who has invited and called us into his kingdom; with whom to you almighty Father, power, rule, and glory are due, now and to eternity. Amen.

The deacon proclaims: Let us in concord pray with faith for our blessed bishop N. To the end that God may vouchsafe him to his Church for a long time, with right teaching and exemplary works to shepherd wisely the Lord's people, conferring imposition of hands on those who are worthy for the uses of the holy table. May he abide with innocent mind, and with spotless conduct stand before the Lord all the days of his life.

Let us also make entreaty for the priest N., that devoutly and irreproachably he may advance and prosper in the work of ministry before the holy altar, and may receive lot and heritage together with all the saints in the kingdom of heaven.

And again for our blessed bishop through faith, for the life and salvation of us all, let us pray to the Lord. Make us to live and have mercy.

Thrice: Lord, have mercy.

And the bishop says the following prayer: Lord God, almighty, of all things that come into being; who sit on a throne not made with hands, and unseen are praised and magnified by deathless holy watchers, who with unresting voices in mutual concert celebrate your thrice holy and princely glory: we, your servants, in concord pray you incline to our petitions; and vouchsafe to us your bounteous compassion. Bestow on your servant the rank of priesthood, that with correct life and spotless conduct he may render to you profitable praise. Pour out upon him plentifully the grace of the Holy Spirit, with the sevenfold gifts of truth, of wisdom, of understanding, and of the weighty mystery, of strength, of reverence for God, and of your fear, O Lord.[7] May there be driven far from him all the subtlety and guile of the crafty enemy; to the end that, living in righteousness and by his own example teaching those who believe in you, he may truly shepherd the people; and for his actions and teaching may be called great in the kingdom of your Christ and worthily glorify you, O Lord. And may we all, having welcomed him with the salutation of holiness, and with thanksgiving and praise being at all times prepared for his all-powerful will, magnify the holy Trinity, now and ever and to eternity. Amen.

And they robe him, saying: Priests—

Reading from Isaiah the prophet: [61:1–6]

Reading from the apostle Peter's first catholic epistle: [5:1–4]

Alleluia. The Lord said to my Lord, sit. . . .[8]

Reading. Gospel according to Matthew: [16:13–19]

The bishop says the following prayer: Lord God, who are strong and pass understanding, God of glory and all honor; you have crowned with glory and honor your saints; you have bestowed prophetic grace among men; you have vouchsafed priestly honor; you have chosen the holy apostles, and have instituted in the catholic Church various orders of direction and government; you have raised up therein chief priests, have advanced and increased priests and orders of deacons, whereby is magnified the name of your advent, Christ God: now, therefore, Lord, Lord, illumine with the grace of your Holy Spirit this your servant, whom you have chosen for the calling of priesthood, that he may live before you a life spotless and free from blemish; and may serve your holy Church and your congregation without scandal and free from all the oppression of the evil one. And may we all, having welcomed him with a spiritual and holy salutation, as always so in this present, with unceasing thanksgiving glorify Father and Son and Holy Spirit, now and ever and to eternity.

Byzantine[1]

After the Trisagion, when the cantors have come down from the ambo, the archbishop stands on the step before the holy table, and there is given to him the scroll on which is written: The divine grace, which always heals that which is infirm and supplies what is lacking, appoints the presbyter N., beloved by God, as bishop. Let us pray therefore that the grace of the Holy Spirit may come upon him.

And he reads it in the hearing of all, having his hand on the head of the ordinand. And after the reading of "The divine grace," the people say, Lord, have mercy, *three times.*

And the archbishop, opening the Gospel, lays it on his head and neck, the other bishops standing around and touching the holy Gospel, and making three crosses on his head and laying his hand on him, he prays thus: Sovereign Lord, our God, who have established by your illustrious apostle Paul the hierarchy of ranks and orders for the service of your venerable and pure mysteries at your holy altar—first apostles, second prophets, third teachers[2]—O Lord of all, strengthen by the advent, power, and grace of your Holy Spirit him who has been elected to undertake the gospel[3] and the high-priestly dignity, by the hand of me, a sinner, and by that of the bishops who minister with me, as you strengthened your holy prophets, as you anointed kings, as you sanctified high-priests. And give him an irreproachable high-priesthood, and adorning him with all sanctity, make him holy so that he may be worthy to pray for the salvation of the people and to be heard by you. For your name is hallowed and your kingdom glorified. . . .

And after the "Amen," one of the bishops present performs the diaconal prayer, thus: In peace let us pray to the Lord.

For peace from above and the salvation of our souls, let us pray to the Lord.

For the peace of the whole world, the welfare of the holy churches, and the unity of all, let us pray to the Lord.

For our archbishop N., his priesthood, succor, perseverance, peace, and his salvation, and the works of his hands, let us pray to the Lord.

For N., now appointed bishop, and his salvation, let us pray to the Lord.

That our loving God will bestow on him a spotless and irreproachable high-priesthood, let us pray.

For our most pious and divinely-protected emperor, for this city, for our delivery, help, save, and have mercy, at the intercession of our all-holy, immaculate Lady, the mother of God.

And while this prayer is being said by the bishop, the archbishop, holding his hand in the same way on the head of the ordinand, prays thus: Lord our God, who, because human nature cannot sustain the essence of your divinity, by your dispensation have established teachers subject to the same passions as ourselves who approach your throne to offer you sacrifice and oblation for all your people; Lord, make him who has been made dispenser of the high-priestly grace to be an imitator of you, the true shepherd, giving his life for your sheep,[4] guide of the blind, light of those in darkness, corrector of the ignorant,[5] lamp in the world, so that, after having formed in this present life the souls who have been entrusted to him, he may stand before your judgment-seat without shame and receive the great reward which you have prepared for those who have striven for the preaching of your gospel. (*Aloud:*) For yours are mercy and salvation. . . .

And after the "Amen," the patriarch takes the Gospel and sets it down on the holy table, and then, having put the omophorion[6] on the newly-ordained, he kisses him, as do all the bishops, and the archbishop ascends with him to the throne, and the rest of the liturgy is completed.

FOR THE ORDINATION OF A PRESBYTER
After the holy gifts have been brought in and placed on the holy table and the mystical hymn is completed, the customary scroll on which is written, "The divine grace," is given to the archbishop, and when he has read it in the hearing of all, the ordinand is presented to him and kneels down, and he, having made three crosses on his head, keeping his hand imposed on him, prays thus: O God, without beginning or end, being older[7] than all creation and having honored with the

name of elder those who have been found worthy to exercise in this order the sacred ministry of the word of your truth[8]; Lord of all, may it please you that this man, whom you have been pleased should be appointed through me in irreproachable conduct and steadfast faith, should receive this great grace of your Holy Spirit; and make your servant perfect, pleasing to you in all things, and conducting himself in a manner worthy of this great dignity of the priesthood which he has received by your providential power. For yours is the might, yours is the kingdom and the power. . . .

And one of the presbyters performs the diaconal prayer, thus: In peace let us pray to the Lord.

For peace from above and salvation.

For the peace of the whole world.

For our archbishop N., his priesthood, succor, perseverance, peace, and his salvation, and the works of his hands, let us pray to the Lord.

For N., now appointed presbyter, and his salvation, let us pray to the Lord.

That our loving God will bestow on him a spotless and irreproachable priesthood, let us pray.

For our most pious and divinely-protected emperor. . . .

And while this prayer is being said by the presbyter, the archbishop, holding his hand in the same way on the head of the ordinand, prays thus: O God, great in power and unsearchable in understanding, wonderful in your counsels beyond the sons of men, Lord, fill this man, whom you have willed to undertake the rank of the presbyterate, with the gift of your Holy Spirit so that he may be worthy to stand blamelessly at your altar, to proclaim the gospel of your salvation, to exercise the sacred ministry[9] of the word of your truth, to offer you gifts and spiritual sacrifices, and to renew your people by the baptism of regeneration; so that, being present at the second coming of our great God and Savior Jesus Christ[10] your only Son, he may receive the reward of the good stewardship of his office in the abundance of your goodness. *(Aloud:)* For blessed and glorified is your most honored and magnificent name. . . .

And after the "Amen," [the archbishop] places the upper part of his orarion[11] *on the lower and puts the phenolion*[12] *on him, and having given him the kiss, he seats him with the rest of the presbyters. And then the deacon says,* Let us complete our prayer to the Lord. *And when the veil has been removed from the holy gifts, and the people have said the "Fitting and right," then the archbishop gives one bread from the paten into the hands of the newly-ordained presbyter, and he bows over the holy table holding in his hands the bread given to him and placing his head over it, and remains thus until the "Holy things for the holy people" is said. Then the newly-ordained returns the bread to the archbishop and communicates before the other presbyters, receiving also the holy blood from him who ordained him.*

FOR THE ORDINATION OF A DEACON

After the holy oblation has been made and the doors are open, before the deacon says, All the saints . . . , *he who is to be ordained deacon is presented to the archbishop, and after "The divine grace" has been said, the ordinand kneels, and the archbishop, making three crosses on his head and laying his hand on him, prays thus:* Lord our God, who by your foreknowledge send down the abundance of your Holy Spirit on those destined by your unsearchable power to be ministers to serve at your immaculate mysteries, Lord, keep this man also, whom you are pleased should be appointed through me to the ministry of the diaconate, in all holiness, holding the mystery of the faith in a pure conscience.[13] Give him the grace which you gave to Stephen your protomartyr, whom you also called first to the work of your diaconate [14] And make him worthy according to your good pleasure to administer the rank given to him by your goodness—for those serving well gain for themselves a good rank[15]—and make your servant perfect. For yours is the kingdom and the power. . . .

And one of the deacons performs the prayer: In peace let us pray to the Lord.

For peace from above and the salvation of our souls, to the Lord.

For the peace of the whole world.

For our archbishop N., his priesthood, succor, perseverance, peace, and his salvation, and the works of his hands, to the Lord.

For N., now appointed deacon, and his salvation, to the Lord.

That our loving God will bestow on him a spotless and irreproachable diaconate, let us pray.

For our most pious and divinely-protected emperor. . . .

And while this prayer is being said by the deacon, the archbishop, holding his hand in the same way on the head of the ordinand, prays thus: God our Savior, who with an incorruptible voice prophesied to your apostles, and proclaimed that he who fulfilled the work of the diaconate would be first of them, as it is written in your holy gospel: whoever wishes to be first among you, let him be your deacon[16]; you, Lord of all, fill this your servant, whom you have deemed worthy to undertake the ministry of a deacon, with all faith and love and power and holiness by the advent of your lifegiving Spirit—for not by the imposition of my hands but by the descent of your abundant mercies is grace given to those worthy of you—so that, free from all sin, he may stand blameless before you on the dreadful day of judgment, and receive the unfailing reward of your promise. For you are our God, God of mercy and salvation. . . .

And after the "Amen," he takes the phenolion[17] from the newly-ordained, and puts on him the orarion[18]; and having given him the kiss, he hands over to him the holy fan, and stands him fanning the holy gifts on the holy table. And then the deacon standing in the ambo says, Having commemorated all the saints. . . . *And after the newly-ordained has received the holy body and the precious blood, the archbishop gives him the holy cup, and he takes it and distributes the holy blood to those who draw near. This [is what happens] when the complete liturgy is celebrated; but the ordination of deacons and deaconesses may happen both at a complete eucharist and at a Liturgy of the Presanctified. When such an ordination happens at a Liturgy of the Presanctified, the chief priest enters and stands before the holy table, and with the ordinand standing near him, says in a loud voice,* The divine grace . . . , *and makes him kneel. And everything happens according to the aforementioned order up to the dismissal.*

PRAYER FOR THE ORDINATION OF A DEACONESS
After the holy oblation has been made and the doors are open, before the deacon says, All the saints . . . , *she who is to be ordained is brought to the bishop. He says aloud,* The divine grace . . . , *and she bows her*

head, and he lays his hand on her head, and making three crosses, he prays thus: Holy and almighty God, who through the birth of your only-begotten Son and our God from the Virgin according to the flesh sanctified the female, and not to men alone but also to women bestowed grace and the advent of your Holy Spirit; now, Lord, look upon this your servant and call her to the work of your diaconate,[19] and send down upon her the abundant gift of your Holy Spirit; keep her in orthodox faith, in blameless conduct, always fulfilling her ministry according to your pleasure; because to you is due all glory and honor. . . .

After the "Amen," one of the deacons makes the prayer thus: In peace let us pray to the Lord.

For peace from above.

For the peace of the whole world.

For our archbishop N., his priesthood, succor, perseverance, peace, and his salvation, and the works of his hands.

For N., now appointed deaconess, and her salvation. That our loving God will bestow on her a spotless and irreproachable diaconate, to the Lord.

For our most pious and divinely-protected emperor.

And while this prayer is being said by the deacon, the archbishop, holding his hand in the same way on the head of the ordinand, prays thus: Lord, Lord, who do not reject women offering themselves and wishing to minister in your holy houses in accordance with what is fitting, but receive them in an order of ministers; bestow the grace of your Holy Spirit also on this your servant who wishes to offer herself to you, and fill her with the grace of the diaconate, as you gave the grace of your diaconate to Phoebe[20] whom you called to the work of ministry. Grant to her, O God, to persevere blamelessly in your holy temples, to cultivate appropriate conduct,[21] and especially moderation, and make your servant perfect, that standing at the judgment-seat of your Christ she may receive the worthy reward of her good conduct. By the mercy and love for humanity of your only-begotten Son. . . .

And after the "Amen," he places the diaconal orarion[22] around her neck under the maphorion,[23] bringing forward the two ends. And then standing in the ambo, [the deacon] says, Having commemorated all the saints. . . . *After she has received the holy body and the precious blood, the archbishop gives her the holy cup, which she receives and places on the holy table.*

PRAYER FOR THE ORDINATION OF A SUBDEACON

When the bishop enters the diaconicon[24] and stands before the holy table, the ordinand is brought to him, and laying his hand on his head and making the sign of the cross, he prays thus: Lord our God, who through the one Holy Spirit have distributed your gifts to each of those whom you have chosen, who have granted diverse operations to your Church, establishing ranks of service in it for the ministry of your saints and of the immaculate mysteries; having destined with your ineffable foreknowledge this your servant to be worthy to minister in your holy Church, Lord, keep him blameless in all things, and grant him to love the beauty of your house, to stand at the doors of your holy temple, to light the lamps of the dwelling of your glory; and plant him in your holy Church like a fruitful olive tree, bringing forth fruit of righteousness; and make your servant perfect, in the time of your appearing enjoying the reward of those who love you; for yours is the kingdom. . . .

And after the "Amen," the newly-ordained subdeacon says three times, Those who are faithful . . . , *and gives to wash to the bishop who ordained him,[25] and so receives from him the lifegiving communion.*

PRAYER FOR THE APPOINTMENT OF A READER AND CANTOR

After he who is to be appointed as reader or cantor has received the tonsure, he is led to the ordaining bishop, and laying his hand on his head and making the sign of the cross, he prays thus: Lord God almighty, choose this your servant and sanctify him, and make him worthy with all wisdom and understanding to perform the meditation and reading of your divine words, preserving him in blameless conduct by the mercy and pity of your only-begotten Son, with whom. . . .

And after the "Amen," there is given to the reader the book of the Apostles, and he reads a little, and [the bishop] gives him the peace; to the cantor is given the Psalter, and he reads what is prescribed.

Byzantine

Coptic[1]

THE ORDER OF THE SETTING APART OF A READER

When he who is to be made a reader is brought in, let him be placed without vestment before the altar, with his neck bowed down. The bishop shall stand on the step of the altar. Those who have brought him into the midst[2] shall make a prostration to him,[3] while the bishop says to them: Do you bear witness that he is truly worthy of this order? *They shall bear witness:* Yes, our father, he is worthy. *Afterwards take a pair of scissors, make five crosses on him, one in the middle and four at the four sides of his head, and you shall pronounce the name of the holy Trinity and offer incense. Say the Thanksgiving and the Prayer of Incense, and this prayer, facing the west:* We ask and beseech you. . . . [A version of the first prayer from the Jacobite rite, p. 174.]

Say this prayer, facing the east: Great God, rich in his gifts. . . . [A version of the second prayer from the Jacobite rite, p. 174.]

Turn to the west, take hold of his temples, then say: Great and loving God. . . . [A version of the third prayer from the Jacobite rite, p. 174.]

Again turn to the east, take hold of his temples, saying: Our Master and Lord, God almighty, who knew from the first the number of his elect in the whole world and who called them from the first, who chose Esdras your servant.[4] You gave him wisdom that he might read your law to your people. You have now chosen your servant N., who is designated a reader. Give him wisdom and a spirit of prophecy that he may might perform the practice of your holy words for your people with blameless conduct, in the grace and compassion of your only-begotten Son, our Lord and our God and our Savior, Jesus Christ, who. . . .[5]

And he kisses the altar and the hand of the bishop and of those who are standing [with him]. And give him of the holy mysteries.

The archdeacon reads over him this catechesis: My son, this is the first rank of the priestly status to which you have been admitted. It is necessary for you to learn each one of the readings of the holy scriptures, the breath of God, which have been entrusted to you to instruct the people thereby. For this is a great work. The one who is assigned to it must be like a lamp shining on the lampstand, lest you fill the ears of those who hear you with what you read, but yourself be rejected. Instead, remember at all times the word of the Lord which said, "let him who reads understand,"[6] so that, through your good progress and your advancement in this rank, your worth might therefore be seen and you might be given approval to be advanced to the higher rank. Therefore, this is so that those who have brought you into the midst[7] might have a boast that they did well to give you a vote of approval in the proper time and order, in Jesus Christ our Lord, who. . . .[8]

Afterwards give him a book so that he may carry it on his breast. He shall kiss the altar and the bishop and those who stand with him. Give him of the holy mysteries.[9]

CONCERNING A SUBDEACON WHO IS TO BE SET APART

When a subdeacon is to be ordained, he is placed before the altar without vestment, with his head bowed down. He shall kneel with those who brought him into the midst[10] *before the bishop on the steps of the altar. Then the bishop offers incense and says the Thanksgiving and the Prayer of Incense and this prayer, with his face turned toward the east:* Lord God of hosts. . . . [A version of a preparatory prayer from the Jacobite rite, also found in the Maronite and Melkite rites, pp. 175, 189, and 204.]

The archdeacon: The grace which fills our deficiency shall come upon this brother whom we have nominated for this rank and order of the subdiaconate in the holy Church of God which has escaped from dangers and afflications. Pray, all of you, that the Holy Spirit might come upon him as we say all together, "Lord, have mercy."[11]

The bishop prays, facing the east: Yea, Lord, make him worthy. . . . [A version of a preparatory prayer from the Jacobite rite, p. 176.]

The bishop turns to the west and takes hold of his temples and prays: Our master and Lord, God almighty, who in the tent of testimony revealed those who adorn the temple as guardians of the holy vessels[12]; now, our master, make your face shine upon your servant N., who has been granted to be a subdeacon by the discriminating vote of those who have brought him into the midst.[13] Fill him with holy spirit so that he might worthily handle the liturgical vessels, that he might stand at the doors of the temple and might light the lamp of the house of your prayers. You shall plant him in your Church as an olive tree laden with fruit, which produces at all times fruit of righteousness, through the grace. . . .[14]

He turns his face to the altar: Look upon us. . . . [A version of the supplementary prayer from the Jacobite rite, p. 176.]

Sign his forehead with your thumb, saying: We ordain you in the holy Church of God. Amen.

The archdeacon: N., a subdeacon of the holy Church of God. Amen.

The bishop proclaims, saying: We ordain you, N., subdeacon of the church of N. in the city of N., in the name of the Father and of the Son and of the Holy Spirit. Amen.

Turn to the west, make three crosses on him, saying: We ordain you, N., subdeacon of the church of N. in the city of N., in the name of the Father and of the Son and of the Holy Spirit. Amen.[15]

Make three crosses on him. Say this prayer, turning to the east: We give thanks to you. . . . [A version of the thanksgiving prayer from the Jacobite rite, p. 177.]

The bishop turns to him and places the orarion[16] on his shoulder, saying: Glory and honor be to your holy name, Father and Son and consubstantial Holy Spirit. Peace and upbuilding of the holy Church. Amen.[17]

He kisses the altar and the bishop and those who stand with him for the communion of the mysteries. Hands shall not be laid on him. Then instruct him with this catechesis.

The archdeacon: My son, you have been entrusted with a good grade which is the subdiaconate. Therefore, you shall perform those things which have been assigned to you. They are: that you should follow after the deacon to assist him in the work of ministry, as he follows after the presbyter. It is necessary for you, therefore, to watch over the doors of the house of God, which is the church, so as not to allow a beast to enter it, neither a dog nor the heretics, at the time of the holy services. When the deacon proclaims, "Let none of the catechumens stand here nor anyone who does not receive of the holy mysteries," then[18] you shall pay attention to watch with great care over the doors of the church. Since, therefore, you have been trusted to touch that which is holy, the holy liturgical vessels, therefore you should realize the measure of the honor and the gift which has been given you as a wise and faithful servant who eagerly does the will of his lord, so that you may receive the fruit of the heavenly calling, through Christ Jesus our Lord, who. . . .

The seventh canon of Hippolytus: He is to have the virtues of the deacon, and hands are not to be laid on him, and he is not to be ordained; and he is to remain without a wife after testimony is given for him and it is certified by his neighbors that he has kept himself away from women. And glory [be] to God for ever. Amen.[19]

CONCERNING THE APPOINTMENT OF A DEACON

The person who is to be brought as deacon shall be chosen from the clergy because they are trustworthy for this ministry. He shall be brought to the bishop and they shall give testimony about him. He will be placed without vestment before the altar in front of the bishop, with his right knee bent on the steps of the altar. The bishop shall offer incense and say the Thanksgiving and the Prayer of Incense. Then say this prayer: Lord God of hosts. . . . [As before, p. 141, with the substitution of "deacon" for "subdeacon."]

The archdeacon: The grace of our Lord Jesus Christ which fills our deficiencies from the beneficence of God the Father and the Holy Spirit shall be upon N., who has approached the holy altar in fear and trembling, prostrate and lifting the eyes of his heart to heaven, to you who are in heaven, awaiting your heavenly gift, so that he might pass from the rank of the subdiaconate into the order of the diaconate in the holy church of N. Pray, all of you, that the Holy Spirit might come upon him as we say all together, "Lord, have mercy."[20]

Turn to the west, place your right hand on his head, and say this prayer of invocation: Our master, Lord God, the almighty, true and faithful in your promises, who are rich in all things to those who pray to you, hear us as we entreat you. Make your face shine on your servant N., who has been given to the diaconate by a vote and judgment of those who have brought him into the midst.[21] Fill him with holy spirit and wisdom and power, as you filled

Stephen the protodeacon and protomartyr, imitator of the sufferings of Christ. Comfort him with your grace. Establish him as a minister of your holy altar so that, having ministered as pleases you, blamelessly and irreproachably, in the diaconate with which he has been entrusted, he might be worthy of a higher rank. For it is not by our hands that grace is given, but by the visitation of your rich mercy it is given to those who are worthy of it. As for me, cleanse me from all sins of others, free me from those which are my very own, through the mediation of your only-begotten Son, our Lord and our God and our Savior, Jesus Christ, who. . . . [22]

The bishop says this prayer facing the altar. Say: Yea, Lord, make him worthy. . . . [A version of a preparatory prayer from the Jacobite rite, p. 178.]

Turn to the east toward the altar. Say this prayer: Look upon us. . . . [A version of the supplementary prayer from the Jacobite rite, p. 179.]

Turn to the west. Sign his forehead with your thumb, saying: We ordain N. deacon for the altar which has been named for its orthodoxy in the church of the city of N., in the name of the Father and of the Son and of the Holy Spirit. Amen. We ordain you, N., in the Church of God. Amen. [23]

Make three crosses on his face, naming the Trinity. Turn to the east. Pray thus: We give thanks to you. . . . [A version of the thanksgiving prayer from the Jacobite rite, pp. 179–180.]

Then the bishop turns and places the orarion[24] on his arm, saying: Glory and honor to the holy, consubstantial Trinity, the Father and the Son and the Holy Spirit. Peace and upbuilding to the one, holy, catholic, apostolic Church of God. Amen. [25]

A catechesis of the deacon: The work of ministry with which you have been entrusted, O my son, [is great[26]]. It is necessary for you, therefore, to fulfill those things which have been assigned you to do, since you have been enrolled as a son of Stephen, the first deacon: to visit the people of the Lord, the widows and the orphans and the afflicted. You shall gladden those whom you are able to help and supply their needs, being an example for them so that they might see your good works and emulate them from your behavior; following the bishop or the presbyter, informing him about the afflicted, so that he might visit them according to the canonical rules; honoring those higher than you in dignity—the presbyters, since they are as a father to you—so that you too might be worthy of the Blessed One who says, "Whoever will serve me my Father will honor"[27]; as the holy apostle Paul also says, "Those who have served well, it is a good rank which they have acquired for themselves and a great confidence in the faith which is in Christ Jesus our Lord."[28] Know, therefore, the measure of the honor which has been given you and bear it, which is the true blood which was given for the salvation of the world, which was given into your hands[29] for the glory of our God, Jesus Christ our Lord. Amen.

The bishop blesses him and gives him of the mysteries. Lay hands on him three times, while the clergy proclaims three times: Worthy.

The bishop says: N., a deacon of the holy Church of God. Amen.

CONCERNING THE APPOINTMENT OF A PRESBYTER

When a presbyter is appointed, let him first receive testimony from the members of the clergy about his good deeds, how he knows the word of doctrine well, is gentle, a comforter, charitable, and that his marriage was lawful according to the canon. But if he is ordained deacon, if he is not one already, let him be made a reader and a subdeacon and let him be given the blessing on another day. Let him be brought in vested as a deacon, with the orarion on his left arm, before the altar. A presbyter shall stand with the bishop. He who will be ordained shall kneel before the altar in front of the bishop; and he shall say the Thanksgiving and offer incense and the Prayer of Incense and this prayer, with his face toward the altar: Lord God of hosts. . . . [As before, p. 141, with the substitution of "presbyter" for "subdeacon."]

The archdeacon says: The grace of our Lord Jesus Christ, who supplies our deficiency through the beneficence of God the Father and the Holy Spirit, shall come upon N., who has approached the altar in fear and trembling and humility, kneeling and lifting the eyes of his heart to heaven, to you who are in heaven, awaiting from it your heavenly gift, so that he might pass from the order of the diaconate to the rank of the presbyterate in the church and the altar of N. Pray, all of you, that the gift of the Holy Spirit might come upon him. Amen.[30]

Pray therefore, facing the east: Yea, Lord, make him worthy. . . . [A version of a preparatory prayer from the Jacobite rite, p. 181.]

Turn to the west. Place your right hand on his head. Pray thus. Say:
Our master, Lord God almighty, who created all things by your
coeternal Word, exercising providence over the universe through
him also, according to your will which looks at all times on your
holy Church, [and makes it increase and those who preside in
it[31]], making them multiply and giving them strength to labor in
word[32] and deed; look upon your servant N., who has been
made a presbyter by the vote and judgment of those who have
brought him into the midst.[33] Fill him with holy spirit and grace
and counsel, fearing you, so that he might help and guide[34] your
people with a pure heart, just as you looked over your people
whom you chose and commanded your servant Moses to choose
for himself presbyters whom you ordained by an uncreated holy
spirit which proceeds from you.

Pray![35]

Yea, Lord, hear us as we beseech you, and preserve in us also
the Holy Spirit of your grace which is uncreated. Grant him the
spirit of your wisdom, so that, filled with works of healing and
instructive speech, he might teach your people in meekness and
serve you in purity with a clean mind and a willing soul, that he
might perform the functions of the priesthood over your people,
those who will approach him that he might renew them through
the regeneration of baptism. As for me, cleanse me from all sins
of others and free me from those which are my own, through
the mediation of your only-begotten Son, our Lord and our God
and our Savior, Jesus Christ, who. . . . [36]

Turn to the altar. Pray thus: Look upon us. . . . [A version of the
supplementary prayer from the Jacobite rite, p. 182.]

Turn to the west. Sign his forehead, saying: We ordain you in the
Church of God. Amen.

The archdeacon proclaims: N., a presbyter of the holy altar of the
holy catholic Church of God of the Christ-loving city of N.

The bishop proclaims: We ordain you, N. as presbyter for the holy
altar which has been named for the orthodox, in the name of the
Father and of the Son and of the Holy Spirit.

*He makes three crosses on his forehead, the symbol of the Trinity. He
clothes him with the vestment, saying:* Glory and honor for the all-
holy consubstantial Trinity, the Father and the Son and the Holy

Spirit. Peace and upbuilding for the holy Church of God. Amen.[37]

Turn to the east. Pray over him thus: We give thanks to you. . . . [A version of the thanksgiving prayer from the Jacobite rite, p. 182.]

A catechesis of the presbyter: Know, O brother, what is the manner of the ordination of which you have been made worthy, that is, the presbyterate with which you have been entrusted, since it is the great mystery of the new covenant in the order of teaching. It is necessary for you, therefore, to act and teach through good deeds rather than by word, remembering the word of the chief, Peter, who says, "I exhort the presbyters who are among you, I your fellow-presbyter and witness of the sufferings of Christ and partaker of the glory which is to be revealed: tend the flock of God which is among you, and supervising not with constraint but willingly, in accordance with God, and eagerly, not domineering those allotted to you, but be an example to the flock, so that, when the chief shepherd will be manifest, you will receive the unfading crown of glory."[38] You shall work, therefore, with the talent which was entrusted to you, that it might be doubled, so that you might receive the reward of the wise and faithful servant,[39] gathering together your people for the word of instruction, as a nurse nourishes her children,[40] that you might save yourself with those who hear you. Go in peace, the Lord be with you.

He who is ordained kisses the altar and the bishop and those who are present. They give him of the mysteries. The bishop shall lay hands on him three times and all shall proclaim three times: Worthy is N., the presbyter of the holy, catholic, apostolic Church of the Christ-loving city of N.

In the peace of God. Amen.

Date 1080 of the Martyrs.[41]

THE APPOINTMENT OF THE BISHOP AND THE ORDER OF HIS ORDINATION

After [it has been established] that his life has been as it should be, he is chosen by the whole people in accordance with the beneficence of the Spirit, being blameless, wise, pure, gentle, kind, free from care, vigilant, not a lover of money, but a lover of the poor, knowing the Scrip-

tures well, merciful, not involved in any business of this world, quiet, prepared for good works, so that he might be designated for an order of God most high. It is good if he does not have a wife, but otherwise, let him be asked if he has been the husband of one wife[42] in a holy marriage and likewise of middle age. And the clergy and all the people together shall bear witness to him. Let his deed of election be written and sent to the archbishop with some of the faithful members of the clergy and the people. If he is a deacon, let him be ordained a presbyter and let him be given of the holy mysteries and the pope[43] communicates him. And his ordination takes place on the Lord's day with the bishops and the clergy gathered together according to the rule. And after the night office and the psalmody and the doxology and the gospel, they begin the synaxis. And they read the Acts and say the Triadic, "Only-begotten."[44] Then the archbishop sits on his throne with the bishops. And the archdeacon takes the deed of election and makes a prostration at the footstool of the pope, and he gives the deed of election into his hands, and he takes it and makes a sign to those who have approached him, saying, Have you brought this? *And they answer submissively,* Yes, our master, *and the pope gives it to one of the deacons, and he reads it before all. As for the ordinand, his head shall be bowed.*

The Deed of Election of the bishop: In the name of the Father and of the Son and of the Holy Spirit, the consubstantial and incomprehensible Trinity. We write to the blessed, orthodox illuminator and father of all peoples, father of fathers and ruler of all [rulers] of Christ, Abba N., the holy patriarch, who became worthy of the throne of Mark the Evangelist, the man of true knowledge, who preached in all the world powerfully and with [the effect of] saving souls—since we too have desired to partake of the grace of your excellent prayers, we, your poor servants, for indeed it is difficult and impossible for a tongue of clay to proclaim [even] a part of your blessed virtues—which [true knowledge] our holy father, the Evangelist Mark, first preached in planting and strengthening the catholic and apostolic Church, [knowledge] about the coming of her true bridegroom, the onlybegotten Son, Jesus Christ, our Savior, who is perfected and who perfects everything, who for our sake looked down from his holy heaven, the God who searches hearts and reins,[45] who gave power to his servants and redeemed them by his precious blood, who in a loving way chose, for the shepherds of his rational lambs, the blessed patriarch on the orthodox throne, who is on the apostolic throne. For this reason he chose for us our honored and pure father. But now we impress on ears which are pure from all defilements and all scandals the griefs which have fallen upon us and the weariness of orphanhood which has found us because of our sins. It happened that our father, the blessed bishop Abba N., went to his rest, he who was seen with the manifestation of his righteous thoughts and his holy commands which draw near to God, and he was removed from us to the dwelling-places of rest by him who said to him, "Good and faithful servant, enter into the joy of your Lord."[46] The Church, therefore, remained without a shepherd. Then the whole council gathered, and they spoke to the multitudes about this matter. We prayed to the holy, perfect Trinity with a pure heart and upright faith, and it revealed to us that N., the servant of God, the presbyter and monk of the monastery of N., is worthy to be bishop of the Christ-loving city N., for his life is indeed filled with virtue, because he is a pious man, purified from the world, hospitable, one who gives instruction, having disregarded the world, hastening to hear the gospel of truth. And for the sake of the man who is of this sort, we make a prostration at your feet, beseeching you to make him bishop for us and a shepherd over us, so that through him those of the holy churches who are bent might be straightened and he might be salvation for souls and might tend us with acts of mercy and compassion. We too with holy and pure prayers scrupulously ask of our Lord Jesus Christ, our Savior, that he preserve you in the holy Church for many years, our holy father, the patriarch, the perfect servant of God, and that he favor you in all your works, as we say with all our people, "Lord, have mercy."

Let the archdeacon make this proclamation: The city which has loved Christ and heeds his law, which loves its father and which was not able to endure orphanhood, instead assembled and took counsel in order to seek after a father. They hastened with exactness to an investigation and went about to find for themselves a shepherd to tend them in a good life; and they prayed earnestly to God and he informed them of his perfect servant N., the presbyter and monk of the monastery of N. And behold, I have sent him to you with the presbyters and Christ-loving clergy, the document of his ordination being with him, according to . . . ,[47] that you might make him bishop of your own and a shepherd for you, and to be a steward of the holy churches. For the clergy and the people have given testimony that he is the replacement for Abba N., and that he remembers him in his prayers. Behold, therefore, we accepted your prayer when we saw your weariness and we did not wish to reject you, the Christ-loving people who asked that he should come into the midst.[48] It is necessary for you, our beloved and our loved ones, that you ask and pray with great force, all you who are assembled, that there may come upon him the gift of heavenly grace of the Holy Spirit, as we say with all the people, "Lord, have mercy."

After this, let the archbishop descend from the throne with the bishops and stand at the altar. The ordinand bends his knees at the altar before the archbishop, while everyone stands in fear and silence, praying with heart and reverence. The pope offers incense and says the Prayer of Incense and joins to it this prayer, facing east, while the new ordinand bends his knees upon the step: Lord God of hosts. . . . [As before, p. 141, with the substitution of "high-priest" for "subdeacon."]

Then let the bishops who are participants in the ordination assemble with him, and the archdeacon says these supplications, while the new ordinand stands: Let us all say, praying strenuously, saying, "Lord, have mercy."

The people: Lord, [have mercy].

Lord almighty who are in heaven, God of our fathers, we beseech you, Lord, hear us and have mercy on us.

Lord, have mercy.

Pray for the peace of the one, only, holy, catholic, apostolic Church, and the salvation of the people. Hear us and have mercy on us.

Lord, have mercy.

Pray for the life and rule and safety of our father Abba N., the patriarch and archbishop, and the rest of the orthodox bishops and the clergy and the Christ-loving people. Hear us, Lord, and have mercy on us.

Lord, [have mercy].

Pray for the forgiveness of our sins and our iniquities, so that the Lord may save us from all affliction and wrath and trial and rising up of our enemies. We pray you, Lord, hear us and have mercy on us.

Lord, have mercy.

Lord, save your people, bless your inheritance, visit the world with mercies and compassions. Raise up the horn of the Christians in the power of the life-giving cross. Pass over our iniquities, set right the works of our hands. Hear the prayer of your people through the intercessions of our Lady, the *theotokos* and holy virgin Mary, and the prayers of our blessed father Mark the Apostle and the choir of your saints. Yea, Lord, hear us, we who are praying to you, for mercy is from you.

Lord, [have mercy].

We beseech you, Lord, forgive our transgressions which we have committed voluntarily and those which we have committed involuntarily. Receive our supplication from us. Send forth on us your mercies and your compassions, for we all seek mercy from you.

[Lord, have mercy.]

And we beseech you, send your Holy Spirit upon this your elect servant N., on whose behalf this supplication comes to you. Lord, God of glory, we beseech you, hear us and have mercy on us. Lord, [have mercy].

The archdeacon: Raise your hands, bishops.

The bishops raise their hands and take hold of the new ordinand on either side and they place their hands on his arms. Let the pope pray, facing the west: Our master, the almighty, and Lord of the universe, father of compassions and God of all power, you are the strength that aids, you are the helper, the physician and the savior, the wall and the firmness, our hope and our refuge, the grace and the ascension, the hope and the life and the resurrection, and with you is the reconciliation and the salvation which is for all of us for ever, as you reconcile everyone. Give us strength, watch over us, guard us, protect us, save us, for you are the Ruler of rulers and Lord of lords, and Master of masters, and King of kings. You are the one who gave authority to him whom you previously caused to sit[49] and granted to bind and loose what is necessary, for you are the one who gives wisdom to him as an instrument through the Church of your Christ, over which you watch as a beautiful bride, for you are God, who is all-powerful and almighty, and yours is the kingdom and the glory, the Father and the Son and the Holy Spirit, now. . . .

The archdeacon makes this proclamation: The grace which gives health to those who lack it, comes on those who are assembled by economy in all the holy churches, and shall come now upon N., the servant of God, the presbyter and monk of the monastery of N., that he may become bishop of the Christ-loving city of N., that he may be in place of N., who went to his rest, whom the Lord has taken to him, and has left us his good remembrance. Pray, all of you, and ask the Lord, you who are assembled, that the grace of the Holy Spirit may come upon him, as we say with all our people, "Lord, have mercy."[50]

Turn your face to the altar. Say this prayer: Yea, Lord, make him worthy. . . . [A version of a preparatory prayer from the Jacobite rite, p. 183.]

Turn to the west, place your right hand on the head of the new ordinand. Let the archdeacon proclaim: Stand well, stand with trembling, stand quietly, stand with humility, stand with fear. Pray, all of you, with us and with the bishops assembled, and raise your hands.

The bishops stretch out their hands and take hold of his arms. The pope prays the prayer of ordination:[51] Great being, our master, Lord, God almighty, father of our Lord and our God and our Savior Jesus Christ, the one alone who is unbegotten and without beginning and ruled over by none; who always is and existed before the ages, who is without end and who alone is most high; alone wise, alone good, who is invisible by nature, the infinite, who possesses knowledge, the boundless and the incomparable, who is cognizant of hidden things, and knows all things before they happen; who dwells on high and looks on those who are lowly; who gave ecclesiastical rules through your only-begotten Son, our Lord Jesus Christ and the Holy Spirit; who appointed priests from the beginning that they might stand for your people; who did not leave his sanctuary without a ministry; who delighted to receive honor from those whom he had chosen: now also pour forth your princely Spirit which you vouchsafed to your holy apostles. Give, therefore, this unique grace to your servant N., whom you have chosen as bishop, that he may feed your holy flock and that he may be to you a blameless minister, entreating your goodness day and night, gathering the number of those who will be saved, offering to you gifts in the holy churches. Yea, almighty Father, give to him through your Christ the unity of your Holy Spirit, so that he may have power to forgive sins according to the command of your only-begotten Son, Jesus Christ our Lord, to provide clergy[52] according to his command for the priesthood, and to loose all ecclesiastical bonds, to make new houses of prayer, and to consecrate altars,[53] and that he may be pleasing to you in gentleness and a pure heart, offering to you blamelessly and irreproachably a pure and bloodless sacrifice, the mystery of the new covenant, a sweet-smelling savor.

The archdeacon: Let us beseech the Lord.

[The archbishop:] Vouchsafe, Lord, to fill him with healing graces and instructive speech,[54] that he may be a guide of the blind and a light of those who are in darkness, teacher of the ignorant,[55] a lamp in the world, dividing the word of truth,[56] being a true shepherd, giving his life for his sheep,[57] so that he may prepare the souls who have been entrusted to him, and may prepare himself also to act according to your holy will, that he may find means to stand with confidence before the dreadful judgment-seat, looking to the great reward which you have prepared for those who have striven for the preaching of the gospel. As for me, Lord, cleanse me from all sins of others and free me from those which are my own, through the mediation of your only-begotten Son, our Lord and our God and our Savior, Jesus Christ, who. . . .

When he has finished, he turns to the east, to the altar, and says, Amen. *Then he says this petition:* Look, Lord, upon us. . . . [A version of the supplementary prayer from the Jacobite rite, p. 184.]

Turn your face to the west. Sign the head of the newly ordained with your thumb three times, saying: We ordain N. bishop in the holy church of N., the Christ-loving city and its diocese, in the name of the Father and of the Son and of the Holy Spirit.

After this, clothe him with the sacerdotal vesture, the white tunic, the white hood, the white omophorion,[58] *saying:* Glory and honor to the holy Trinity, the Father and the Son and the Holy Spirit. Peace and upbuilding of the one, holy, catholic, apostolic Church. Blessed be the Lord God for ever. Amen.

Turn your face to the west, sign the head of the newly ordained with your thumb three times, saying: We ordain N., the elect of God, bishop in the one, only, holy, indissoluble Church of the unseen and living God, of the Christ-loving city of the orthodox N. and its diocese, to the glory and honor of the all-holy Trinity. Peace and upbuilding of the holy Church, to the vindication of sound judgments and holy manifestations and pure gifts, to a resurrection of the dead, to an imperishable pledge for ever. Amen.

The people: Worthy *(three times).*[59]

The archdeacon says these supplications: Let us all say, praying, "Lord, have mercy."

Pray for the one, only, catholic, Church, which is from end to end of the inhabited world, praying to the Lord, saying "Lord, have mercy."

Pray for mercy and peace for our souls, praying [and] saying, "Lord, have mercy."

Pray for our holy father, honored by God, the archbishop N., beseeching the Lord for him, saying, "Lord, have mercy."

Pray that the Holy Spirit may come upon this elect bishop with the imposition of hands at the coming into the midst.[60] Pray to the God of glory strenuously, all saying, "Lord, have mercy."

Pray that God make us worthy of the heavenly calling, all we who are assembled and those who are not assembled with us, saying, "Lord, have mercy."

After this, let the pope say: Peace to all.

And let him say this prayer, facing the east: We give thanks to you. . . . [A version of the thanksgiving prayer from the Jacobite rite, p. 186.]

After this the pope says: Peace to all.

And they set the new bishop at the right of the altar, the gospel on his breast. And the pope returns to the throne and sits, and they read the epistle and the psalm and the gospel according to custom. And [the pope] goes up [to the altar] and celebrates the holy Anaphora, and he partakes of the holy mysteries, and he gives to the bishops. And afterwards let him break the bread with the new bishop and give him of the holy mysteries [and] of the blood. Then he gives him his nose, and let him put his right hand on his head, all proclaiming, Worthy, worthy, worthy [is] N., bishop of the city of N. *They give [him] the Peace, and the pope stands [and] removes from him the sacerdotal vesture, and he clothes him with a black robe, and while he clothes him, the clergy chant what is appropriate. When they have finished, they sit according to rank on entering the sacristy, and they recite the praises and the acclamations. They give [him] the Peace a second time. The pope gives him the Peace and the bishops and the presbyters, to the glory of the Lord. Amen.*

[An exhortation to the bishop follows.]

East Syrian[1]

[After preliminary rubrics and prayers:]

The bishop recites in a low voice this prayer, which is to be recited before all ordinations, with his hands stretched out in a supplicating posture, saying: The grace of our Lord Jesus Christ, which always supplies what is lacking, by the will of God the Father and the power of the Holy Spirit, be with us always, and perfect through our feeble hands this high and awful service for the salvation of our souls *(and he raises his voice)* now and always and for ever and ever. *And they reply:* Amen.

And he signs himself, and not those about to be ordained; for he says that prayer for himself, just like the first prayer before the altar at the beginning of all services.

THE RITE OF ORDINATION OF READERS

The archdeacon proclaims: The readers are about to be ordained; pray for them. *And he raises them to the first step. He delivers into the hands of the ordinands the book of the psalms of David.*

The bishop says this blessing in a low voice, placing his hand on their heads: Sanctify these your servants, O Lord God, mighty and omnipotent, and by the abundance of your grace elect them with a good election, and by your mercy make them worthy to be entrusted with the reading of the holy Scriptures and divine words before your chosen people in your holy Church, while they are preserved blameless all the days of their life, through the grace and mercy of your only-begotten, to whom and to you and to the Holy Spirit we ascribe glory and honor and praise and adoration *(and he raises his voice)* now. . . . *And he signs the ordained from the front of their face through the middle of their head to the back, and from right to left. He replies:* Amen.

The archdeacon hands over to the bishop the oraria,[2] and he lays them over the outstretched arms of the ordained, and he delivers to them one of the volumes of readings or one of the two parts of the book of life.[3]

Here ends the rite of ordination of readers.

THE RITE OF ORDINATION OF SUBDEACONS

[After preliminary prayers:]

The archdeacon proclaims: The subdeacons are about to be ordained; pray for them.

The ordinand stands up, and the ordainer raises him from the bottom step to the middle step; but the bishop himself goes up and stands on the top step.

The bishop says this prayer for subdeacons, placing his right hand on them and extending his left: Look upon these your servants, Lord God, mighty and omnipotent, and according to the abundance of your grace elect them with a holy election, and by your mercy make them worthy to supply what is lacking in your holy Church; and grant to them, Lord, by your pity, that they may minister blamelessly before you, with a pure heart and a good conscience, while your wisdom perfects in them every virtue, through the grace and mercy of your only begotten, to whom and to you and to the Holy Spirit we ascribe glory and honor and praise and adoration *(he raises his voice when he says)* now. . . .

And he makes the sign [of the cross] over their heads. And he takes the book from the hand of him who is being ordained, and kisses him on the head, and hands the book to the archdeacon. Then he takes the orarion⁴ and places it round his neck.

You ought to know that readers and subdeacons are not to be signed on the forehead nor does the Spirit descend on them, but a special prayer [is said] which separates them from lay people for the closing of doors, for service before the Levites, and for reading the prophetic books.

Subdeacons are to be admitted as far as the lamp which is in the middle of the sanctuary, that is, outside the altar. And he shall instruct them to ascend the steps holding on to one another, and he who is first is to hold the edge of the bishop's vestment, but he himself is to stand at the door of the altar and instructs them to say: Let us pray, peace be with us.

Here ends the rite of ordination of subdeacons.

THE RITE OF ORDINATION OF DEACONS

[After preliminary prayers and psalms:]

Then the archdeacon instructs the ordinands to kneel on the right knee and keep the left upright; [this] signifies that they have received one talent. And they place both their hands on their ears in a humble manner and with face bent downwards; and they raise the forefingers of each hand upward. You ought to know that the extended hands of the deacon and the fingers over the ears and the pointing upward signify that he stands upright in service but obedient before the priest and bishop.

The ordainer hands over his pastoral staff to the archdeacon. And the archdeacon says: Let us pray, peace be with us.

The bishop says this "gehanta," that is, this formula of ordination of deacons, priests, bishops, and metropolitans, laying his right hand on the head of him who is being ordained, and extending his left in a supplicatory manner, and he says in a low voice: Our good God and our merciful king, *(repeat)* who are rich in mercy and abounding in compassion, you, Lord, in your ineffable goodness have placed me as a mediator of your divine gifts in your holy Church, that I may give in your name to the ministers of your holy mysteries the talents of the ministry of the Spirit, and according to the apostolic tradition, Lord, which has descended to us by the imposition of hands of the ecclesiastical ministry, behold, we present before you these your servants, that they may be elect deacons in your holy Church, and we all pray for them, *(repeat)* that the grace of the Holy Spirit may come upon them, and perfect and complete them for the work of this ministry for which they are presented, through the grace and mercy of your only-begotten, to whom and to you and to the Holy Spirit we ascribe glory and honor and praise and adoration *(and raising his voice)* now. . . .

And he makes the sign [of the cross] over the heads of those who are ordained. They respond: Amen.

The archdeacon says in an audible voice: Lift up your eyes to the heights of the highest, and ask for mercy from the compassionate God for the subdeacons N.N., who are being ordained and made deacons for the church of God to which they are appointed. Pray for them. *And he recites their names one after the other in order.*

The bishop say this ordination [prayer] for deacons, laying his right hand on their heads and extending his left in a supplicatory manner, and says in a low voice: Lord God, mighty, omnipotent, *(repeat)* holy and glorious, who keeps covenant and grace and truth with those who fear him and keep his commandments, you, who gave through your grace knowledge of the truth to all men in the manifestation of your only-begotten son, our Lord Jesus Christ, which was made in the flesh, and chose your holy Church, and established in it prophets and apostles and priests and teachers for the perfecting of the saints,[5] and placed in it also pure deacons for the service of your glorious and holy mysteries; and as you chose Stephen and his companions, so now also, Lord, according to your mercy give to these your servants the grace of the Holy Spirit, that they may be elect deacons in your holy Church, and serve at your pure altar with a clean heart and good conscience, and may shine in works of righteousness, serving at your life-giving and divine mysteries, and be worthy to receive from you the heavenly reward in the day of retribution for this pure and holy ministry which they minister before you, through the grace and mercy of your only-begotten, to whom and to you and to the Holy Spirit we ascribe glory and honor and praise and adoration *(and raising his voice)* now and always and for ever and ever.

And he makes the sign [of the cross] over their heads. They respond: Amen.

Next he instructs them to prostrate themselves on the ground and to rise again. Then he takes the orarion[6] from their neck, and places it over the left shoulder, saying: Adorn, Lord our God, your servant with the splendor of righteousness, and make his soul shine with pure works of holiness.

Afterwards the archdeacon delivers the book of the Apostles to the bishop, who offers it to be held by each of those who are being ordained; and he makes the sign [of the cross] on the forehead with his forefinger, beginning from below and moving upwards, and from right to left, and he says in an audible voice: Set apart, sanctified, perfected, and complete is N. for the work of the diaconate in the Church, and for the execution of the Levitical and Stephanite office, in the name of the Father and of the Son and of the Holy Spirit for ever. *And he kisses him on the head.*

The bishop takes the book from their hands and delivers it to the archdeacon.

[A hymn follows, during which the archdeacon takes the new deacons to kiss the altar and the bishop's hand. The bishop blesses them individually, and then they salute those standing around the altar, who kiss their heads and bless them. Concluding prayers are said if the eucharist is not being celebrated.]

THE RITE OF ORDINATION OF PRIESTS

[After preliminary prayers and psalms:]

The archdeacon approaches the ordinands and instructs them to kneel on both knees, extending their hands and placing them over their eyes in a supplicatory manner, their heads bent downwards and their vestment over the shoulder in the manner of deacons. And it is to be noted that the priest kneels on both knees to signify that he has received two talents; and the priest extends both hands above his eyes to signify that he has been given by God the ability and power of invoking the Holy Spirit, and of bestowing blessing, and of begetting spiritual sons, and of feeding them with spiritual food.

The bishop gives his staff to the archdeacon. The archdeacon proclaims: Let us pray, peace be with us.

The bishop says in a low voice: The grace of our Lord Jesus Christ. . . . [As before, p. 156.]

The archdeacon proclaims: Peace be with us.

The bishop recites this imposition of hands, laying his right hand on the head of the ordinand, and saying in a low voice: Our good God and our merciful king. . . . [As above, p. 158, with the substitution of "priest" for "deacon."]

The archdeacon says: Lift up your eyes to the heights of the highest, and ask for mercy from the compassionate God for the deacons N.N., who are being ordained and made priests for the church of God to which they are appointed. Pray for them.

The bishop says over them in a low voice this prayer for priests, laying his right hand on their heads and extending his left: Lord God, mighty, omnipotent, *(repeat)* creator of heaven and earth and all that is therein,[7] who chose your holy Church and established in it prophets and apostles and teachers and priests for the perfecting of the saints, and for the work of ministry and for the upbuilding of the ecclesiastical body[8]; you therefore, great God of hosts and king of all the ages, look also now upon your servants, and elect them with a holy election by the indwelling of the Holy Spirit, and give them the word of truth in the opening of their mouth,[9] and elect them to the priesthood, Lord, mighty God,[10] that they many lay their hands on the sick and heal them,[11] and may serve at your holy altar with a pure heart and good conscience, offering to you oblations of prayers and sacrifices of praises in your holy Church; and by the power of your gift may sanctify the forgiving bosom for the mystical birth of those who by your grace are called to participation in the adoption of sons of your majesty, and may adorn with works of righteousness the sons of the holy catholic Church for the praise of your holy name, so that for this pure ministry which they offer before you, they may obtain approval in the new age, and stand confidently before the dreadful seat of your majesty, through the grace and mercy of your only-begotten; to you and to him and to the Holy Spirit we ascribe glory and honor and praise and adoration, now

And he makes the sign of the cross over the heads of those who are being ordained. And they respond: Amen.

And he instructs them to prostrate themselves on the ground and to rise again. Next the bishop takes the vestment which had been placed on the shoulder of each one, and clothes him in it, and says: May the Lord our God clothe you with the vestment of righteousness, that you may be pleasing before him, pure, clean, and holy all the days of your life on earth, for ever and ever.

And he takes the orarion[12] from their shoulder, [and] places it on their breast. And the bishop takes the venerable gospel book and delivers it into the hand of him who has received the imposition of hands, and signs him with the sign of the cross with the right thumb on the forehead, saying: Separated, sanctified, perfected, consecrated is N. for the work of the priesthood in the Church and for ministry of the Aaronic priesthood, in the name of the Father and of the Son and of the Holy Spirit for ever. *And he kisses him on his head.*

Then the bishop takes the Gospel and delivers it to another. So he does to each one, however many there are. When all have been signed, the bishop takes the Gospel from them, and delivers it to the archdeacon.

[A hymn follows, during which the archdeacon takes the new deacons to kiss the altar and the bishop's hand. The bishop blesses them individually, and then they salute the priests and deacons around the altar, who kiss their heads. Concluding prayers are said if the eucharist is not being celebrated.]

THE RITE OF BLESSING OF DEACONESSES

[After preliminary prayers and psalms:]

Then the bishop recites: The grace of our Lord Jesus Christ. . . . [As before, p. 156.]

The archdeacon proclaims: Peace. . . .

The bishop prays: Our good God and our merciful king. . . . [As before, p. 158.]

The archdeacon proclaims: Peace. . . .

The bishop prays, laying his hands on her head, not in the manner of ordination but of blessing: Lord God, mighty, omnipotent, who created all things by the power of your word, and by your command chose pure and holy women, who were pleased with men and women alike, so as to give the gift of grace of the Holy Spirit to them: you, Lord, now also through your mercy choose this your maidservant for the good work of the diaconate, and give to her through your mercy the grace of the Holy Spirit, so that without stain she may minister before you with a pure heart and a good conscience, keeping without stain every virtue of good morals; and that she may instruct the assembly of women and teach chastity and good works; and may receive from you the consummation, the reward for all her good works in the great and glorious day of your coming; by the grace and mercy of your only-begotten, that we may offer glory, thanksgiving and adoration, now *(he raises his voice, saying:)* now and always. *They respond:* Amen.

[Psalms, hymns, and concluding prayers follow.]

Then she stands up straight, and the bishop lays his hand on her head, not in the manner of ordination but he imparts a blessing to her; and he recites over her a secret prayer for her strength, and commands her to avoid pride.

She does not approach the altar, because she is a woman, but only the oil of chrism. This is her function, to pray from her heart at the head of the nuns at the time of services and at the end of the prayers to say

Amen *aloud, and the others with her; to anoint women coming to baptism and to lead them under the hand of the priest, for it is not right for men to anoint women—even if they do it in our day—since a priest should never let his eyes fall on a woman.*

Here ends the ordination of deaconesses.

THE RITE OF ORDINATION OF BISHOPS
[After preliminary prayers and psalms:]

The archdeacon spreads the cover of the Gospel over the back of the ordinand, and the patriarch places the holy book on it, arranging the Gospel so that it faces the one who is to read from it. Then the archdeacon says: Let us stand ready. . . .

He reads the Petrine passages which he takes from Matthew and John [Mt 16:13–19; Jn 21:15–17]. Other passages are to be read on the backs of two or more bishops, which are taken from Luke, Mark, Matthew and John [Lk 10:1–2, Mk 16:15; Mt 10:16; Jn 13:34; Mt 10:8; 18:19–20; Lk 10:19–20, 23–24; Jn 20:22–23; Mt 18:18; Jn 20:21; Mt 28:19–20]. And the people respond: Glory to Christ our Lord.

The bishops place the closed Gospel on the back of the ordinand; and they place their right hands on his two sides until the ordination is finished.

The archdeacon intones: Peace.

The patriarch says this prayer in a low voice: The grace of our Lord Jesus Christ. . . . [As before, p. 156.] *He signs himself and not the ordinand.*

The archdeacon intones: Peace.

The patriarch says this prayer, laying his right hand on the head of him who is being ordained, and extending his left hand: Our good God and our merciful king. . . . [As before, p. 158, with the substitution of "bishop" for "deacon."]

Next the archdeacon says: Lift up your minds to the heights of the highest, and ask for mercy from the compassionate God for the presbyter and monk N., who is being ordained and made bishop over the city of N., *or* over the church of God of the place N. and all its region, to which he is appointed. Pray for him.

They respond once: It is worthy and just.

And the patriarch recites this imposition of hands over the bishop in a low voice, extending his right hand over his head and extending his left in a supplicatory manner: Great God, eternal, knower of hidden things, who created all things by the power of your word, and hold and rule all by the calm and sweet command of your will, who at all times do for us much more than we ask for and imagine, according to your power which is at work in us[13]; you who by the precious blood of your beloved Son, our Lord Jesus Christ, have redeemed your holy Church and established in it apostles and prophets, teachers and priests, by whose work might be multiplied the knowledge of the truth which your only-begotten Son gave to the human race; Lord, now also let your face shine on this your servant, and elect him with a holy election by the unction of the Holy Spirit, so that he may be for you a perfect priest, who will imitate the true high-priest who lays down his life for us; and confirm him by the Holy Spirit in this ministry to which he accedes. You, God, father of truth, holy and glorious, grant to him that he may feed your flock with uprightness of his heart; with his tongue may he preach the right word of truth, so that he may be a light to those who sit in darkness, the teacher of those who lack understanding, the instructor of children and the immature.[14] Clothe him, Lord, with strength from on high, so that he may bind and loose in earth and in heaven,[15] and by the imposition of his hand the sick may be healed, and wonders may be done through him in your holy name to the praise of your glorious divinity; and by the power of your gift he may make presbyters and deacons and subdeacons and readers and deaconesses for the ministry of your holy Church, and may gather and increase your people and the sheep of your pasture,[16] and may perfect the souls entrusted to him in the fear of God and all purity, and may stand confidently before your awful judgment-seat and be worthy to receive from you the reward which has been promised to faithful laborers; by the grace and mercy of your only-begotten Son. To you and to him and to the Holy Spirit we offer praise and honor, praise and adoration *(And he raises his voice)* now and always and for ever and ever.

And he makes the sign [of the cross] on the head of the ordinand. And they respond: Amen.

The bishops remove their right hands from his sides, and lift the gospel book from his back; and he worships and rises. Then the archdeacon takes the cross and the ring, the Ma'epra and Birona[17] *from the altar, and gives them to the patriarch, who puts the Ma'epra around him and clothes him with the Birona, etc., and says:* May the Lord clothe you with heavenly vesture, arm you with mystical and spiritual weapons, adorn you with works of righteousness, and beautify you with the gifts of chastity, that without stain or blemish you may feed the sheep entrusted to your reverence in the fear of God and all holiness, for ever. Amen.

He delivers the staff into his right hand and says: The rod of power, which Jesus Christ the Lord sent out of Sion.[18] May he himself feed you and through you lead those whom you will feed. Amen.

Then he makes the sign [of the cross] on his forehead with his forefinger, from below upwards, and from right to left, saying: Set apart, sanctified, perfected is N. for the great work of the episcopate of the city of N., *or* the place N. and all its region, in the name of the Father and of the Son and of the Holy Spirit. *They respond:* Amen.

Then he kisses his head and says: May Christ, who chose you to feed his sheep, strengthen you that you may make yourself acceptable to the will of his majesty even to the end. Amen.

Then he bows before the patriarch and kisses his right hand. The patriarch puts him in his proper place, where all present in the sanctuary salute him. Next they pray, chanting the song of the sanctuary, and they proceed to the bema, and the newly-ordained reads the gospel, preaches, and consecrates. If two are ordained at the same time, one reads and the other consecrates; if three, the third preaches.

Georgian[1]

*EKTENIA ON CONSECRATION AS BISHOP,
PRESBYTER, AND DEACON:*

Let us pray to the Lord: we beseech you for the salvation out of heaven.

For the forgiveness by God out of heaven of our reverend father in Christ Svimion, Catholicos of Karthli, and for the prospering of the works of his hands, let us pray to the Lord.

For the faith of him on whom hands are now firmly laid, let us pray to the Lord.

That the Lord may grant him a holy and blameless, unprofaned service, [let us pray] to the Lord.

For the acceptance of our prayers and the remission of our transgressions.

All-holy, glorious, blessed, incorruptible, cherished, our queen *theotokos.* . . .

The bishop gives thanks, and the deacon cries in a loud voice: By the good will of the Father, Son, and Holy Spirit, the intercession of the holy *theotokos,* perpetually virgin Mary; by the power of the life-giving and precious Cross of Mtzkhetha[2]; by the grace and faith of the holy catholic Church; by the intercession of St. John the Baptist, of St. Stephen the holy protodeacon and protomartyr; by the prayers of all the prophets, apostles, evangelists, patriarchs, and martyrs; by the authority and election and laying on of hands of our reverend father in Christ, Svimion, Catholicos of Karthli, by the witness and cooperation of *(if a Bishop, his name is here mentioned, and if not)* these presbyters: is consecrated this our brother *(here shall be named of what church it is)* from layman to reader/from reader to subdeacon/from subdeacon to archdeacon/ from archdeacon to presbyter/from presbyter to chorepiscopos/ from chorepiscopos to bishop, in the heritage of the holy catholic Church to minister to the holy churches, to pray for all Christians. Let us pray that the Lord may have mercy upon him.

This he says three times: Lord, have mercy and make him worthy.

And when hands are imposed for a bishop, presbyter, and deacon, the bishop first recites this prayer: The grace of God heals the sick, satisfies them that are in need: hands are laid on this our child.

Here shall be named of what church it is. And he [the bishop] pronounces a charge over those who have elected him [the person ordained] and have witnessed for him:

CONSECRATION AS READER

The first rank of the holy Church is the rank of reader, wherefore it is incumbent on you to have in [your] hands with reverence the divine books and walk in the first road so that they who hear you may find edification, and you yourself may receive a greater rank through never disgracing this your ordination, to the end that you may conduct your life heedfully, in purity and righteousness, and please God who loves humanity, and attain to greater service.[3]

PRAYER 2[4]

Sanctify, O almighty Lord, this your servant N.; set him apart, you who are holy and glorious, and make him worthy of all wisdom and understanding so that he may read your divine words, and observe them entire blamelessly, by the mercy and love for humanity of your Christ, with him to you glory, with the Holy Spirit, now, henceforth, and for ever.

On ordination of a subdeacon: on Sunday the bishop says in the hearing of all: Equal of deacons, O son,[5] emulate the gospel of the great God, behave yourself holily, strive after holiness with understanding, school yourself in meekness, be zealous in adoration, and be not remiss in fasting, to the end that the Lord God may give you peace and endow you with the greatest honor. *And the people say:* So be it, so be it.[6]

BENEDICTION FOR APPOINTMENT AS SUBDEACON

O God of hosts, God of truth, God of Abraham, Isaac and Jacob and all his righteous seed: God and Father of our Lord Jesus Christ, Father of mercies, O God, giver of all consolation,[7] look upon this your servant N., who is sealed as subdeacon, and favor him with the seal of the subdiaconate, to the end that he may serve unabashed the door of your holy Church, that being proved he may advance to greater [honor], for to you is fitting all glory, honor, and worship, to the Father and Son and Holy Spirit, now, henceforth, and for ever.

SECOND BENEDICTION OF SUBDEACON

Look upon and set apart for yourself this your servant, O almighty God, and make him prominent in good works through your mercy, and account him worthy unabashed to perform this service by your will and deed, by the grace and clemency of your Christ, with him and with the Holy Spirit to you glory [is fitting] now and henceforth and for ever.

BENEDICTION OF A DEACONESS[8] I

O Lord God of hosts, who before all women commanded Miriam the sister of Moses to invoke you,[9] who gave the grace of prophecy to Deborah,[10] who also ordained in this new dispensation by your Holy Spirit that deacons should not be double-tongued, nor too much addicted to wine,[11] but instructing in godliness, so that they might be an example of all that is pleasing: you yourself promote this your maidservant to the grade, to the end that she may anoint with oil those who come to your holy baptism and bring them to your holy font, and that she may become a deacon of your Church after the order of Phoebe, whom the apostle ordained as ministrant at Cenchrea[12]; grant also to her with vigilance to convince and instruct the young in the performing of your duties; give grace to her to utter all things in your name; to the end that serving worthily and without sin she may find herself emboldened to intercede in the appointed hour[13] of your Christ, with whom you are blessed, with the all-holy Spirit, now and henceforth and for ever.

BENEDICTION OF A DEACONESS II

You who created all things by the word of your command, and by the incarnation and labor of your only-begotten Son sanctified and equalized man and woman as seemed pleasing to you; you who gave the grace of your Holy Spirit not only to men but to women: manifest now also this your maidservant in this service, O Lord almighty, and give to her the grace of the Spirit, so that she may walk pleasingly and blamelessly in works of righteousness by the mercy and pardon of your Christ; with him to you glory [is fitting], with your Holy Spirit, now, henceforth, and for ever.

THIRD BENEDICTION OF A DEACONESS

Almighty Lord, who have adorned your Church with the ministry of the diaconate and have filled with the grace of your Holy Spirit the multitude of churches: you yourself, O Lord, promote to the grade of the ministration of the diaconate this your maidservant N. and vouchsafe to her reverently and holily to accomplish this fair ministry; accept her vow for good, grant to her the power to endure; for to you always is fitting glory, to the Father and the Son and the Holy Spirit, now and henceforth and for ever.

He that is ordained as archdeacon must have an attestation from the priests of that church on the holy altar of which he is elected to serve: he must be the husband of one wife, chaste, blameless and uncalumniated, tried in the nurture of the sick, zealous for orphans and widows, vigilant in night-watching, patient in prayer and fasting, reverently heedful of the teaching of pastors and observant of ecclesiastical ordinances in their entirety, and when he has fulfilled all this, let him be accounted worthy to stand in the order of deacon.

ORDINATION OF AN ARCHDEACON I

By you, O Lord, various forms of grace are bestowed on all the ministry of your Church—teachers, deacons, presbyters, ministers—grant also the grace of the diaconate to your servant *(name)*, make him worthy to serve your holy altar with true faith and perfect love, acceptably and unashamedly to fulfill your command, and enable him, confirmed continually in the perfection of Christ, to advance to the higher grade; for blessed, holy and glorious is your name, of Father, Son, and Holy Spirit, now and henceforth and for ever.

ORDINATION OF AN ARCHDEACON II

O God who created and adorned. . . . [Prayer for a deacon from the *Testamentum Domini*, p. 120.]

O Lord God, sovereign of all, who have maintained your grace toward those who fear your name, who favored men with the understanding of your truth by the advent and incarnation of your only-begotten Son, and manifested the apostles to confirm your saints and manifested deacons for the service of your holiness by your counsel: first of all Stephen and them that were with him you consecrated and appointed for this service, and now also set apart and manifest by the grace of the Holy Spirit [this] your servant for the ministry of your holiness, so that he may serve at your altar with pure intention, so that he may be notable in good works for the glory of your holy name, so that in the day of retribution he may find your goodness from above by the mercy and pardon of your Christ; with him to you glory [is fitting] with the most holy Spirit, now, henceforth, and for ever. Amen.

He who is appointed presbyter or bishop must have a credential from the whole people to the effect that the aforesaid is the husband of one wife, pure, spotless, and blameless,[14] experienced in laboring among the sick, a guardian of orphans and widows; and that he is worthy to be a father of the Church, a gentle and pure minister (to be said three times). He must manifest that kindliness which shall be required, so that they may merit the favor of remission, so that they may be vessels of the most holy Spirit, must have and bear the cross of the only-begotten Son of God, Jesus Christ.

But let the appointment of a presbyter be as follows: they are led up in front of the holy altar, and the bishop lays his hands on their heads, and they bend their necks and are blessed with this blessing:

CONSECRATION AS PRESBYTER I

You whom the celestial thousands and myriads wait upon,[15] O Lord; you have instituted an earthly ministry and have established for the people presbyters to be directors of good service; and now, Lord, we ask you, give to your servant N. your Holy Spirit, so that he may fulfill apostolic service by true teaching to present to you your Church,[16] may restrain himself together with his appetites by the power of your grace and by the loving kindness of your Christ; to him belongs glory together with the Holy Spirit, now and henceforth and to ages of ages.

CONSECRATION TO THE PRIESTHOOD II

God and Father of our Lord Jesus Christ. . . . [Prayer for a presbyter from the *Testamentum Domini*, p. 119.]

CONSECRATION TO THE PRIESTHOOD III

O Lord, sovereign of all, holy, glorious, who created heaven and earth, the sea and all that is therein,[17] who have established your holy Church and manifested therein apostles and prophets and presbyters for the edification and perfecting of your saints[18]; O God of hosts and king of glory, seek out now also and look upon your servant, and elect him with the election of the advent of the Holy Spirit to dwell in him, give him the word of teaching, for the opening of his mouth,[19] and perfect him as an elect presbyter, O Lord, sovereign of all, to the end that he may lay his hands on the sick and heal them,[20] may serve at your holy altar with pure and worthy heart and mind, to offer you this bloodless and reasonable sacrifice; and enlighten him in the doing of righteousness, for the edification of your holy Church, to the glory of your terrible name, O Lord, so that he whom you have made worthy to stand before this your holy altar may be enabled to serve joyfully in that day of your manifestation, by the mercy and grace of your only-begotten Son, with whom be glory to you, together with the Holy Spirit, now and evermore and to ages of ages.

[Then follow two prayers for the consecration of a *chorepiscopos*.]

CONSECRATION OF A BISHOP AND CATHOLICOS I

O God, who made all things. . . . [Prayer for a bishop from the *Testamentum Domini*, pp. 117–118.]

CONSECRATION OF A BISHOP II

O God who are great and eternal, and from whom nothing is hidden, who created all things by the word of your command, who have exceeded all we asked for or understood,[21] who by the precious blood of your only-begotten Son have established churches and manifested in them teachers, by whom has been spread over the whole earth the knowledge of your truth, vouchsafed to those born of men by the Prince your only-begotten

Son, whom from generation to generation you manifested your chosen ones: now also, O Lord God, look down on this your servant, and elect him with the election of the Holy Spirit, so that he may become a perfect priest after the example of the true shepherd who lays down his life for his sheep[22]; establish him by the Spirit of your only-begotten in this holy and glorious ministry, so that he may feed your flock with a right mind; and prosper him in the words of truth, and give to him the word when he shall open his lips,[23] so that he may be the light of those who sit in darkness, the teacher of those who lack understanding, the instructor of children.[24] Arm him and clothe him with strength from on high, to the end that, when he lays hand on the sick, he may work signs and wonders among your people, so that he who has been chosen by your will as a witness of your bounty to him and a shepherd of your people from our wretchedness may teach perfectly and edify all spiritually; so that he may stand before your holy altar, and in the terrible day of your manifestation he may receive, together with your faithful laborers, a goodly reward; through the loving-kindness, grace, and forgiveness of your only-begotten Son, with whom to you glory [is fitting] together with the Holy Spirit, now and henceforth to the ages of ages.

CONSECRATION OF A BISHOP III

And if they consecrate as bishop, let this prayer be offered by the archbishop; and if a Catholicos be appointed, then the [Bishop of] Manglis offers the prayer: You who conferred the gift of high-priesthood and bodily ministry on Israel, and have appointed for us a spiritual priesthood: hear us, O Lord, and establish your servant N. as a pastor to minister truly and guard the faith; to watch over your Church; to gather together the strangers, and to be overseer of your holy and faithful ones, so that he may receive the grace of your Christ and make your Church grow by the aid of the Holy Spirit, and stand before the glory of your Christ; to whom is due glory, to the Father, Son, and Holy Spirit, now and from henceforth and for ever.

After the imposition of hands on bishop, presbyter, and deacon, while the three prayers are recited and the honor is conferred, this prayer is recited: O Lord God of hosts, who have fairly adorned with beauty your Church, and through it those who minister therein:

seal him also upon whom our hands have just now been laid with the spirit of peace and all gracious order; for you are the enlightener and to you is fitting glory, to Father, Son, and Holy Spirit, now and henceforth and evermore. Amen.

Jacobite[1]

READER

[After introductory prayers, canticles, and Scripture reading, the bishop says secretly:]

We ask and beseech you, Lord God, accept this your servant as a reader in your holy Church; instruct him in your commandments; give him understanding of your justifications; and grant to him that with fear he may show obedience to you, rendering him worthy to be a chosen vessel and an honorable reader before you, that he may also find your mercy with those who through the ages have pleased you; (*And he raises his voice*) for you are a God who wills mercy and kindness; and to you is due glory, honor, and adoration from all, Father, Son, and Holy Spirit, now. . . .

People: Amen.

Bishop: Peace be with you all.

People: And with your spirit.

The bishop (secretly): Great God, and rich in gifts, who have granted orders to your Church and established grades of ministry in it, and poured out your gifts on your servants: sanctify this your servant also, and appoint him as reader, and make him worthy with all wisdom and understanding to perform the meditation and reading of divine words; and fill him with your gift, while he is preserved in blameless conduct; (*And he raises his voice*) by the mercies of your only-begotten Son, through whom and with whom glory, honor, and dominion are due to you, with your good, life-giving, and consubstantial most-holy Spirit.

Then the bishop turns to him, and holding both his temples with both hands, prays in silence this prayer: Great and loving God, in whose hands all things are held, and by whose command all things are controlled, who are near to all, and stand by all: look upon this your servant, who is presented by us to be a proclaimer of your holy words of the Old and New Testament, that he may expound to the people your holy words and your right precepts, and proclaim your divine and salutary doctrines, which you have appointed for the help and salvation of our souls. (*And he raises his voice*) O God, instruct him in your commandments and make him understand your justifications, and illuminate the eyes of his mind to the light of the knowledge of your commandments; and grant to him that with purity of heart and unfeigned faith he may perform their meditations and readings for the upbuilding of those who hear; to the praise and glory of your kingdom, Father, Son, and Holy Spirit, now. . . .

And he gives him the book; and carrying this, [the reader] gives the peace to the altar and to the priests while they sing the hymn; and [the bishop] gives communion from the holy mysteries to the newly-ordained together with the clergy.

SUBDEACON

[After introductory prayers, canticles, and Scripture reading, the bishop says this prayer secretly:]

Lord God of hosts, who have set us in the inheritance of this ministry, who know the minds of men and examine hearts and reins,[2] hear us according to the multitude of your mercies, and cleanse us from every defilement of body and spirit[3]; take away our sins like a cloud and our iniquities like darkness; fill us with your power and the grace of your only Son and the working of your most-holy Spirit; make us sufficient that we may be ministers of your New Covenant, so that we may be able, as befits your holy name, to stand before you to perform the priestly ministry for your divine mysteries; and do not abandon us to participate in the sins of others, but rather wipe out our own; and grant to us, Lord, that we may do nothing wrong through error, but give us knowledge to choose those who are worthy and to present [them] to you; (*And he raises his voice*) and accept as a subdeacon and make perfect this your servant who is here present and awaits your heavenly gift; for you are kind and very merciful toward all who call upon you, and strong is your power and that of your only Son and of your most-holy Spirit, both now. . . .[4]

People: Amen.

Bishop: Peace be with you all.

People: And with your spirit.

The archdeacon makes this proclamation: The grace of our Lord Jesus Christ, which always supplies our deficiencies, presents from the order of the brethren to the rank of subdeacon N., to be a subdeacon in the holy church of N. at the risk of those who presented him. Let us all now pray, that there may come upon him the grace of the Holy Spirit; and let us cry out and say three times, Lord, have mercy.

And the bishop says secretly: O Lord, make your servant worthy of the calling of the subdiaconate, so that he may deserve through your kindness, as befits your holy name, to labor and serve in the temple of your glory, and find mercy before you; (*And he raises his voice*) for you are a merciful and compassionate God, and to you is due glory, honor, and dominion, and to the Son and to the Holy Spirit.

People: Amen.

The bishop applies the two fingers next to the thumbs to the edge of the paten and chalice while they are brought round, and turns to him who is being ordained subdeacon, and while he places his fingers on his temples, he prays this prayer of invocation silently: God, who are from eternity, who anointed kings, who sanctified prophets, who called just ones, Lord, call this your servant with holy callings, and sign him with the sign of the subdiaconate; and appoint him as a good servant of your holy Church, bestowing on him the gift of your Holy Spirit. Grant to him, Lord, that he may love communion and the beauty of your house, and stand at the doors of your holy temple, to light the lamps of your house of prayer, and with fear, zeal, and a good conscience may fulfill the ministry to which you have called him. (*And turning to the altar, he raises his voice*) And plant him like a fruitful olive tree, which brings forth fruit of righteousness, through Jesus Christ our Lord, with whom is due to you glory, and honor, and dominion, and with your good and most-holy Spirit.

People: Amen.

Bishop: Peace [be with you all].

People: And with [your] spirit.

The bishop prays secretly: Look upon us, O Lord, and on our ministry, and cleanse us from every stain, while you give grace from heaven to this your servant, so that he may deserve by your kindness blamelessly to be occupied in this ministry to which you have called him, and find your mercy with all who through the ages have pleased you; (*And he raises his voice*) for you are a God who wills mercy and kindness, and from all is due glory, honor and adoration to you, and to the Son, and to the Holy Spirit, now. . . .

The bishop, turning, signs him with his finger on the forehead [with the sign] of the glorious cross three times, and says: He is ordained in the holy Church of God.

And the archdeacon cries out, saying: N., subdeacon in the holy church of N.

The bishop again says: N., subdeacon in the holy church of the orthodox which was previously named, in the name of the Father, Amen, and of the Son, Amen, and of the Holy Spirit in eternal life. Amen.

And the bishop again turns to the east, and prays this prayer secretly: We give thanks to you, almighty Lord, in all and for all, and we praise and glorify your holy name, because you have deigned to do with us, and sent your blessing on this your servant. And we ask and beseech you, O Lord, hear us according to the multitude of your mercies, and may the blessing of the subdiaconate be pleasing to you which has been performed by us on this your servant through your kindness; and grant to him that purely and innocently he may fulfill all his ministry; (*he raises his voice*) so that he may find your peace through the mercy of your only Son, through whom and with whom is due to you glory. . . .

People: Amen.

The bishop again turns to the newly-ordained, and places the orarion[5] on his shoulder, taking it around his neck and returning it to his left shoulder, and he says, with [? the clergy] responding after him: For the praise and honor of the holy and consubstantial Trinity, and for the glorification and upbuilding of the holy Church.

Then the bishop receives the oil for the lamps, and gives it to him, saying, with [? the clergy] responding after him: I am as a glorious olive tree in the house of God for the peace and upbuilding of the holy Church of God.

Then they begin the hymn and bring him near, and he gives the peace to the altar, and the bishop and the clergy give him the peace.

[After introductory prayers, canticles, and Scripture reading, the bishop says secretly, "Lord God of hosts. . . ." (as on p. 175, with the substitution of "deacon" for "subdeacon"), and then the archdeacon proclaims:]

The grace of our Lord Jesus Christ, which always supplies our deficiencies through the will of God the Father, with the power of the Holy Spirit, advances from the order of subdeacons to the rank of deacons this man standing here, who with fear, trembling, and true faith bows his soul before the holy altar and with the mind's eye looks up to the height to you, who dwell in the heavens, and awaits your heavenly gift, N., to be a deacon at the holy and divine altar of the holy church of N. at the risk of those who presented him. Let us all pray, therefore, that there may come upon him the grace and descent of the Holy Spirit; and let us cry out and say three times, Lord, have mercy.

People (thrice): Lord, have mercy.

The bishop prays secretly: Lord, make him worthy. . . . [A version of the preparatory prayer found in the rite for the subdiaconate, p. 176.]

Then the bishop puts his hands side by side and places them on the mysteries, and also extends his arms, and joins them three times over the body and blood, and when he has received his extended palms from the chalice, he turns to the ordinand and places his hands on his head. And again the bishop raises his hands, extending his arms and lowering them trembling on the head of the ordinand three times, while his eyes look up with fear. And afterwards he places his right hand on his head, and hides his hands and the head of the ordinand in his phenolion.[6] And when the bishop's hands have been hidden, and his right hand placed on his head and his left hand moving here and there, with his mouth the bishop prays this prayer silently: God, who build your Church and make it firm, who increase it, supplying those things which are lacking to it through your holy ones who in all generations have been ordained for its leadership; you, Lord, also at this time look upon your servant and send on him the grace of your Holy Spirit, and fill him with faith, love, power, and holiness; and just as you gave grace to Stephen, whom you called first to the work of this ministry,[7] so grant that upon this your servant may come aid from heaven. For not by the imposition of the hands of us sinners, but by the operation of your abundant mercies is grace given to those who are worthy of it. Therefore we ask and beseech you, free us from participation in sins, because you are he who renders to each according to his works.[8] Grant to us, Lord, that we may do nothing wrong through error, but give us knowledge to choose those who are worthy and to present them at your holy altar, that they may blamelessly exercise your ministry[9] for the growth and increase of your people,[10] and may not be a scandal to your Church; that they themselves may avoid eternal damnation, and we also may escape the terrible penalty of those who sin at your altars; (*And turning to the altar, he raises his voice*) so that, standing before your holy altar with purity of heart, we may obtain mercy with this your servant on the day of your just retribution; for you are a merciful and compassionate God, and to you is due glory, honor, dominion, and to the Son and to the Holy Spirit.

People: Amen.

Bishop: Peace [be with you all].

People: And with [your] spirit.

Deacon: Let us bow our heads before the Lord.

People: Before you, [O Lord].

Bishop (secretly): Look upon us, O Lord. . . . [A version of the supplementary prayer found in the rite for the subdiaconate, p. 176.]

And the bishop again turns to him who is being ordained, and places his right hand on his head, saying: He is ordained in the holy Church of God.

The archdeacon cries out: N., deacon at the holy altar of the holy church of N.

And the bishop again says: N., deacon at the holy altar of the holy church of the place of the orthodox previously named, in the name of the Father. Amen. And of the Son. Amen. And of the Holy Spirit in eternal life. Amen. *And he signs his forehead.*

And when he has made three crosses, he turns to the east, and prays the prayer of thanksgiving secretly: We give thanks to you, our almighty Lord, and we praise and glorify your holy name, because you have deigned to do with us, and poured out your gift on this your servant. Again we ask and beseech you, O Lord, hear us according to the multitude of your mercies, and may this ordination to the diaconate be pleasing to you which has been performed on this your servant through the coming of your most-holy Spirit. To the calling, add also the election, the sanctity, and grace of your goodness; and choose us and him for good, and grant to him that he may labor for you in the talent which he has received[11]; (*And he raises his voice*) so that with all who have done your will he may receive the reward of faithful and wise deacons, at the second coming from heaven of our Lord, our God and our Savior, Jesus Christ, with whom glory, honor, and dominion are due to you, with your good and most-holy Spirit. . . .[12]

And immediately taking the right hand of the newly-ordained, the bishop raises him up and places on his head the orarion[13] which he has received, saying: For the praise and honor and adornment and exaltation of the holy and consubstantial Trinity, and for the peace and upbuilding of the holy Church of God.

And he repeats it a second time, and the clergy make the same response; he lowers the orarion and places it over his left shoulder. The bishop also receives the thurible, and again says a third time, and they respond after him: To the praise, *etc. And he gives him the thurible to swing. And then they begin the hymn, and they bring him near, and he gives the peace to the altar, and the bishop puts incense in the thurible, and the deacon goes round to all, and they give him the peace, and he partakes of the holy mysteries.*

PRESBYTER

[After introductory prayers, canticles, and Scripture reading, the bishop says secretly, "Lord God of hosts. . . ." (as on p. 175, with the substitution of "presbyter" for "subdeacon"), and then the archdeacon proclaims:]

The grace of our Lord Jesus Christ, which always supplies our deficiencies through the will of God the Father, with the power of the Holy Spirit, calls and advances from the rank of deacons to the rank of presbyters this man standing here, who with fear and trembling bows the neck of his soul before the holy altar and with spiritual eyes looks to you, who dwell in the heavens, and awaits your heavenly gift, N., to be a presbyter at the holy altar of the holy church of N. at the risk of those who presented him. Let us all pray, therefore, that there may come upon him the grace of the Holy Spirit; and let us sing and say, Lord, have mercy.

The bishop prays secretly: O Lord, make him worthy. . . . [A version of the preparatory prayer found in the rite for the subdiaconate, p. 176.]

The bishop immediately places his palms on the holy body and extends his arms and joins them, receiving [grace] from the body and placing on the chalice; and again a second time he moves his arms over the body and receives [grace] with his palms and places on the chalice; and a third time he extends his arms and moves them over the chalice, and then he receives [grace] from the chalice, and with palms together and covered with the veil, he turns to the ordinand, and he places his hands on his head, and consecrates; again he raises his hands and spreads out his arms, and moves them and lowers them on his head. When this has been done three times, then he places his right hand on his head, and moves his left hand here and there; and when he has his hands covered with his phenolion,[14] he moves his left hand around his neck and face three times.

Prayer of invocation of the Holy Spirit silently: Great and wonderful God, who do glorious and wonderful things, of which there is no number, great and unsearchable in understanding, wonderful in counsel more than the sons of men; you are our God, who know the secrets of hearts, who observe thoughts and examine reins,[15] because nothing is hidden from the eye of the justice of your judgments; you, O God, know also the life of this your servant, you who know the future. You are he who in all generations appoint for the sacred ministry those who please you: appoint also this your servant as a presbyter and grant to him that with blameless conduct and unwavering faith he may receive the great gift of your Holy Spirit, so that he may be worthy to exercise the priesthood according to the gospel of your kingdom, to stand before your holy altar, to offer gifts and spiritual sacrifices, to renew your people by the baptism of regeneration. May he show himself to all as a lamp of the light of your only-begotten Son, who is co-eternal with you, to order and adorn your holy Church, to do good by the imposition of his hands; so that the word of your gospel may spread, and your name may be glorified in every creature just as in the Church which is entrusted to this your servant; (*and turning to the holy altar and raising his voice*) so that when he is present at the second coming from heaven of our Lord, the great God and our Savior Jesus Christ, in the order of presbyters he may receive the good reward of good steward-ship, through the abundance of the grace of your only-begotten Son, through whom and with whom is due glory, honor, and power, with your most-holy and good Spirit. . . .

People: Amen.

Bishop: Peace [be with you all].

Deacon: Let us bow our heads.

Bishop (secretly): Look upon us, O Lord. . . . [A version of the supplementary prayer found in the rite for the subdiaconate, p. 176.]

And turning to the ordinand, and placing his right hand on his head, he says: He is ordained in the holy Church of God.

The archdeacon cries out: N., priest at the holy altar of the holy church of N.

The bishop again adds: N., presbyter at the holy altar of the holy church of the place of the orthodox previously named, in the name of the Father. Amen. And of the Son. Amen. And of the Holy Spirit in eternal life. Amen. *At each invocation making on his forehead with his finger the sign of the venerable cross.*

And when he has completed three crosses, turning to the altar, he prays this prayer secretly: We give thanks to you. . . . [A version of the thanksgiving prayer found in the rite for the diaconate, p. 179.]

Again turning to the newly-ordained, the bishop takes him by his right hand, and raises him. The archdeacon says, Bless, sir. *The bishop takes the orarion*[16] *which has been placed on him and draws it over his right shoulder to the front, and says*: For the praise and honor of the holy and consubstantial Trinity; for the tranquillity and upbuilding of the holy Church of God. *And the clergy make the same response*: To the praise. . . .

And again the bishop receives the phenolion,[17] *and puts it on him, and a third time says the same*: To the praise. . . . *And they respond after him. He immediately begins the hymn. While the clergy recite the hymn, the bishop takes the newly-ordained by his hand, and brings him near, and he gives the peace to the altar, that is the table, and kisses the hand of the bishop. And afterwards the bishop himself gives him the peace, and he tells the others to give him the peace. And after this they give him the incense, and he begins to intone the general Sedro. And immediately the bishop signs a piece of the holy body in the chalice, and gives him communion, and then he commands him to give communion to the assembly.*

BISHOP

[After introductory ceremonies, prayers, canticles, and Scripture reading, the patriarch says secretly, "Lord God of hosts. . . ." (as on p. 175, with the substitution of "bishop" for "subdeacon"), and then directs one of the bishops to make the proclamation:]

The divine grace, which heals infirmities and supplies deficiencies, and to which belongs the care of the churches, calls and promotes N., the pious priest present, to the episcopate of the blessed flock of the city of N. Let us all pray, therefore, that there may come upon him the grace and descent of the Holy Spirit; and let us cry out and say three times, Lord, have mercy.

The patriarch prays this prayer secretly: O Lord, make him worthy. . . . [A version of the preparatory prayer found in the rite for the subdiaconate, p. 176.]

The patriarch, putting both his hands on the holy body, both extends his arms and gathers [grace] three times, while each time he also draws his extended palms over the chalice, and he stretches out and returns, he receives [grace] and draws back to the body; then he also moves round with a trembling movement three times over the chalice, and in the same way each time he brings his palms to the body, and he stretches out and returns, he receives [grace] and draws back to the chalice. And when he has done it three times and three times, then they cover his hands with the veil, and he turns to him who is to be promoted and stretches out over his head and consecrates. And two bishops hold with their hands the holy gospel book open over the hands of the patriarch. Then the patriarch lifts his hands and extends his arms, and raises and lowers three times over the head of the candidate, while the bishops lower it together with the hands of the patriarch, and they wave fans over the Gospel. And then the patriarch puts his right hand on the head of him who is being promoted, and moves his left hand here and there in a circle, while the patriarch himself prays this prayer, which is an invocation of the Holy Spirit, secretly, that is in silence, and he says: God, who created all things by your power, and have founded the world by the will of your only-begotten Son; who have bestowed on us the knowledge of truth, and made known to us your kindly Spirit, you who are holy, you who are princely,[18] you who gave your beloved Son, the only-begotten Word, Jesus Christ, Lord of glory, as pastor and medicine for our souls; and by his precious blood established your Church and instituted every priestly order in it; who gave us leaders so that we might please you by making the knowledge of the name of your Christ multiplied and glorified throughout the world: send on this your servant your holy and spiritual Spirit, so that he may feed and visit your Church which has been entrusted to him; may ordain priests, and consecrate deacons, and sanctify altars and churches, and bless houses, make effective invocations, heal, judge, greet, free, loose, bind, deprive, apportion, and separate. And give him all the power of your saints, which you gave to the apostles of your only-begotten Son, so that he may be a praiseworthy chief-priest in the honor of Moses, in the rank of Aaron, in the power of your disciples, in the works of bishop James,[19] in the seat of the patriarchs, so that the sheep of your heritage may be strengthened with you through this your servant. Give him wisdom and knowledge, that he may teach the will of your majesty, may recognize sins, and may know the limits of justice and judgments, may remove difficult crafts and release all bonds of iniquity[20]; (*He turns to the east, and raises his voice, saying*) for you are the giver of good things, the bestower of wisdom and divine gifts, and to you we give glory, Father, Son, and Holy Spirit, now. . . .

People: Amen.

Patriarch: Peace be with you all.

People: And with your spirit.

The patriarch prays this prayer secretly: Look upon us, Lord. . . . [A version of the supplementary prayer found in the rite for the subdiaconate, p. 176.]

Then the patriarch again turns to the newly-ordained, and the bishops remove the Gospel and turn away from him, and the patriarch signs him with his finger on the forehead, saying: He is promoted in the holy Church of God. *And they respond*: N., bishop of the holy church of the blessed diocesan city of N.

The patriarch again repeats the same proclamation: N., bishop of the holy church of the place of the orthodox previously named, in the name of the Father. Amen. And of the Son, Amen. And of the Holy Spirit. Amen. *At each invocation making a cross on his forehead.*

Then the patriarch takes his right hand and raises him, while one of the bishops says three times: Lord, bless. *And they respond*: Lord, bless. *Then the patriarch places on his head the cidarim and says*: For the praise and honor, adornment and exaltation of the holy and consubstantial Trinity; for the tranquillity and upbuilding of the holy Church of God.

The bishops and the whole clergy repeat this after him. And again the patriarch takes the phenolion[21] *and clothes him, and says*: For the praise. . . . *And again he takes the orarion*[22] *and places it on his back, saying*: For the praise. . . . *And they repeat it after him.*

Then they lead him to the throne and make him sit with his face turned toward the west; and the bishops and presbyters take hold of the throne and lift it and carry it round three times. Each time the patriarch begins and they respond after him: Axios. Worthy and just.

And the whole assembly cries out: Worthy and just.

Then one of the bishops reads the gospel from John: Truly, truly, I say to you, he who does not enter by the door. . . . *And ends where it says*: and they will be one flock and one shepherd.[23]

And after the gospel, one of the bishops leads this litany: Let us all stand up, and with diligence and voices pleasing to God:

For the one holy catholic and apostolic Church, which [exists] from one end of the world to the other, let us make request from the Lord.

For this our assembly let us make request from the Lord. That our election may be without offense and with grace, let us pray to the Lord.

For this bishop here present, to the Lord.

For his firm stand and for the fear of God, which [is] in the Holy Spirit, let us pray to the Lord.

That he may please God, let us beseech the Holy One.

For the church entrusted to him, let us make request from the Lord.

For the beauty of his life and service and his humility and right knowledge, let us beseech God.

That we may all deserve the victory of the heavenly calling, let us make request from the Lord.

Let us all earnestly pray the Lord for ourselves and for one another.

And again the patriarch turns to the east and prays this prayer of thanksgiving secretly: We give thanks to you. . . . [A version of the thanksgiving prayer found in the rite for the diaconate, p. 179.]

And the patriarch again turns to him who has been promoted, and taking his hand, he raises him from the seat; and they bring the staff, and the patriarch takes the top of it, and beneath the hand of the patriarch each of the bishops in turn takes hold of it, and beneath them all he who has been promoted takes hold of it.

And the patriarch sings aloud: The Lord send forth to you the rod of his power from Sion, and it will rule over your enemies.[24] *And the bishops and all the clergy likewise repeat this after him. And when the patriarch has said it again and a third time, and they have repeated it after him, then they leave the staff in the hand of him who has been ordained.*

After this they lead him to the table, and the patriarch says quietly to him while he listens:

[An exhortation follows.]

Prayer over him: God, who chose Moses and made him great, and by the rod in his hands worked signs and wonders in the land of Egypt; who also chose David from following the sheep to shepherd Jacob his people and Israel his heritage; who chose divine apostles and made them heralds of the proclamation of the gospel, and by their hands worked all glorious signs and all wonders; may he also now take your right hand and shepherd with you the rational sheep which are entrusted to you, equipping you with the clothes of an approved pastor and beautiful guidance; and may he level before you every height and stumbling-block; through the prayers of Mary the mother of God and of the divine apostles and holy fathers and orthodox teachers for ever. Amen.

And immediately one of the bishops leads this litany, all the clergy stand-ing in silence before the altar:

[A litany follows.]

After the litany they begin the hymn of one of the teachers with whose name he who is ordained is called. And the patriarch and the bishops give him the peace. The rest of the assembly is blessed with his right hand, and they give him the peace. And they lead him to the door of the altar, and he signs the whole people three times with the sign of the cross with the staff which [he holds] in his hand. And the whole people is blessed by him; and then they partake of the life-giving mysteries, and he who is promoted completes the oblation, and the patriarch commends [him to the divine favor].

Maronite[1]

N.B.: Because of the length and late date of extant manuscripts of these rites, only an outline of the principal formularies is here given. All are said by the bishop, unless otherwise indicated.

READER

The Lord God bless you. . . .
[An expanded version of the introductory blessing found in the Melkite rite, p. 201.]

[Then follow preliminary prayers, after which the candidate reads Ez 43:1–11.]

Lord of the heavenly hosts. . . .
[Said secretly: a version of the first half of the preparatory prayer, "Lord God of hosts," found in the Coptic, Jacobite, and Melkite rites, pp. 141, 175, and 201.]

[The archdeacon leads a litany.]

Grant to us, Lord God. . . .
[Second half of the above prayer.]

We present to your holiness. . . .
[Said by a deacon: an expanded version of the presentation/ bidding found in the Melkite rite, p. 201.]

The divine grace. . . .
[Said with the candidate kneeling on his left knee and the bishop's hands on his temples; a very much expanded version of the Byzantine proclamation/bidding, p. 133.]

We ask you and pray. . . .
[Said secretly, the bishop moving his hand over the candidate's head; a version of the first prayer for a reader in the Jacobite rite, p. 174.]

Great God, and rich in gifts. . . .
[Said secretly, the bishop moving his hands around in a trembling manner; a version of the second prayer for a reader in the Jacobite rite, p. 174.]

Great and loving God. . . .
[Said secretly, the bishop holding the candidate's temples; a version of the third prayer for a reader in the Jacobite rite, p. 174.]

We ask you, Lord God. . . .
[The bishop having first placed his hand on the consecrated elements and then on the candidate's head; another version of the first prayer for a reader in the Jacobite rite, p. 174.]

O Lord, who are great and rich in gifts, and marvelous in all your wonders, and exceed all in your hidden nature, and are exalted in your glory, and who instituted the venerable orders of your Church; grant and magnify in him the rank of your holy Church and all its sons, Father. . . .
[A prayer with no exact parallels.]

[Then follow vesting with the sticharion (alb/tunic) and orarion (stole)—accompanied by formularies resembling those used for the vesting of the higher orders in the Jacobite rite—a hymn, a reading from Isaiah by the new reader, further prayers, and a procession with a hymn. The new reader kisses the altar and the bishop, and receives communion. The rite concludes with a thanksgiving prayer, with some resemblance to that in the Jacobite rite (p. 177), and a dismissal prayer.]

SUBDEACON
The Lord God bless you. . . .
[An expanded version of the introductory blessing found in the Melkite rite, p. 203.]

[Then follow introductory prayers, including a litany.]

We present to your holiness. . . .
[Said by the archdeacon; an expanded version of presentation/ bidding found in the Melkite rite, p. 203.]

The divine grace. . . .
[Said with the candidate kneeling on his left knee and the bishop's hands on his temples; a very much expanded version of the Byzantine proclamation/bidding, p. 133.]

O Lord, make him worthy. . . .
[Said secretly, the bishop moving his hand over the candidate's head; a version of the short prayer of the Jacobite rite, p. 176.]

Lord God of hosts. . . .
[Said secretly; a version of the preparatory prayer found in the
Jacobite and Melkite rites, pp. 175 and 203.]

God, who are from eternity. . . .
[Said secretly, the bishop having placed his forefingers on the
edge of the paten and chalice and then on the candidate's temples; a version of the Jacobite ordination prayer, p. 176.]

God, who entrusted the priesthood to the renowned tribe of the
sons of Levi and the high-priesthood to Aaron and his sons;
you, Lord, by your command and your will chose priests and
Levites; you, Lord, also by your grace and deep knowledge
chose and constituted in your holy Church high, middle, and
low ranks of priesthood, that they might be for the glory of your
holy name and for the adornment and upbuilding and exaltation
of the holy Church, keeping and preserving all the service of
your holy house and of your holy mysteries and of your holy
dwelling by priestly sacrifices, that the priests might serve you
with their sacrifices, that the Levites might honor you in their
orders, and that these also might minister to you and keep the
door of your temple and the entrance of your holy dwelling, so
that they also, Lord, might be worthy of the high and honorable
rank of those who have gone before them. You also, Lord, be
pleased with this your servant and grant and make him worthy,
that he may minister to you and honor you in an admirable type
of the Levites and may have a place in your house and a clear
path to your holy altar; and you, Lord, send down upon him
your power and let your Holy Spirit come upon him, and may
your great compassion and your will rest on him, and through
your mercy may be fulfilled and consummated in spiritual service; *(and turning to the altar, he says:)* and we shall offer glory and
adoration to Father and Son and Holy Spirit, now. . . .
[The bishop having first placed his hand on the consecrated elements and then on the candidate's head; a prayer with no
known parallels.]

[A litany follows.]

Lord God, merciful and kind, God of truth and true, God of
Abraham. . . .
[The bishop having first placed his hand on the consecrated elements and then on the candidate's head; an expanded version of
the first Melkite prayer, p. 204.]

Look upon us. . . .
[Said secretly; a version of the supplementary prayer found in the Jacobite rite, p. 176.]

[Then follow vesting with the sticharion (alb/tunic) and orarion (stole)—accompanied by formularies resembling that used in the Jacobite rite (p. 177)—the delivery of the ewer of water, and a procession around the church, during which the subdeacon lights and extinguishes a candle and open and closes the church door, and after which he reads from the Acts of the Apostles. There are further prayers, a declaration that the candidate is ordained, similar to that in the Jacobite rite (p. 177), and a thanksgiving prayer, with some resemblance to that in the Jacobite rite (p. 177). The subdeacon receives a lighted candle, kisses the altar and the bishop, and receives communion. The rite concludes with a dismissal prayer.]

DEACON
The Lord God bless you. . . .
[An expanded version of the introductory blessing found in the Melkite rite, p. 205.]

[Then follow introductory prayers, including a litany.]

We present to your holiness. . . .
[Said by the archdeacon; an expanded version of presentation/ bidding found in the Melkite rite, p. 206.]

The divine grace. . . .
[Said with the candidate kneeling on his right knee and the bishop's hand on his head; a very much expanded version of the Byzantine proclamation/bidding, p. 133.]

O Lord, make him worthy . . .
[Said secretly; a version of the short prayer of the Jacobite rite, p. 178.]

Lord God of hosts. . . .
[Said secretly; a version of the preparatory prayer found in the Jacobite and Melkite rites, pp. 178 and 205.]

God, who build your Church. . . .
[Said secretly; a version of the Jacobite ordination prayer, the bishop having first placed his hand three times on the consecrated elements and then on the candidate's head, as in the Jacobite rite, p. 178.]

You are holy, Lord God, who dwell in holy ones, and in the holy
your will rests and you are worshiped by holy and spiritual ministers; who bestowed on this our lowly human nature those holy
and spiritual mysteries which by your goodness and grace were
conferred on the weak human race, that made partakers of this
spiritual ministry of holy angels, we might be filled with your
holiness, hope, love, faith, and piety. And just as grace was
given to your holy servants who were appointed by your apostles and elected deacons in holy churches and in faithful monas-
teries, so may your servant N. be pleasing to you, Lord God,
and grant him help and grace from your heaven; for not by the
imposition of our sinful and tiny hands but by the descent of
your divine mercy is the grace of your Holy Spirit conferred on
all those whom you have made suitable, that by it they may be
worthy to approach you. As we sinners pray and beseech your
many mercies for this your servant, confirm him in orthodox
faith and plant in him your truth, and may be strengthened in
this mystic ministry for which you have made him suitable and
worthy, and may he be, Lord, a mirror of good works for your
blessed and faithful people, while he stands before you and your
holy altar all the days of his life purely, justly, chastely, reverently, splendidly, and carefully, and show forth the perfect and
correct ministry which the kindness of your mercy has prepared
for him through this rank which he has received by your grace;
and grant to him in this age and the age to come, that with
honor and your holiness he may perform all things fittingly for
your praise and for the upbuilding of your faithful people, Lord,
in everything which he says, does, and works, that he may be
the light and salt of your holy Church; (and turning to the altar, he
raises his voice and says:) through your grace and through the love
for humanity of your only-begotten Son and through the descent
of your most-holy Spirit, now. . . .
[Said secretly, the bishop having first placed his hand on the
consecrated elements and then on the candidate's head; a prayer
with no known parallels.]

[The archdeacon leads a litany, with a concluding prayer said by
the bishop.]

You are holy and glorious, Lord, who made your angels spirit
and your ministers a burning fire,[2] before whom stand a thousand thousand, and myriads of myriads glorify the honor of
your dominion; cherubim with the great sound of their voices

bless your eternity, and seraphim with the movement of their wings sanctify your hidden nature; fire is contained in your ministry and a swift spirit is for your honor. Thus since by your good will through your perpetual mercy from the beginning you concerned yourself with the weak and lowly human race, Lord, while you made for yourself glorifiers and ministers from the earthly race, we acknowledge your mercy, Lord, who kindly brought yourself down to us, that your greatness might be served by earthly as well as spiritual beings. May it be pleasing to you, Lord, and by your great mercy grant us forgiveness which is from you, and grant a spiritual ministry to this your servant N., who has poured out his soul before you in the hope of your grace, that he may receive from you the splendid yoke of your spiritual ministry. Fill him, Lord, with your hidden power, let your Holy Spirit descend upon him, and may he receive through this imposition of hands a good gift, that he may be a deacon of your spiritual mysteries and therein may glorify your holy name and adorn your propitiatory altar and through him gladly and joyfully the ministry of the most-holy Trinity may be shown forth and in him the will of your divinity may be fulfilled and he may serve your mysteries reverently and may stand splendidly before your altar and praise you; *(and turning to the altar, he says:)* and let us offer praise to the name of the praiseworthy Trinity, Father. . . .
[The bishop having first placed his hand on the consecrated elements and then on the candidate's head; a prayer with no known parallels.]

Look upon us. . . .
[Said secretly; a version of the supplementary prayer found in the Jacobite rite, p. 179.]

Lord God, upholding all and ruling all, who by this diaconal ministry. . . .
[The bishop having first placed his hand on the consecrated elements and then on the candidate's head; a version of the first Melkite prayer, p. 206.]

Lord God of all, who by the goodness of your knowledge gave a holy gift to those. . . .
[The bishop having first placed his hand on the consecrated elements and then on the candidate's head; a version of the first Byzantine/third Melkite prayer, pp. 136 and 207.]

Christ, God, Word, who are holy and the redeemer of all who
fear you, you, Lord, who prophesied to your blessed apostles . . .
[The bishop having first placed his hand on the consecrated elements and then on the candidate's head; a version of the second
Byzantine prayer, p. 137.]

[The rite continues with a signing with the cross, vesting with
the sticharion (alb/tunic) and orarion (stole)—accompanied by formularies resembling that used in the Jacobite rite (p. 180)—a
hymn, a reading from 1 Timothy by the new deacon, and further
prayers and hymns, during which the new deacon performs actions which symbolize the liturgical duties of his office—
incensing, carrying the Epistle book in procession, and waving
the chalice veil. Two further prayers are said by the bishop with
his right hand on the deacon's head and holding in his left hand
the paten during the first prayer and the chalice during the second. Then follow a declaration that the candidate is ordained,
similar to that in the Jacobite rite (p. 179), and a thanksgiving
prayer, with some resemblance to that in the Jacobite rite (p.
179). The deacon kisses the altar and the bishop, and receives
communion. The rite concludes with a second, longer version of
the thanksgiving prayer, a dismissal prayer, and an exhortation
to the deacon.]

PRESBYTER

The Lord God bless you. . . .
[An expanded version of the introductory blessing found in the
Melkite rite, p. 208.]

[Then follow preliminary prayers, including a litany.]

We present to your holiness. . . .
[Said by the archdeacon; an expanded version of the
presentation/bidding formula found in the Melkite rite, p. 209.]

The divine grace. . . .
[Said with the candidate kneeling on both knees and the bish-
op's hand on his head; a very much expanded version of the
Byzantine proclamation/bidding, p. 133.]

O Lord, make him worthy. . . .
[Said secretly; a version of the short prayer of the Jacobite rite, p.
181.]

Lord God of hosts. . . .
[Said secretly; a version of the preparatory prayer found in the Jacobite and Melkite rites, pp. 180 and 208.]

Great and wonderful God. . . .
[Said secretly; a version of the Jacobite ordination prayer, the bishop having first placed his hand three times on the consecrated elements and then on the candidate's head, as in the Jacobite rite, p. 181.]

Great and wonderful God. . . .
[The bishop having first placed his hand on the consecrated elements and then on the candidate's head; a further, expanded, version of the above prayer.]

Lord, mighty God and Lord of all, to the honor of whose dominion thousands of thousands and myriads of myriads of celestial powers are joined in fear and trembling, and with great excitement minister, glorify, sanctify, and bless and cry out without rest; you also by your grace and your many mercies have constituted earthly and sinful men for your ministry and made and raised up from them priests and chief-priests to rule your people and shepherd your rational sheep. Now also, Lord God, we pray you and beseech your many mercies, that you would look on us with the eye of your mercy and strengthen this your servant N., who bends his neck before your holy altar and before our lowliness, that he may receive from us sinners this imposition of hands of your Holy Spirit, that he may fulfill this angelic ministry and be worthy to minister your true and divine doctrine for the strength and stability of the holy Church. You, our Lord God, perfect him through this priesthood and imposition of hands, which he receives from you today through us sinners and the indwelling of your Holy Spirit and the help of your grace; *(and turning to the altar, he says:)* for you are a god of many gifts and rich in mercy, and to you we offer glory and adoration and to your only-begotten Son and your living, holy, good, venerable, life-giving and consubstantial Spirit, now. . . .
[The bishop having first placed his hand on the consecrated elements and then on the candidate's head; a prayer with some slight similarity to the first Georgian/second Melkite prayers for a presbyter, pp. 170 and 210.]

Lord God, who comprehend all things by your will, who created man and filled him the breath of your spirit and perfected him

with all his properties, understanding and wisdom and divine
knowledge; who distributed to us divine and magnificent and
wonderful gifts and constituted us in your holy Church pastors,
priests and reverend teachers and rulers, when we were not worthy to set foot on the threshold of its doors because of our sins
and wickednesses: and now, Lord God, we pray and beseech
you that you would send your Holy Spirit on this your servant
N., and through participation in it he may be worthy of the rank
of the presbyterate to which, Lord, you have called him and constituted him before the holy altar of your glory, that he may do
your good and acceptable will, performing and fulfilling the pure
services of all your holy Church, and may offer good sacrifices
and perfect burnt-offerings and spiritual oblations; and grant to
him, Lord, that in this spiritual rank he may prosper in all your
commandments and keep your laws, following every way of righteousness, and may be pleasing to you, Lord, in all his works
and his excellent deeds, *(and turning to the altar, he says:)* giving
thanks to you and adoring and glorifying all the days of his life,
Lord, giver of good things and of excellent and heavenly gifts,
Father. . . .
[The bishop placing his hand on the candidate's head; a prayer
with no known parallels.]

[A hymn follows.]

Holy God, Father of truth. . . .
[Said while the bishop anoints the hands of the new presbyter—
a ceremony added under Roman influence; a prayer with no
known parallels.]

Look upon us, O Lord. . . .
[Said secretly; a version of the supplementary prayer found in
the Jacobite rite, p. 182.]

[Then follow a signing with the cross, a declaration that the candidate is ordained, similar to that in the Jacobite rite (p. 182), a
thanksgiving prayer, with some resemblance to that in the Jacobite rite (p. 182), and the vesting of the newly-ordained. After
readings and a litany, the presbyter performs actions which symbolize the liturgical duties of his office—incensing, and carrying
the Gospel book and then the paten in procession while hymns
are sung.]

O Lord God, from you we ask and beseech your mercy. . . .

[The bishop placing his hand on the presbyter's head together with the paten; a prayer with no known parallels.]

Blessed are you, Lord God. . . .
[The bishop placing the cross on the presbyter's head; an expanded version of the fourth prayer for a presbyter in the Melkite rite, p. 211.]

[After the exchange of the kiss and the reception of communion, the rite concludes with further prayers, including a second, longer version of the thanksgiving prayer, and an exhortation to the new presbyter.]

BISHOP
[Preliminary prayers.]

Lord of heavenly and divine hosts. . . .
[Said secretly; a version of the preparatory prayer found in the Jacobite and Melkite rites, pp. 183 and 201.]

[The ordinand reads a lengthy declaration of obedience to the canons.]

We present to your holiness. . . .
[Said by one of the two bishops who present the candidate; a presentation/bidding formula with similarities to that in the Melkite rite for a presbyter, p. 209.]

The divine grace. . . .
[Said with the candidate kneeling on both knees and the patriarch's hand on his head; a very much expanded version of the Byzantine proclamation/bidding, p. 133.]

O Lord God, make this your servant worthy. . . .
[Said secretly, with the patriarch's hands on the consecrated elements; a version of the short prayer of the Jacobite rite, p. 183.]

God, who adorn your universal Church by these high-priests through the imposition of hands; who can do all things; adorn this your servant also, whom you have made worthy to receive the high order of bishops from you, with all virtues and keep him in stability and peace and fill [him] with all the attributes of faith and charity and power and holiness through the illumination of your living and holy and life-giving Spirit, and not now by the imposition of my weak hand but by the descent of the

Holy Spirit, that we may be free from all our sins on the terrible
day of judgment and may stand without stain before you and
receive the true reward through your coming; by your grace and
the mercies and kindness of your only-begotten Son and of your
good and most-holy Spirit.
[Said with the patriarch's hand on the candidate's head, while
some bishops hold the gospel book over his hands and others
hold fans over the book; a prayer with no known parallels.]

God of gods and Lord of lords, who sit on the chariot of your
glory in the highest and your will is done in the lowest depths,
who have joined to the honor of your ministry assemblies burning with flame, wonderful in appearance, and amazing in like-
ness, and have established innumerable worlds of light and infinite hosts of the Spirit, which offer sanctifications and send up
praises and lift up glorification to you, Lord, to the place in
which your tabernacle rests; and because your mercies are many,
you have also made weak and lowly earthlings to be participants
in the glorification of your majesty and your divine ministry, and
from these you have established prophets and then apostles, and
after these teachers and workers of miracles,[3] to be participants
in the service of your greatness and joined to the assemblies of
light and the mysteries of your divinity. And we also your weak
and sinful servants, who have received the rank of the highest
priesthood, when we were not worthy to set foot on the threshold of your holy temple, we humbly pour out prayers to you
and ask you through the prayers of Mary, mother of God, that
you incline the mercy of your divinity to us and accept this ministry and this ordination which is performed on this your servant
through our poverty. O Lord, may he be our ruler day and night
and at all times and our liberator and redeemer from the deceits
of the adversary; grant that he may be pleasing to you in all his
conduct and not deviate to the right or to the left from your way,
which leads to eternal life; may he in no way grieve your Holy
Spirit, but by your grace, Lord, may be established and strengthened and complete the course of his contest reverently and justly
all the days of his life, and also in the last day of your terrible
and dreadful coming may he meet you carrying as lamps of light
his good works and enter with you to rest and sing glory to your
venerable name, Father. . . .
[The patriarch having first placed his hand on the consecrated

elements and then on the candidate's head; a prayer with no known parallels.]

[A litany follows.]

Blessed are you, Lord God. . . .
[The patriarch having first placed his hand on the consecrated elements and then on the candidate's head; a variant form of the prayer used for the presbyterate, p. 197.]

Incline your ear, Lord, and hear the prayers of your sinful and poor servants, and accept through your mercy our petitions and give to this your servant N. faith and wisdom in the things which are entrusted to him by your grace and by your rational flock, that he may do your will and be worthy of your heavenly kingdom; for you are to be adored and our glorious God and your living and Holy Spirit.
[Said with the new bishop standing; a prayer with no known parallels.]

Look upon us . . .
[Said with the patriarch's hand on his head; a version of the supplementary prayer found in the Jacobite rite, p. 184.]

[The new bishop is led in procession three times around the church, during which hymns are sung. In the more recent manuscripts, at the end of each procession, a lengthy prayer is said, and then follows a version of the ordination prayer for a bishop from the *Apostolic Constitutions* (pp. 113–114), accompanying the unction of the candidate which was introduced under Roman influence. In the older manuscripts, the three prayers are placed in an appendix: the first (a version of the Jacobite ordination prayer, pp. 183–184) is for the ordination of a bishop, the second for the ordination of a metropolitan, and the third for the ordination of a patriarch. After further prayers, readings, and a hymn, there follow a declaration that the new bishop is ordained and a vesting, with formularies resembling those in the Jacobite rite (pp. 184–185). He is then enthroned, and all cry out three times: "*Axios*, worthy and just." The bishop delivers to him the staff and all cry out: "The Lord shall send you the rod of power from Sion, and you will rule among your enemies."[4]]

Lord, who gave to Moses . . .
[A prayer with some similarity to that accompanying the delivery of the staff in the Jacobite rite, p. 186.]

[The rite concludes with an exhortation, and several further prayers, among them a version of the Jacobite thanksgiving prayer, p. 186.]

Melkite[1]

In the name of the Father and of the Son and of the Holy Spirit.

PRESENTATION OF A READER
The chief deacon presents him who is receiving the imposition of hands. He kneels before the bishop and says: Lord bless. *The high-priest says:* The Lord bless you to readers of the most holy church of this place, now. . . .

And the chief deacon causes him to rise, and makes him stand opposite the altar, while placing with the imposition [of hands]. And the high-priest says this prayer for his soul, his face toward the east, secretly: Lord God of hosts. . . . [A version of the preparatory prayer found also in the Coptic, Jacobite, and Maronite rites, but here without the reference to the particular order being conferred: see pp. 141, 175, and 188].

It is necessary that you should know that this prayer, the writing of which has preceded, is said at the beginning of every imposition of hands.

And then the chief deacon presents him upon whom the imposition of hands is taking place, while he says as follows: We bring forward our brother N., sub-cantor, to readers of the most holy church of this place. Let us say on his behalf. *Then he answers him,* Lord, have mercy *(three times).*

The high-priest says as follows, within the hearing of all: The divine grace, which heals that which is infirm and supplies what is lacking, and always provides for her holy churches, appoints the servant of God N., sub-cantor, to the readers of the holy church *(and he names the church)* of the place. Let us pray, therefore, that there may come upon him the grace of the Holy Spirit, now and always and. . . .

And all of them answer him: Hear, Lord.

The chief deacon says three sections from the prayers of the deacon: In peace let us pray and make request to the Lord.

For the peace of the whole world. . . .

The holy, pure, blessed mother of God, and the chaste virgin, my lady Miriam, along with all the saints and just ones, whom we commemorate, while we remember their souls, and all life; Christ our God do we praise.

And the high-priest, laying his hand on the head of the candidate for the imposition of hands, says this prayer: Lord God, who [are] omnipotent and omniscient; before they were born, he who selected this your servant to those who read of this church, who is outstanding in his holiness, adorning him, Lord, by the grace of your divinity: and make him worthy,[2] that he may labor in the reading of your divine word, and guide him in the company of wisdom and discernment, that you may keep him in a way in which there is no fault; by the grace and compassion and the love of your only Son to the son of man, with whom you [are] blessed and praised, and with your living and good and holy Spirit, now be it and for ever and ever, Amen.

And he says again: Lord, the mighty God, appoint this your servant and sanctify him, and make him worthy, with all wisdom and understanding, for the reading of your divine word; and guide him and cause him to enter upon the elect, the ancient[3] among ranks, [who is] excelling in our Lord Jesus Christ, that one with whom you [are] blessed and praised with your living and good and holy Spirit, now be it and for ever and ever, Amen.

And he hands to him the First Epistle of Paul to the Romans: Paul, a servant of Jesus Christ, called and sent, separated to the gospel of God, that which he promised beforehand by the prophets of the holy scriptures which concern his Son, who was of the seed of the house of David according to the flesh.[4]

Then the bishop bestows on him the salutation. He says to him, Peace to all. *Then he puts on him the phenolion[5] and says:* In the name of the Father and of the Son and of the Holy Spirit, now and always. . . .

And he exhorts him, saying as follows: My son, behold the first rank of the ranks of the Church, that excels in its holiness, is the rank of the reader. It is incumbent on you that you should be entrusted with the divine scriptures and look in them every day; and that you should make your methods likewise pure, in order that those who listen to you may receive with clearness; and that you should discipline yourself for a higher rank; for you need by no means be ashamed on account of the reckoning which will be your portion. For when you conduct yourself with purity, piety, and righteousness, behold, the God who is gracious to men will be merciful to you, and you will be worthy of the greater rank.[6]

End. Finished is the imposition of hands on the reader; and the chant to God, for ever and ever, Amen, Amen, Amen.

PRESENTATION OF A SUBDEACON

The chief deacon, in whom authority to give the imposition of hands is invested,[7] presents him. He makes a prostration in the presence of the bishop, saying: Bless, my Lord. *Then the bishop says, while he signs him with signs, praying over him:* The Lord bless you to subdeacons of the holy Church of God of this place of the city, now. . . . Amen.

And he places the orarion[8] on the altar, and the chief deacon causes him to rise, and makes him stand before the altar. The high-priest, placing with the imposition [of hands], while he says, praying the prayer on behalf of his soul; petition at the beginning of the imposition of hands, Lord God of hosts, he . . . , *petition at the beginning of the imposition of hands in the prayer of the reader.*

Then the chief deacon presents him in the presence of that one, saying: We bring forward our brother N., the most pious sub-reader, to subdeacons of the most holy church of this place. Let us say on his behalf, "Lord, have mercy." *He answers him,* Lord, have mercy *(three times).*

Then he kneels on his left knee, and the bishop lays his hand on the head of the one receiving the imposition of hands and makes the sign [of the cross] over him, saying: In the name of the Father and of the Son and of the Holy Spirit, for ever and ever, Amen.

Then he says in prayer, within the hearing of all: The divine grace, which heals that which is infirm and supplies what is lacking, and always provides for her holy churches, appoints the servant of God N., sub-reader, to the subdeacons of the most holy church of this place. Let us pray, therefore, that there may come upon him the grace of the Holy Spirit, now and always and. . . .

Then they answer three times: Hear, Lord! Hear, Lord! Hear, Lord!

Then chief deacon says from the prayers of the deacon: In peace let us pray and make request to the Lord.

For the peace of the whole world. . . .

For the salvation and peace and succor of our holy fathers. . . .

For our pious and divinely protected emperor, along with all the court and their forces, let us pray and make request to the Lord.

For the salvation and peace and succor of this subdeacon who is being ordained at this time, let us pray and make request to the Lord.

The holy, pure, blessed mother. . . .

Then the bishop places his hand upon the head of the candidate for the imposition of hands, and says this prayer: God of hosts, the true God, the God of Abraham and of Isaac and of Jacob [and of] all their righteous seed, God and Father of our Lord Jesus Christ, Father of mercies and God of all consolation,[9] look upon this your servant who is now being appointed subdeacon, and make him worthy of the ordination to service which he will serve with boldness at the door of your Church; and that he may light the lamp of your prayer; and loving the beauty of your house, and being an adornment in everything in your hallowed Church; and that he may enter among those, upon the elect and ancient[10] of outstanding ranks; for to you is all-seemly the glory and the honor and the adoration, to the Father and the Son and the Holy Spirit, now be it and for ever and ever, Amen.

And the chief deacon praying, From the Lord let us make request, *and the high-priest praying this second prayer:* Everlasting God, who anoint priests and kings, who sanctify prophets and call just ones, Lord our God, call this your servant, the pure Reader, by ordination to service, and make him worthy, that, loving the beauty of your house, he may also stand in fear before the door of the holy Church, and may also light the lamp of the house of your prayer. And plant him like an olive tree and make him a flourishing plant which gives good fruit; by the grace and mercy and love of your Christ to the son of man, with whom you are blessed and glorified along with your Spirit living and good and holy and life-giving, now be it, for ever and ever, Amen.

Then he causes him to rise and clothes him with the sticharion,[11] and he takes the orarion from upon the altar and makes the sign of the cross upon him; and he places it upon his left shoulder and puts it round his neck and says: There is put upon this servant of God the orarion of the subdiaconate, in the name of the Father and of the Son and of the Holy Spirit, now and always. . . .

And the candidate for the imposition of hands receives the vessel and pours upon the hand of the bishop, while the chief deacon says: Let us bow our heads to the Lord.

Then the bishop puts his hand upon him and says: Lord our God, you who have given to your congregations varied gifts[12] and set among them ranks and deacons, and pour out your splendid[13] gifts: upon this your servant, Lord, also bestow [them] in the ordination upon him. Reckon him in the roll of subdeacons and make him worthy, that we may be well-pleasing to you and glorify you and your only Son and your living and good and Holy Spirit, now be it, for ever and ever, Amen.

End. And the bishop exhorts him as is agreeable to the canon and the becoming divine service, and dismisses him with the salutation. Ended is the imposition of hands on the subdeacon. The praise is to God, who is to everlasting. O God, have mercy on your servant, the writer of this book, and on both his parents and all his kin, and the reader and those who hear and those who say this prayer, by the intercessions of those who make intercession and of all saints. Amen.

PRESENTATION OF A DEACON

The bishop takes the scroll in which is written as follows: The divine grace appoints the deacons of this place, now. . . . Amen. *And he names the place.*

And he clothes with the orarion of the diaconate him who is receiving the imposition of hands; and he makes a prostration in the presence of the bishop, and says: Lord, bless. *The bishop says:* God bless you to deacons of the holy church (*and he names the church; if it is a city he says,* of the city, *and if it is a village, he says,* of the country), now and always and to the. . . .

Then the chief deacon makes him stand before the altar, while he lays the gospel and the paten and the chalice and the two fans on the altar; and placing with the imposition [of hands], while the high-priest prays the prayer on behalf of his soul and says: Lord God of hosts, he who has set us . . . , *petition at the beginning of the imposition of hands; and thereafter the prayer.*

The chief deacon says as follows: We bring forward our brother, the subdeacon here, to deacons in the most holy church of this place. Let us all say on his behalf, "Lord, have mercy," three [times].

Then he who is receiving the imposition of hands makes obeisance on his right knee, and the chief deacon says: In peace let us pray and make request to the Lord.

For the peace of the whole world. . . .

For the salvation and peace and succor of our holy fathers N. and N.

For a pious and divinely protected emperor. . . .

Again for this deacon who is being ordained at this time, and for his salvation, let us pray and make request to the Lord.

That loving God may give him the grace of a ministry in which is neither flaw nor blemish, let us pray and make request to the Lord.

The pure, holy, blessed mother of God. . . .

Then the bishop places his hand upon the head of the candidate for the imposition of hands, and makes the sign of the cross over him and says secretly to himself: In the name of the Father and of the Son and of the Holy Spirit, for ever and ever, Amen.

And he raises his voice and says: The divine grace, which heals that which is infirm and supplies what is lacking, and always provides for her holy churches, appoints the servant of God N. from subdeacons to deacons of the holy church *(and he names the church)* of this place. Let us pray, therefore, that there may come upon him the grace of the Holy Spirit, now and always. . . .

And he makes over him the sign of the cross. Then he answers him, Hear, Lord! Hear, Lord! Hear, Lord! *three times, while the high-priest says this prayer:* [You] who by the diaconal ministry adorn your Church, almighty God, and who complete her varied beauty by the gifts of your Holy Spirit, who have chosen, by the hands of your holy apostles, Stephen, a man full of faith and grace and the Holy Spirit, and Philip and Prochorus and Nicanor and Timon and Parmenas and Nicolaus, the prosylete of Antioch,[14] the seven deacons: enroll in the diaconal ministry your servant N., to fulfill the solemn and holy service of your holy sanctuary; to hold forth the cup of your Christ and to give communion to your people; to protect widows, to help orphans. And order his purpose to good, and supply him with power, to the right ordering of the whole ecclesiastical economy; for to you glory is fitting, Father and Son and Holy Spirit, now and always. . . .

The chief deacon praying, says, From the Lord let us make request. *And the high-priest says, making petition:* From you, Lord of many counsels, grace is given for every need of your Church; You also, who have introduced the diaconal ministry, fitting members to members, teachers to deacons, to priests ministers, grant the grace of the diaconate to your servant N., and save him as servant to your sanctuary, with true faith and perfect love, acceptably and unashamedly to fulfill your command, to make progress to the greater gifts, being empowered always to perfection in Christ Jesus, with whom you are blessed and glorified, with your all-holy and good and life-giving Spirit, now and always and to. . . .

And he makes this [petition] until he receives it. Three [times]. Lord our God, who by your foreknowledge send down the abundance of the Holy Spirit on those destined by your unsearchable greatness to be ministers and to serve at your immaculate mysteries, Lord, keep this man also, whom you are pleased should be appointed through me to the ministry of the diaconate, in all holiness, holding the mystery of the faith in a pure conscience.[15] Ordain him deacon, O God, and give him the grace which you gave to Stephen your protomartyr, whom you also called first to the work of your diaconate. And make him worthy to please you in the rank of the diaconate which you have given him. And make him your perfect servant, a partner of those who have served you well and have gained for themselves a good rank,[16] by the grace and pity and love for humanity of your only-begotten Son, with whom you [are] blessed with your all-holy and good and live-giving Spirit, now and always and to the ages of ages, Amen.

Then he makes him stand and spreads the orarion on his left shoulder and says: There is put upon the servant N. the orarion of the diaconate, in the name of the Father and of the Son and of the Holy Spirit, now and always and to. . . .

And he gives to him the holy gospel, from John, and the chief deacon brings the man forward, saying, Wisdom, erect! Let us hear from the holy gospel. *The bishop says,* Peace to all. *Then he who is receiv-*

ing the imposition of hands says, From the gospel of John. *And he reads:* In the beginning was the Word, and the Word was with God, and the Word was God. He was in the beginning with God. All things were made by him, and without him there was not anything made.[17]

The bishop says, Peace to all. *Then he places the gospel on the altar. The bishop gives him the paten. He kisses it and raises it upon his head, then places it on the altar. He gives him likewise the chalice. He kisses it and places it on the altar. Then he takes the fans and gives him them. He kisses them and places them at the side of the altar. Then he makes the sign of the cross on them three times, and says,* Let us attend! *And he kisses them and places them on the blessed altar. If it is not an assembly for the eucharist, he draws near the blessed sacrament. Then when afterwards the bishop has kissed them, he inclines his head. Then he lays his hand on him. The chief deacon says,* Lord, bless. *And the high-priest says as follows:* Holy One, served by holy servants, give the spirit of faith to N. your servant, so that he may faithfully serve the mystery of your liturgy. Keep him blameless, without accusation in your Church; guard his progress to a higher rank and the everlasting presence, in the presence of your Christ, with whom yours [is] the power and the kingdom with your all-holy Spirit, now and always and to the ages of ages. . . .

Then he answers him Amen. *The high-priest says,* Blessed [is] the Lord. Behold you have become a deacon. *Then he answers him three times,* Worthy! *three [times]. And he acquaints him with the canon and dismisses him with the salutation. Ended is the presentation of the deacon, and the chant to God, everlasting, Amen*

IMPOSITION [OF HANDS] ON A PRESBYTER

The bishop takes the scroll in which is written as follows: N. appoints N. from deacons to presbyters. *And he who is deemed worthy for the imposition of hands makes a prostration, saying,* Lord, bless. *And the high-priest says:* The Lord bless you to presbyters of the most holy church of the city now. . . . *And if it is a village, he says,* of the country.

Then the bishop enters in front of the blessed altar, holding the scroll. Then he casts the incense, and thereafter the prayer over the incense. He says the prayer which is on behalf of his soul—find it in the prayers of the Reader—and it is: Lord God of hosts, he who has set us. . . .

And thereafter the prayer.

One of the presbyters lifts up his voice, saying as follows: We bring forward our brother N., the deacon, to presbyters of this holy church of God of this place. Let us all say on his behalf, "Lord, have mercy." *Then he answers him,* Lord, have mercy.

Then the candidate kneels on his knees and the bishop places his hand on his head and makes over him the sign of the cross and says: The divine grace, which heals that which is infirm and supplies what is lacking, and always provides for her holy churches, appoints the servant of God N., the deacon, to presbyters of this most holy church *(and he names the church).* Let us pray, therefore, that there may come upon him the grace of the Holy Spirit, now and always. . . .

And he answers him three times, Hear, Lord! *three times; and a presbyter says the prayers of the deacon in three verses:* In peace let us pray and make request.

For the peace of the whole world. . . .

For the salvation and peace and succor of our holy fathers N. the patriarch, and N. the metropolitan, with all the servants of the sanctuaries and the mercies of Christ, let us pray and make request to the Lord.

For a pious and divinely protected emperor, with all the court and his forces, let us pray and make request.

Again for our brother N. who is being ordained presbyter at this time, and for his salvation, let us pray and make request.

That loving God may give him a priesthood in which is neither flaw nor blemish, let us pray and make request to the Lord.

The holy, pure, blessed mother of God, and the chaste virgin, my lady Miriam, along with all the saints and just ones, whom we commemorate, as we remember them, each and all, and all life; Christ our God do we praise.

Then the bishop prays, placing his hand on the candidate for the imposition of hands, and he says as follows: Holy One, served by holy angels, Lord, the God who does glorious things by authority, of which there is no number, great in power and unsearchable in understanding, wonderful in counsels beyond the sons of men; you are our God, he who in each generation have chosen the holy ones who have exercised the priestly ministry for you: now also choose your servant N. and grant him, in irreproachable conduct and steadfast faith, to receive the great and rich grace of your Holy Spirit, that he may be worthy to exercise the sacred ministry of the gospel of your kingdom, so that he may become a perfect priest offering you gifts and spiritual sacrifices, and renewing your people by the baptism of regeneration; to all holding forth this lamp of light, so that, by your counsels, having obtained the safety of your faithful peoples, he himself may also be present, in the order of presbyters, at the coming from heaven of your only-begotten Son, and receive the reward of the faithful and wise stewards,[18] in the abundance of your kindness; for kind you are and full of pity for all who call upon you in truth, and glory is fitting to you, to your only-begotten Son, and to your all-holy, good, life-giving Spirit, now and always and to the. . . .

The presbyter says: From the Lord let us make request.

The high-priest says: To you the heavenly beings minister, Lord, in thousands and ten thousands of well-pleasing ministers.[19] You have also instituted a ministry on earth, having established for your people presbyters for these offices of piety. From you also do we now ask that there be given to N. your servant the Holy Spirit, so that he may fulfill for you the apostolic ministry in true teaching, to the presenting of your Church,[20] bringing with him his zeal in your power. For yours is the glory, Father and Son and Holy Spirit, now and always and to the ages. . . .

And the presbyter says: From the Lord let us make request.

The high-priest says the third prayer: You who have brought together the Church and who have established the priesthood, give the gift of the Spirit to the presbyter, [one] of ministers who have been perfected to the holy gifts by the Spirit of your Christ, for the discharging of the services[21] on behalf of your Church, and for teaching the commandments, and to beseech your propitiation for all and the grace of your favor to the benefit of your people; by the grace and love for humanity of your Christ, with whom you are blessed and all-praised, with the all-holy and good and live-giving Spirit, now and always and to the ages. . . .

Then he folds the orarion and places it on his neck, saying: There is put upon the servant of God the orarion of priesthood, in the name of the Father and of the Son and of the Holy Spirit, now and always. . . .

And he puts on him the phenolion[22] and says: There is put upon N. the phenolion of the priesthood, in the name of the Father and of the Son and of the Holy Spirit, now and. . . .

And he signs him on his forehead, saying—with [the sign of] the cross—and he says: There is sealed the servant of God N. from deacons to presbyters of the holy catholic Church of God of the *(and he names the church)* in the name of the Father and of the Son and of the Holy Spirit, now. . . .

And he gives to him the holy gospel, and a presbyter says, Wisdom, erect! Let us hear from the holy gospel. *He who is receiving the imposition of hands says,* Peace to all. *They answer him,* And of the Spirit. *He says,* From the holy [gospel] according to John: In the beginning was the Word, and the Word was with God, and the Word was God. He was in the beginning with God. All things were made by him, and without him there was not anything made.[23]

The bishop says, Peace to you. *Then when he who is receiving the imposition of hands has kissed the gospel, he lays it on the altar, and the bishop gives [him] the paten, I mean the salver, and on it the blessed body. And he who is receiving the imposition of hands raises the paten, while another presbyter announces, saying,* Let us attend! *The candidate for the imposition of hands says,* Holy things for the holy people![24] *Then he answers him,* One [is] holy. One [is] Lord, Jesus Christ, to the glory of God the Father, Amen.

And he on whom is taking place the imposition of hands inclines his head, and the bishop places his hand on his head and says this prayer: Blessed are you, the God who by diverse gifts have adorned your Church, and chose in the Old Covenant seventy presbyters and filled them with the gift of prophecy,[25] and in the New Covenant first apostles, second prophets, then teachers[26]; this one also your servant N., make him a presbyter. Ordain him, Lord, by the coming of your all-holy Spirit. Grant him to offer to you gifts, offerings, and sacrifices, for a sweet-smelling savor.[27] Give him grace and utterance in the opening of his mouth.[28] Give him to pray on behalf of your sick servants.[29] Grant to him to bring to the second birth those who approach you, by the baptism of the second birth. Grant him to care for widows, to help orphans,[30] to adorn in all things your Church; by the grace and pity and love for humanity of your only-begotten Son, with whom you [are] blessed, with your all-holy and good and life-giving Spirit, now and. . . .

And the bishop says, making the sign of the cross on the head of the candidate for the imposition of hands, Blessed [is] the Lord. Behold you have become a presbyter. *Three [times]. He says this three times, and he answers him three times,* Worthy! Worthy! Worthy! *Then he and all those who are present in the place kiss the bishop. Then the bishop exhorts him in his duties and dismisses him with the salutation.*

Finished is the imposition of hands on a presbyter, by the help of God—may he be exalted—and the chant to God, everlasting, eternal, Amen, Amen, Amen. Have mercy, O God, on him who reads and on him who writes and on him who hears and recites, Amen, Amen, Amen.

PART IV
WESTERN TEXTS

Roman

CONSECRATION OF BISHOPS

Hear, Lord, the prayers of your humble people, that what is to be carried out by our ministry may be established further by your power; through. . . .

[Then follow texts for the Secret and the Hanc Igitur of the ordination mass.]

Assist [us], merciful God, so that what is done by our obedient office may be established by your blessing; through. . . .

Be gracious, Lord, to our supplications, and with the horn of priestly grace inclined over these your servants pour out upon them the power of your benediction; through. . . .[2]

God of all the honors, God of all the worthy ranks, which serve to your glory in hallowed orders; God who in private familiar converse with Moses your servant also made a decree, among the other patterns of heavenly worship, concerning the disposition of priestly vesture; and commanded that Aaron your chosen one should wear a mystical robe during the sacred rites, so that the posterity to come might have an understanding of the meaning of the patterns of the former things, lest the knowledge of your teaching be lost in any age; and as among the ancients the very outward sign of these symbols obtained reverence, also among us there might be a knowledge of them more certain than types and shadows. For the adornment of our mind is as the vesture of that earlier priesthood; and the dignity of robes no longer commends to us the pontifical glory, but the splendor of spirits, since even those very things, which then pleased fleshly vision, depended rather on these truths which in them were to be understood.

And, therefore, to these your servants, whom you have chosen for the ministry of the high-priesthood, we beseech you, O Lord, that you would bestow this grace; that whatsoever it was that those veils signified in radiance of gold, in sparkling of jewels, in variety of diverse workmanship, this may show forth in the conduct and deeds of these men. Complete the fullness of your mystery in your priests, and equipped with all the adornments of glory, hallow them with the dew of heavenly unction. May it flow down, O Lord, richly upon their head; may it run down below the mouth; may it go down to the uttermost parts of the whole body, so that the power of your Spirit may both fill them within and surround them without. May there abound in them constancy of faith, purity of love, sincerity of peace. Grant to them an episcopal throne to rule your Church and entire people. Be their strength; be their might; be their stay. Multiply upon them your blessing and grace, so that fitted by your aid always to obtain your mercy, they may by your grace be devoted to you; through. . . .

BLESSING OVER DEACONS

Lord God, mercifully hear our prayers, that you may favorably attend with your assistance the things that are to be carried out by our service, and may justify the more by your choice those whom we believe according to our judgment should be offered for the holy ministries about to be sought; through. . . .[3]

Let us pray, dearly beloved, to God, the almighty Father, that on these his servants, whom he deems worthy to call to the office of deacon, he may mercifully pour the benediction of his grace and favorably preserve the gifts of the consecration bestowed; through. . . .[4]

O God, glorious bestower of sacred dignities, we beseech you that you would grant that these your servants, whom you deem worthy to call to the office of Levites, may rightly fulfill the ministry of the holy altar, and that you would make them, abounding in all gifts of grace, both to obtain for themselves boldness before your majesty and to furnish to others an example of perfect devotion; through. . . .[5]

Assist us, we beseech you, almighty God, giver of honors, distributor of orders, and bestower of offices; who, abiding in yourself, make all things new, and order everything by your Word, Power, and Wisdom, Jesus Christ, your Son our Lord—by everlasting providence you prepare and apportion to each particular time what is appropriate—whose body, your Church, you permit

to grow and spread, diversified by a variety of heavenly graces
and knit together in the distinction of its members, united
through the wondrous law of the whole structure for the increase of your temple, establishing the service of sacred office in
three ranks of ministers to do duty in your name, the sons of
Levi having been chosen first, that by remaining in faithful vigilance over the mystical workings of your house, they might obtain by a perpetual apportionment an inheritance of everlasting
blessing.

Look favorably also on these your servants, we beseech you,
Lord, whom we humbly dedicate to serve in your sanctuaries in
the office of deacon. And although indeed being men we are
ignorant of divine thought and highest reason, we judge their
life as best we can; but things unknown to us do not slip by
you, Lord, things hidden do not escape you. You are the witness
of sins, you are the discerner of minds, you are able truly to
bring heavenly judgment on them or else grant to the unworthy
what we ask. Send upon them, Lord, we beseech you, the Holy
Spirit, by whom, faithfully accomplishing the work of ministry,
they may be strengthened with the gift of your sevenfold grace.[6]
May the pattern of every virtue abound in them: discreet authority, unfailing modesty, purity of innocence, and the observance
of spiritual discipline. May your commandments be reflected in
their conduct, so that by the example of their chastity they may
win the imitation of the holy people, and displaying the testimony of a good conscience, may persevere strong and stable in
Christ, and by fitting advancements from a lower rank may be
worthy through your grace to take up higher things;
through. . . .

CONSECRATION OF A PRESBYTER

Let us pray, dearly beloved, to God the Father almighty that
upon these his servants, whom he has chosen for the office of
presbyter, he may multiply heavenly gifts, with which what they
have begun by his favor they may accomplish by his aid;
through. . . .

Hear us, O God of our salvation, and pour forth the benediction
of the Holy Spirit and the power of priestly grace on these your
servants, that you may accompany with the unfailing richness of

your bounty these whom we present before your merciful countenance to be consecrated; through. . . .

Holy Lord, almighty Father, everlasting God, bestower of all the honors and of all the worthy ranks which do you service, you through whom all things make progress, through whom everything is made strong, by the ever-extended increase to the benefit of rational nature by a succession arranged in due order; whence the priestly ranks and the offices of the Levites arose and were inaugurated with mystical symbols; so that when you set up high-priests to rule over your people, you chose men of a lesser order and secondary dignity to be their companions and to help them in their labor. Likewise in the desert you did spread out the spirit of Moses through the minds of seventy wise men, so that he, using them as helpers among the people, governed with ease countless multitudes.[7] Likewise also you imparted to Eleazar and Ithamar, the sons of Aaron, the richness of their father's plenty, so that the benefit of priests might be sufficient for the salutary sacrifices and the rites of a more frequent worship. And also by your providence, O Lord, to the apostles of your Son you added teachers of the faith as companions, and they filled the whole world with these secondary preachers.

Wherefore on our weakness also, we beseech you, O Lord, bestow these assistants, for we who are so much frailer need so many more. Grant, we beseech you, Father, the dignity of the presbyterate to these your servants. Renew in their inward parts the spirit of holiness. May they obtain and receive from you, O God, the office of second dignity, and by the example of their conduct may they commend a strict way of life. May they be virtuous colleagues of our order. May the pattern of all righteousness show forth in them, so that, rendering a good account of the stewardship entrusted to them, they may obtain the rewards of eternal blessedness; through. . . .

ORDO XXXIV[8]

In the name of the Lord. The order by which an acolyte is ordained in the holy Roman church.

1. *While the mass is being celebrated, they vest the cleric in chasuble[9] and stole.*

2. *And when the bishop or the pope himself comes to the communion, they lead him to him and he delivers a saccula[10] into his hands over the chasuble, and he prostrates himself on the ground with the saccula itself, and he says a prayer for him thus:* At the intercession of the blessed and glorious and ever-virgin Mary and of the blessed apostle Peter, may the Lord save and guard and protect you. *Response:* Amen.

3. *And if he wishes to promote him to the office of the subdiaconate, he is led into the middle and takes an oath before the four holy gospels of Christ concerning the four* capitulae,[11] *according to the canons. And then the archdeacon or the bishop delivers the holy chalice into his hands outside the chasuble,[12] and he prostrates himself on the ground, and he says a prayer for him, as we said above.*

4. *And if he wishes to promote him to the order of the diaconate, while the introit of the mass is intoned, the subdeacon himself, vested in a white tunic and holding his stole in his hand, stands before the chancel barrier.*

5. *The Kyrie eleison is not said then, but, when the introit has been completed, the bishop says the prayer and the Epistle to Timothy is read:* Brothers, deacons ought to be virtuous, not double-tongued, *ending at,* which is in Christ Jesus our Lord.[13] *And the gradual psalm is sung.*

6. *Then the subdeacon's own chasuble is removed by a deacon.*

7. *And the bishop says this prayer:* Let us pray, dearly beloved, to God, the almighty Father, that on this his servant, whom he deems worthy to assume the sacred order, he may mercifully pour the grace of his benediction and bestow on him the gift of consecration; through which he may lead him to eternal rewards.

8. *And then the choir begins the Kyrie eleison. And the bishop prostrates himself before the altar and behind him the subdeacon himself.*

9. *When the litany is finished, they rise from the ground and he immediately says the prayer of consecration for him.*

10. *When he has thus been consecrated, he gives the kiss to the bishop and priests and stands on the right of the bishops, now vested in a dalmatic.*

11. *If he wishes to consecrate him as a presbyter, the archdeacon takes hold of him and leads him outside the chancel barrier, removes his dalmatic from him, and then vests him in a chasuble and leads him back to the bishop.*

12. *And then he says another prayer for him and consecrates him as a presbyter. He gives the kiss to the bishop and the rest of the priests and stands in the order of the presbyterate.*

13. *And then is said the Alleluia or tract and the gospel and what follows, and the mass is completed in its order.*

14. *Again [the order] by which a bishop is ordained. When the bishop of a city or place has died, another is chosen by the people of the city and a decree [of election] is made by the priests, clergy, and people.*

15. *And they come to the pope, presenting with him also the* suggestio, *that is the document requesting that he consecrate him as their bishop, which they have brought with them.*

[Instructions for the examination of the candidate by the pope then follow.]

32. *On the next day which is a Sunday, the pope goes to the church, and there the bishops and presbyters and the other orders of clerics assemble with him.*

33. *And the pope enters the sacristy and signals the choir to sing the psalm.*

34. *And he proceeds with great splendor from the sacristy into the church itself, as is the custom.*

35. *When the introit is completed, they do not then say the Kyrie eleison, but the pope immediately says the collect.*

36. *Next is read the Epistle to Timothy:* Dearly beloved, [this is] a true saying: if anyone desires the episcopate, he desires a good work, *and so on.*[14]

37. *And while the gradual psalm is sung, the archdeacon comes out with the acolytes and subdeacons and vests him in the dalmatic, chasuble, and ceremonial shoes, and leads him in.*

38. *When he has been led in, the pope addresses him thus:* The clergy and people of the city of N., with the consent of the neighboring dioceses, have chosen N., the deacon or presbyter, to be consecrated bishop. Therefore let us pray for this man, that our God

and Lord Jesus Christ will bestow on him the episcopal throne to rule over his church and all its people.

39. *Then the choir begins the Kyrie eleison with the litany, while the pope prostrates himself with the priests and the elect on the ground before the altar.*

40. *When the litany is completed, they rise, and then he blesses him.*[15]

41. *When the blessing is finished, the pope gives him the kiss and the archdeacon takes him and leads him, and so he gives the kiss to the bishops [and] presbyters.*

42. *And then the pope orders him to sit above all the bishops.*[16]

43. *And when he is seated, the Alleluia is said, then the gospel, and the mass is completed.*

44. *But when he comes to the communion, the pope delivers to him the* formata[17] *and the consecrated oblation, and receiving it, the bishop communicates himself from it at the altar and keeps the rest of it for communion for forty days.*[18]

45. *And afterwards at the command of the pope he communicates all the people.*

Gallican

90. *When a bishop is ordained, let two bishops put the book of the gospels on his head*[2] *and hold it, and while one says the blessing over him, let all the rest of the bishops who are present touch his head with their hands.*

91. *When a presbyter is ordained, as the bishop blesses him and holds his hand on his head, let all the presbyters who are present also hold their hands beside the hand of the bishop on his head.*

92. *When a deacon is ordained, let only the bishop who blesses him put his hand on his head, since he is consecrated not for the priesthood but for the ministry.*[3]

93. *When a subdeacon is ordained, since he does not receive the imposition of hands, let him receive from the hand of the bishop the empty paten and the empty chalice, and from the hand of the archdeacon let him receive the ewer with the basin and towel.*

94. *When an acolyte is ordained, let him be taught by the bishop how he ought to conduct himself in his office, but from the archdeacon let him receive a candlestick with a candle, so that he may know that he is responsible for lighting the lamps of the church; let him also receive an empty cruet for the presentation of the wine in the eucharist of the blood of Christ.*

95. *When an exorcist is ordained, let him receive from the hand of the bishop the book in which are written the exorcisms, the bishop saying to him:* Receive and keep, and have power to lay hands on an energumen, whether baptized or catechumen.

96. *When a reader is ordained, let the bishop say a word about him to the people, indicating his faith and life and ability; after this, in the sight of the people, let him hand him the book from which he will read, saying to him:* Receive, and be a narrator of the word of God, and you will have, if you fulfill the office faithfully and profitably, a share with those who have ministered the word of God.

97. *When a doorkeeper is ordained, after he has been instructed by the archdeacon how he ought to act in the house of God, when he is pre-*

sented by the archdeacon let the bishop hand him the keys of the church from the altar, saying: So act as if you are to render to God an account for the things which are opened by these keys.

98. *A psalmist, that is a cantor, is able, without the knowledge of the bishop, simply by the command of the presbyter, to undertake the office of singing, the presbyter saying to him:* See that what you sing with your mouth you believe in your heart and what you believe in your heart you show in your deeds.

MISSALE FRANCORUM[4]

BLESSING OF A DOORKEEPER
Let us humbly beseech God the Father almighty that he may vouchsafe to bless this his servant whom he has deigned to choose for the office of doorkeeper, that it may be his steadfast care day and night at the division of the fixed hours to invoke the name of the Lord.

Holy Lord, almighty Father, eternal God, vouchsafe to bless this your servant as doorkeeper, that among the doorkeepers of the Church he may perform his duties and among your elect may deserve to have a share of the reward; through. . . .

BLESSING OF AN ACOLYTE
Holy Lord, almighty Father, eternal God, who instructed Moses and Aaron that lamps were to be lit in the tent of witness: vouchsafe to bless and sanctify this your servant that he may be an acolyte in your Church; through. . . .

BIDDING FOR A READER
Your brothers choose you to be a reader in the house of your God; may you know your duty so that you may fulfill it, for God is able to increase his grace to you; through. . . .

BLESSING OF A READER
Holy Lord, almighty Father, eternal God, vouchsafe to bless this your servant N. in the office of reader, that distinguished by the constancy of his readings and adorned with. . . .[5]

BIDDING FOR AN EXORCIST

Let us humbly beseech God the Father almighty that he may vouchsafe to bless this his servant N. in the office of exorcist, that he may be a spiritual champion to drive away demons from bodies beset with all their manifold wickedness; through. . . .

BLESSING OF AN EXORCIST

Holy Lord, almighty Father, eternal God, vouchsafe to bless this your servant N. in the office of exorcist, that by the office of the imposition of hands and mouth [you may deign to choose him, and]⁶ he may have power to curb unclean spirits and be an acceptable physician of your Church, strengthened by the power of the grace of healing.

ALLOCUTION AT THE ORDINATION OF A SUBDEACON

Let the empty paten and chalice be displayed in the sight of the bishop, and let the bishop say to him:

See what ministry is bestowed on you. And thus, if until now you have been late to church, from now you ought to be constant; if until now sleepy, from now alert; if until now a drunkard, from now sober; if until now dishonorable, from now pure. May the offerings which come to the altar be called the bread of the presence. Of the offerings themselves only as much ought to be placed on the altar as is able to suffice for the people, lest anything decaying remains in the sanctuary. The underlying cloths ought to be washed in one vessel, the corporals in another. Where the corporals have been washed, no other linen ought to be washed there; the water itself ought to be poured out in the baptistery. Thus I admonish you: so conduct yourself, that you are able to please God.

And you hand him the chalice and paten.

BIDDING AT THE ORDINATION OF A SUBDEACON

Let us pray to our Lord God, that upon his servant N., whom he has vouchsafed to call to the office of subdeacon, he may pour his blessing and grace, so that serving faithfully in his sight he may attain the rewards destined for the saints; through our Lord. . . .

BLESSING OF A SUBDEACON

Holy Lord, almighty Father, eternal God, vouchsafe to bless this your servant N., whom you have deigned to choose for the office of subdeacon, that you may make him active in your holy sanctuary and concerned for the heavenly host; and may he faithfully assist at your holy altar, and may there rest on him the spirit of wisdom and understanding, the spirit of counsel and strength, the spirit of knowledge and godliness; and may you fill him with the spirit of your fear to strengthen him in the divine ministry,[7] that obedient and subject to your command he may attain your grace; through our Lord. . . .

ALLOCUTION TO THE PEOPLE AT THE ORDINATION OF A DEACON

Dearly beloved brethren, the prerogatives themselves of priests would be sufficient for them to put under way at their pleasure the ordination for ecclesiastical service; yet because both our conduct is more pleasing to the Lord and also their favor is greater whose honor is increased, if the consent of your approval confirms what our wishes have decided, accordingly I desire for our son N. advancement by divine aid to the office of the diaconate for our assistance; I wish to know whether you judge him worthy of this office; and if your choice agrees with mine, show aloud the testimony which you wish; through our Lord. . . .[8]

FOR CONSUMMATING THE OFFICE OF THE DIACONATE[9]

Let the prayer of all follow the wish of all; so that, at the supplication of the whole Church, this man who is prepared for the ministry of the diaconate, [may be resplendent in the order][10] of levitical blessing, and being glorious in spiritual conduct, may shine with the grace of holiness; through. . . .[11]

THE BLESSING FOLLOWS

Holy Lord, bestower of faith, hope, grace, and increase, who pour forth your good will through all the elements by the ministries of angels constituted everywhere in heaven and earth, vouchsafe also to shed the light of your countenance especially on this your servant N., that enabled by your favor he may grow as a pure minister at the holy altars, and by [your] indulgence [being] more pure, he may become worthy of the rank of those whom your apostles, at the direction of the Holy Spirit, chose in sevenfold number, with blessed Stephen as their chief and leader, and being equipped with all the virtues required for your service, may find favor; through our Lord Jesus Christ. . . .

ALLOCUTION TO THE PEOPLE AT THE ORDINATION OF A PRESBYTER

Since, dearly beloved brethren, those who rule a ship and those engaged in the voyage share the same purpose for reason of safety or of fear, there should be a common agreement among those who have a common cause. Nor is it in vain that we recall the ordinance of the Fathers, that the people also be consulted concerning the choice of those who are to be appointed to the regulation of the altar, since concerning his activity and present conduct what is sometimes unknown to most people is known to a few, and it is inevitable that someone will more readily yield obedience to the ordained man to whom he has given consent when he was being ordained. The conduct of our brother and fellow-presbyter, as far as I know, is approved and pleasing to God, and worthy (I think) of the increase of ecclesiastical honor. But lest either favor lead astray or feelings deceive one perhaps or a few persons, the opinion of many must be sought. And so we ask your counsel, with God as witness, regarding what you may know concerning his actions and behavior, what you may judge concerning his merit. Your charity, which according to the teaching of the gospel you ought to show both to God and to your neighbor, should have this truthfulness, that you should give testimony to this priest more for merit than for any affection. And we who await the sentence of all cannot understand those who are silent. We know, however, that what is most acceptable to God, the single consent of the minds of all, will come through the Holy Spirit. And therefore you ought to declare your election with a common voice.

[BIDDING]

May it be our common prayer, brethren, that this man, who is chosen for the aid and furtherance of your salvation, may by the mercy of divine assistance secure the blessing of the presbyterate, in order that he may obtain by the privilege of virtue the sacerdotal gifts of the Holy Spirit, so that he be not found wanting in his office; through. . . .

BLESSING

Author of all sanctification, of whom is true consecration, full benediction: you, Lord, spread forth the hand of your blessing on this [your][12] servant N., whom we set apart with the honor of the presbyterate, so that he may show himself to be an elder by the dignity of his acts and the righteousness of his life, taught by these instructions which Paul presented to Titus and Timothy: that meditating on your law day and night, O almighty one, what he reads he may believe, what he believes he may teach, what he teaches he may practice. May he show in himself justice, loyalty, mercy, bravery; may he provide the example, may he demonstrate the exhortation, in order that he may keep the gift of your ministry pure and untainted; and with the consent of your people may he transform the body and blood of your Son by an untainted benediction; and in unbroken love may he reach to a perfect man, to the measure of the stature of the fullness of Christ, in the day of the justice of eternal judgment with a pure conscience, with full faith, full of the Holy Spirit; through. . . .

CONSECRATION OF THE HAND[13]

May these hands be consecrated and hallowed by this unction and our blessing, so that whatever they bless may be blessed and whatever they hallow may be hallowed; through. . . .

ANOTHER

May these hands be anointed with hallowed oil and the chrism of holiness. As Samuel anointed David to be king and prophet, so may they be anointed and perfected, in the name of God the Father and the Son and the Holy Spirit, making the image of the holy cross of the Savior our Lord Jesus Christ, who redeemed us from death and leads us to the kingdom of heaven.

Hear us, gracious Father, almighty, everlasting God, and grant what we ask and pray of you; through. . . .

Dearly beloved brethren, at the death of priests the custom also
of the ancient Church is to be kept, that when others have
passed away, whoever are most worthy should be elected in
their place, through whose teaching the Catholic faith and the
Christian religion may stand fast, lest a violent robber break into
the sheepfold of the Lord and, when the shepherd is absent, a
thief in the night attack the scattered sheep. Since by the disposition of God your priest has thus been taken away, you must act
carefully, in order that, into the place of the deceased, such a
successor may be provided for the Church, that by his constant
watchfulness and unceasing care, the order of the Church and
the faith of the believers may, in the fear of God, grow stronger;
a man who, as the Apostle teaches, may himself show in all his
teaching the pattern of good works[14]; whose character, speech,
countenance, presence, teaching may be a source of strength;
who as a good shepherd may instruct you in the faith, teach the
example of patience, impart the doctrine of religion, and enforce
the example of charity by means of every good work.[15]

By the will of the Lord, therefore, in place of N., of pious mem-
ory, with the testimony of the presbyters and of the whole clergy
and with the advice of the citizens and of those assembled, we
believe that the reverend N. should be elected, a man honorable
in his birth, as you know, exemplary in his demeanor,
unblamable in religion, firm in faith, rich in mercy, humble, just,
peaceful, patient, having charity, steadfast, abounding in all the
good things together that are to be desired in priests. Therefore,
dearly beloved brethren, acclaim this man, chosen by the testimony of good works, as most worthy of the priesthood, crying
out your praises together, and say: He is worthy.

[BIDDING][16]

Dearly beloved brethren, let us beseech God, conveyor of all holiness and piety, who has established his propitiation and sacrifices and rites, for this his servant whom he has willed to exalt
in the Church and to place in the seat of the elders,[17] by the
harmonious decisions which he has inspired and by the loyal
wishes spread forth among his people and by the testimony of
their voices, setting him with the princes of his people[18]; at their

unanimous prayer may he now adorn this same man with the high priesthood, in the fullness of deserved honor, in the grace of spiritual gifts, in the abundance of sacred endowments, and especially in the virtue of humility; as a ruler may he not lift up himself too much, but humbling himself with regard to all, though he be greater, may he be among them as one of them,[19] trembling at all the judgments of our Lord, not for himself alone but for the whole people entrusted to his care; may he be mindful of the souls that will be required of the hands of all who watch over them[20]; may he keep watch for the safety of all, ever proving himself most zealous in his pastoral diligence on behalf of the sheep of the Lord entrusted to him.

That he who is to be raised up over the elect, chosen by all, may be made fit by each and every hallowed and hallowing rite, may we be aided by the most earnest and unanimous prayers of all in this rite of his consecration and of our supplication, which is a most complete and perfect blessing, the highest given to man through man. May the prayer of all rest on him, on whom is placed the burden of praying for all. May the yearning of the whole Church obtain for him virtue, piety, holiness, and the other sacred endowments of the high priesthood which are useful to the whole Church, of our Lord God, who is the flowing wellspring of holy gifts, who gives to all abundantly, bestowing most swiftly and most fully upon the priest what is asked with devout desire for the superabundant holiness of all his people; through our Lord himself.

[ORDINATION PRAYER][21]
. . . May their feet, by your aid, be beautiful for bringing good tidings of peace, for bringing your good tidings of good.[22] Give them, Lord, a ministry of reconciliation[23] in word and in deeds and in power of signs and of wonders.[24] May their speech and preaching be not with enticing words of human wisdom, but in demonstration of the Spirit and of power.[25] Grant to them, O Lord, that they may use the keys of the kingdom of heaven[26] for upbuilding, not for destruction, and may not glory in the power which you bestow.[27] Whatsoever they bind on earth, may it be bound also in heaven, and whatsoever they loose on earth, may it be loosed also in heaven.[28] Whose sins they retain, may they be retained; and whose sins they forgive, do you forgive.[29] Who-

ever blesses them, may he be blessed; and whoever curses them, may he be filled with curses.[30] May they be faithful and wise servants, whom you, Lord, set over your household that they may give them food in due season,[31] in order that they may show forth an entire perfect man.[32] May they be unwearied in watchfulness; may they be fervent in spirit.[33] May they hate pride, love truth, and never be so overcome by faintness or fear as to abandon it. May they not put light for darkness nor darkness for light; may they not say evil is good nor good evil.[34] May they be debtors to the wise and to the unwise, and may they have fruit of the benefit of all. . . .[35]

Mozarabic

XIII. BLESSING FOR ORDAINING A SUBDEACON

First is given to him by the archdeacon the vessels for washing hands, and the paten and chalice. Then is said for him this prayer:

PRAYER

God, who commanded ministers to prepare unceasingly in your tabernacle and, kindest rewarder, showed yourself to be their heritage, so that thinking nothing about the world, they might remain in your sacristy day and night and there occupy themselves constantly in the duty of their office in the sacred ministry; look, we pray, on this your servant N., whom we advance to the office of the subdiaconate by the testimony of his elders. Lord, illuminate him with your blessing and sanctify him by the infusion of your Holy Spirit; so that he may always stand as a worthy minister in the sight of your majesty, and may deserve, with your assistance, to ascend to the rank of a higher office and be fit, with your guidance, to attain the reward of eternal blessedness.

COMPLETION OF THE SAME

Lord God almighty, sanctify this your servant N., whom we consecrate, with your favor, to the ministry of the subdiaconate by the office of our hands. May he be humble, calm, and peaceful in the sight of your majesty. Afford him your aid, that he may serve you with a pure heart. May he retain in himself, with your help, the reward of charity, so that having mortified his faults he may grow in virtues, and by good behavior may attain, with your assent, to a higher rank. Amen.

This being completed, the bishop gives him the book of the apostle Paul, and says to him this exhortation:

EXHORTATION AFTER THE SUBDEACON IS ORDAINED

Receive the apostolic documents and proclaim them in the Church of God. See also that what you proclaim with your mouth you believe in your heart; that what you believe in your heart you fulfill in your deeds. Amen.

XIIII. BIDDING FOR ORDAINING A DEACON

As soon as he comes to be ordained, the bishop puts a stole on him on his left shoulder, and thus says over him these three prayers.[2]

COLLECT[3]

Let the prayer of all follow the wish of all; so that, at the supplication of the Church, this man who is prepared for the ministry of the diaconate, being helped by the Lord, may be resplendent in the office of levitical blessing, and being glorious with spiritual benediction among the blooming lilies of the holy altar, may shine with the grace of holiness.

ANOTHER BLESSING

God, author of the universe, bestower of life, discerner of minds, sanctifier of spirits, look down upon this your servant, N., and vouchsafe to assist him whom we dedicate to the office of deacon, humbly offering him to you and to your most sacred altar. And, Lord, inasmuch as we are men, knowing not divine thought and certainly ignorant of the human conscience, reckoning the innocence of this man as well as we are able, we propose our judgment for a brother of what ever sort he is. Unknown things do not slip by you; hidden things do not escape you. You are the witness of hearts, the discerner of minds. All things work for you, everything does you service. You are able to show heavenly judgment in this matter, to abide by the comforting Spirit, to give what we ask to the worthy or unworthy; that, lifted up from what is small and raised to what is great, by your wondrous right hand he may obtain the degree of ecclesiastical dignity, like theirs, whom your apostles, choosing in sevenfold number, dedicated as messengers of peace and ministry.

With preparation let him attend your altars as Joshua attended Moses your servant, and as Samuel ministered growing up in the temple. Let there abound in him the perfect order of virtues: modesty, authority, innocence discipline. Let him continue in Christ strong and stable, and may he ever be worthy by fitting advancement to be raised from the small to greater things; so that with the assistance of the grace of the Holy Spirit, being faithful in the judgment of your Son our Lord, he may rejoice to render a good account of himself. We beseech your glory, most merciful Father, who as one God are glorious in Trinity, world without end. Amen.

ANOTHER COLLECT

God, who have established the service of your temple in the choice of Levi; who have willed that the order of Levites be for the ministry of serving your name, bless we beseech you, this your servant, N., being joined unto the order of Levites. May he meditate day and night upon your law and teach it, and like Saint Stephen, endowed with special grace, may he ever overcome and conquer the enemies of the Catholic faith. May he have the power of the Holy Spirit, so that, made worthy of grace, he may ever fitly deliver your chalice to the thirsty. Amen.

COMPLETION OF THE SAME

Accomplish, Lord, what we ask and finish what we seek; and be ever thus gracious, that, having been called upon, you may not in any respect fail us. Amen.

This being completed, the bishop gives him the gospel book, and says to him this exhortation:

EXHORTATION AFTER THE DEACON IS ORDAINED

Behold, son, receive the Gospel of Christ, that from it you may proclaim good grace to the faithful people; and have the power of ministering all the ceremonies of the divine ministry at the altar of God. Observe, therefore, the degree of your order, and know yourself to be the minister of the presbyter as also of the bishop. Have modesty and restraint of tongue, chastity and sobriety, and a ministry of faith and a pure conscience. And so minister that you may have bestowed by God, whose minister you have been made, the promise of this life and of that to come.

This being done, he who has been ordained kisses the bishop.

XVII. BIDDING FOR ORDAINING A PRESBYTER

When he who is to be ordained presbyter comes, a stole is hung around his neck, and he is vested in a chasuble; and, while he remains before the altar on his right knee, the presbyters lay hands on him, and he is thus blessed by the bishop with these three blessings:[4]

May it be our common prayer to God, brethren, that this man, who is chosen for our aid and the furtherance of your salvation, may by the mercy of divine assistance secure the blessing of the presbyterate, and may be made fruitful by the bountifulness of the Holy Spirit, and may obtain the dignity of honor and virtue, that he be not found blameworthy in anything. Amen. With the support of the Lord.

PRAYER FOR ORDAINING A PRESBYTER

God, who commanded that the order of elders who were to be set over your Church be constituted in the tabernacle of your temple; sanctify this your servant, N., whom by the action of our hands we consecrate with the honor of the presbyterate for N. church. May he keep the discipline of holy Church with the custody of a good life. May he fill his accepted office without blame, and may he be radiant with the tokens of a most honest life. As a teacher of the people and a ruler of those under him, may he hold the Catholic faith rightly, and may he proclaim the true salvation to all. May he also educate himself in his own mind, and make his body chaste. May he carry out his reading in his work, and may he improve his work by reading. May faith be sufficient to him for his life; chastity, for his presbyterate; quiet, for his humility: so that leading his life in chastity and faith, he may instruct with the doctrines committed to him as well as impart the examples of his deeds. Amen. By your permission, O Savior. . . .

COMPLETION

Complete now, Lord, the fullness of your mystery, and having equipped your priest with adornments of every honor, hallow him with the odor of heavenly ointment. Amen.

Mozarabic

This being done, he gives him the manual, and says to him this exhortation:

EXHORTATION AFTER THE PRESBYTER IS ORDAINED

Behold, brother, you have become a colleague of our order for teaching the mysteries of Christ. Have, therefore, access and power to approach the altar of God. See to it that sanctifying in your heart the holy mysteries, and confessing them with your mouth, you dispense them to all the faithful for their sanctification. Amen.

This being done, the bishop kisses him, and he stands in his order.

An Ordination Prayer Used in England: The Leofric Missal[1]

CONSECRATION

Holy Father, almighty God, who through our Lord Jesus Christ have from the beginning formed all things and afterwards at the end of time, according to the promise which our patriarch Abraham had received, have also founded the Church with a congregation of holy people, having made decrees through which religion might be orderly ruled with laws given by you; grant that this your servant may be worthy in the services and all the functions faithfully performed, that he may be able to celebrate the mysteries of the sacraments instituted of old. By you may he be consecrated to the high priesthood to which he is elevated. May your blessing be upon him, though the hand be ours. Command, Lord, this man to feed your sheep, and grant that as a diligent shepherd he may be watchful in the care of the flock entrusted to him. May your Holy Spirit be with this man as a bestower of heavenly gifts, so that, as that chosen teacher of the Gentiles[2] taught, he may be in justice not wanting, in kindness strong, in hospitality rich[3]; in exhortation may he give heed to readiness, in persecutions to faith, in love to patience, in truth to steadfastness; in heresies and all vices may he know hatred, in strifes may he know nothing; in judgments may he not show favor, and yet grant that he may be favorable. Finally, may he learn from you in abundance all the things which he should teach your people to their health. May he reckon priesthood itself to be a task, not a privilege. May increase of honor come to him, to the encouragement of his merits also, so that through these, just as with us now he is admitted to the priesthood, so with you hereafter he may be admitted to the kingdom; through. . . .

The Later Composite Rite: The Sacramentary of Angoulême[1]

THE ORDER OF A DOORKEEPER

When a doorkeeper is ordained. . . .
[Rubric from *Statuta Ecclesiae Antiqua* 97, pp. 222–223.]

BIDDING FOR A DOORKEEPER

Let us humbly beseech . . . of the Lord; who. . . .
[The Gallican bidding, p. 223.]

BLESSING OF THE SAME

Holy Lord . . . of the reward; through our Lord. . . .
[The Gallican blessing, p. 223.]

THE ORDER OF A READER

When a reader is ordained. . . .
[Rubric from *Statuta Ecclesiae Antiqua* 96, p. 222.]

BIDDING FOR A READER

Your brothers choose you. . . .
[The Gallican bidding, p. 223.]

BLESSING OF A READER

Holy Lord . . . through our Lord. . . .
[The Gallican blessing, p. 223.]

THE ORDER OF AN EXORCIST

When an exorcist is ordained. . . .
[Rubric from *Statuta Ecclesiae Antiqua* 95, p. 222.]

BIDDING FOR AN EXORCIST

Let us humbly beseech. . . .
[The Gallican bidding, p. 224.]

BLESSING OF AN EXORCIST

Holy Lord . . . grace of healing; through our Lord. . . .
[The Gallican blessing, p. 224.]

THE ORDER OF AN ACOLYTE

When an acolyte is ordained. . . .
[Rubric from *Statuta Ecclesiae Antiqua* 94, p. 222.]

BLESSING OF AN ACOLYTE

Holy Lord, almighty Father, eternal God, who through Jesus Christ your Son sent the light of brightness into this world and on the triumphant cross of his passion deigned to pour from his side blood and water for the human race and through your apostles in this age have sent the light of spiritual grace; so deign to bless this your servant N. in the office of acolyte that he may faithfully minister at illuminating the brightness of your church and at presenting the wine and water for the confecting of your blood in the offering of the eucharist at your holy altar; illuminate, Lord, his mind and heart with your love of heavenly grace, strengthen him with the power of your mercy; through. . . .[2]

THE ORDER BY WHICH IN THE ROMAN CHURCH OF THE APOSTOLIC SEE SUBDEACONS, DEACONS, AND PRESBYTERS ARE TO BE APPOINTED

In the first, fourth, seventh, and tenth months on Wednesday and Friday the candidates are to be tested according to the canons [to ascertain] whether they are worthy to discharge this duty. On the Saturday of Twelve Readings at St. Peter's, where mass is celebrated, after they have sung the antiphon to the introit, and the collect has been said, the pope makes an announcement to the people, saying:

With the help of the Lord God and our Savior Jesus Christ.

Again he says:

With the help of the Lord God and our Savior Jesus Christ, we choose for the order of the diaconate *or* presbyterate N., subdeacon of the title N./N., deacon of the title N./N., presbyter of the title N. If anyone has anything against these men, before God and for the sake of God let him come forth with confidence and speak. However, let him be mindful of his communion.

And after a short while all begin the ninefold Kyrie eleison with the litany. When this is finished, all the candidates go up to the pope's chair and he blesses them, after which they are called and come down, and when the blessing has been received, they stand in their orders.
[Variant form of rubrics that appear in the Gelasian Sacramentary.]

THE ORDER OF A SUBDEACON

When a subdeacon is ordained . . .
[Rubric from *Statuta Ecclesiae Antiqua* 93, p. 222.]

THE ORDER OF A SUBDEACON

Let the empty paten and chalice . . . hand him the chalice and paten.
[The Gallican rubrics and allocution, p. 224.]

BIDDING AT THE ORDINATION OF A SUBDEACON

Let us pray . . . for the saints; through. . . .
[The Gallican bidding, p. 224.]

BLESSING OF A SUBDEACON

Holy Lord . . . through our Lord. . . .
[The Gallican prayer, p. 225.]

THE ORDER OF A DEACON

When a deacon is ordained, let only the bishop who blesses him put his hand on his head. The rest of the priests, however, should touch his head beside the hand of the bishop, since he is consecrated not for the priesthood but for the ministry. Through. . . .
[Rubric from *Statuta Ecclesiae Antiqua* 92 (p. 222), but with the inserted concession that the priests also may touch him, proba-

bly copied by scribal error from the rubric for a presbyter. It is also carelessly concluded as if it were a prayer!]

FOR A DEACON
Let us pray . . . consecration bestowed; through. . . .
[The Roman bidding, p. 216.]

THE COLLECT FOLLOWS
O Lord God almighty . . . to be sought; through. . . .
[The first Roman collect, with the word "almighty" added, p. 216.]

CONSECRATION
Assist us . . . higher things; through. . . .
[The northern recension of the Roman ordination prayer, pp. 216–217.]

FOR CONSUMMATING THE OFFICE OF THE DIACONATE
Let the prayer of all . . . of holiness; through. . . .
[The Gallican bidding, p. 225.]

THE BLESSING FOLLOWS
Holy Lord . . . may find favor; through our Lord. . . .
[The Gallican ordination prayer, pp. 225–226.]

THE ORDER OF A PRESBYTER
When a presbyter is ordained. . . .
[Rubric from *Statuta Ecclesiae Antiqua* 91, p. 222.]

ALLOCUTION TO THE PEOPLE AT THE ORDINATION OF A PRESBYTER
Since, dearly beloved . . . with a common voice; through. . . .
[The Gallican allocution, p. 226.]

FOR ORDAINING A PRESBYTER
Let us pray, dearly beloved . . . by his aid; through Christ. . . .
[The Roman bidding, p. 217.]

THE COLLECT FOLLOWS
Hear us . . . to be consecrated; through. . . .
[The Roman collect, pp. 217–218.]

CONSECRATION
O Lord, holy Father . . . of eternal blessedness; through. . . .
[The northern recension of the Roman ordination prayer, p. 218.]

CONSUMMATION FOR PRIESTS
May it be our common prayer . . . in his office; through. . . .
[The Gallican bidding, pp. 226 227.]

BLESSING
O God, author of all sanctification . . . the Holy Spirit;
through. . . .
[The Gallican ordination prayer, p. 227.]

HERE YOU VEST HIM IN THE CHASUBLE
The blessing of the Father and of the Son and of the Holy Spirit
descend upon you, and may you be blessed in the priestly order
and offer acceptable sacrifices for the sins and offenses of the
people to almighty God, to whom be honor and glory.

CONSECRATION OF THE HANDS
May these hands be consecrated. . . .
[The first Gallican formulary for anointing, p. 227.]

THE ORDER OF A BISHOP
When a bishop is ordained. . . .
[Rubric from *Statuta Ecclesiae Antiqua* 90, p. 222.]

EXHORTATION TO THE PEOPLE WHEN A BISHOP IS ORDAINED

Dearly beloved brethren . . . He is worthy. Amen.
[The Gallican allocution, p. 228.]

COLLECTS CONCERNING THE ORDINATION OF A BISHOP

Let us pray, our dearly beloved, that the goodness of almighty God may bestow the abundance of his grace upon these men appointed for the service of the Church; through our Lord. . . .[3]

Hear, O Lord. . . .
[The first Roman collect, p. 215.]

Be gracious, O Lord. . . .
[The second Roman collect, p. 215.]

CONSECRATION

God of all the honors . . . sincerity of peace. May their feet . . . benefit of all. Grant to them an episcopal throne. . . .
[The Roman ordination prayer with the Gallican material interpolated into it, pp. 215–216 and 229–230.]

CONSECRATION OF THE HANDS

May these hands be anointed. . . .
[The second Gallican formula for anointing the hands of presbyters, p. 227.]

Appendix A: The Relationship Between Eastern Ordination Prayers

	Armenian	E. Syrian	Georgian	Melkite	Byzantine	Jacobite
B I S H O P			GEO 1 = TD		BYZ 1	
		Esyr————	GEO 2 – – – – – – –		BYZ 2	JAC
			GEO 3			
P R E S B Y T E R	ARM 1				BYZ 1	
	ARM 2			MEL 1——BYZ 2——JAC		
	ARM 3		GEO 1——MEL ?			
			GEO 2 = TD	MEL 3		
		Esyr————	GEO 3	MEL 4		
D E A C O N	ARM 1			MEL 1		
	ARM 2		GEO 1——MEL 2			
			GEO 2 = TD	MEL 3——BYZ 1		
		ESyr————	GEO 3	MEl 4	BYZ 2——JAC	
S U B	ARM		GEO 1——MEL 1			
		ESyr	GEO 2	MEL 2——BYZ——JAC		
				MEL 3		
R E A D E R		ESyr		MEL 1		JAC 1
	ARM————————GEO – – – –MEL 2– – –BYZ——JAC 2					
						JAC 3

A broken line indicates some similarity between prayers; a solid line indicates close verbal parallels.

The Coptic rite combines the Jacobite prayers with those from *Apostolic Constitutions;* the Maronite rite has been omitted from this table because of its complexity.

Appendix B: Synopsis of Eastern Ordination Prayers for a Bishop

Byzantine: Prayer 2	*Coptic*	*Georgian: Prayer 2*	*East Syrian*	*Jacobite*
Lord our God,		O God . . . who created all things by the word of your command. . .	God . . . who created all things by the power of your word. . .	God, who created all things by your power . . . who gave your beloved Son . . . and by his precious blood
who . . . by your dispensation have established teachers.		who by the precious blood of your only-begotten Son have established churches and manifested in them teachers, by whom has been spread over the whole earth the knowledge of your truth vouchsafed to those born of men by the Prince, your Only-begotten Son . . . now also, O Lord God,	who by the precious blood of your beloved Son . . . have redeemed your holy Church and established in it . . . teachers and priests, by whose work might be multiplied the knowledge of the truth which your only-begotten Son gave to the human race;	established your Church and instituted every priestly order in it; who gave us leaders so that we might please you by making the knowledge of the name of your Christ multiplied and glorified throughout the world;
Lord, make him . . . to be an imitator of you the true shepherd, giving his life for your sheep, guide of the blind, light of those in darkness, corrector	Vouchsafe, Lord, to fill him with healing graces and instructive speech, that he may be a guide of the blind and a light of those who are in darkness, teacher of	Look down on this your servant, and elect him with the election of the Holy Spirit, so that he may become a perfect priest after the example of the true	Lord, now also let your face shine on this your servant and elect him with a holy election by the unction of the Holy Spirit, so that he may be for you a	send on this your servant your holy and spiritual Spirit,

246

of the ignorant, a lamp in the world,

so that, after having formed in this present life the souls who have been entrusted to him,

he may stand before your judgment-seat without shame and receive the great reward which you have prepared for those who have striven for the preaching of your gospel. . . .

the ignorant, a lamp in the world, dividing the word of truth, being a true shepherd, giving his life for his sheep,

so that he may prepare the souls who have been entrusted to him . . . that he may find means to stand with confidence before the dreadful judgment-seat, looking to the great reward which you have prepared for those who have striven for the preaching of the gospel. . . .

shepherd who lays down his life for his sheep . . . prosper him in the words of truth . . . so that he may be the light of those who sit in darkness, the teacher of those who lack understanding, the instructor of children . . .

so that he may stand before your holy altar and in the terrible day of your manifestation he may receive, together with your faithful laborers, a goodly reward. . . .

perfect priest, who will imitate the true high-priest who lays down his life for us . . . may he preach the right word of truth, so that he may be a light to those who sit in darkness, the teacher of those who lack understanding, and the instructor of children . . . that he may gather and increase your people and the sheep of your pasture, and may perfect the souls entrusted to him . . . and may stand confidently before your dreadful judgment-seat, and be worthy to receive from you the reward which has been promised to faithful laborers. . . .

so that he may feed and visit your Church

which has been entrusted to him. . . .

Select Bibliography of Secondary Literature

GENERAL

Bernard Botte, "Holy Orders in the Ordination Prayers," in *The Sacrament of Holy Orders* (London/Collegeville, MN, 1962), pp. 5–23.

P. M. Gy, "Ancient Ordination Prayers," *SL* 13 (1979), pp. 70–93.

——, "La théologie des prières anciennes pour l'ordination des évêques et des prêtres," *Revue des sciences philosophiques et théologiques* 58 (1974), pp. 599–617.

A. G. Martimort, *Deaconesses: An Historical Study* (San Francisco, 1986).

PATRISTIC

O. Bârlea, *Die Weihe der Bischöfe, Presbyter und Diakone in vornicänischer Zeit* (Munich, 1969).

P. van Beneden, *Aux origines d'une terminologie sacramentelle: "ordo," "ordinare," "ordinatio" dans la littérature chrétienne avant 313* (Louvain, 1974).

Paul F. Bradshaw, *Liturgical Presidency in the Early Church*, GLS 36 (Nottingham, 1983).

——, "Ordination," in G. J. Cuming (ed.), *Essays on Hippolytus*, GLS 15 (Nottingham, 1978), pp. 33–38.

——, "The participation of other bishops in the ordination of a bishop in the Apostolic Tradition of Hippolytus," *SP* 18 (forthcoming).

Alexandre Faivre, *Naissance d'une hiérarchie: les premières étapes du cursus clérical* (Paris, 1977).

Roger Gryson, *The Ministry of Women in the Early Church* (Collegeville, MN, 1976).

Joseph Lécuyer, "Note sur la liturgie du sacre des évêques," *EL* 66 (1952), pp. 369–372.

——, "Episcopat et presbytérat dans les écrits d'Hippolyte de Rome," *Recherches de science religieuse* 41 (1953), pp. 30–50.

E. C. Ratcliff, "Apostolic Tradition. Questions concerning the appointment of the Bishop," *SP* 8 (1966), pp. 266–270 and in A. H. Couratin and David Tripp (eds.), *E. C. Ratcliff. Liturgical Studies* (London, 1976), pp. 156–160.

K. Richter, "Zum Ritus der Bischofsordination in der "Apostolischen Überlieferung" Hippolyts von Rom und davon abhängigen Schriften," *ALW* 17 (1975), pp. 7–51.

W. Rordorf, "L'ordination de l'évêque selon la Tradition apostolique d'Hippolyte de Rome," *Questions Liturgiques* 55 (1974), pp. 136–150.

Eric Segelburg, "The ordination prayers in Hippolytus," *SP* 13 (1975), pp. 397–408.

EASTERN

P. Antoine, "L'ordination sacerdotale chez les coptes unis," *ROC* 28 (1931/1932), pp. 362–374.

Bernard Botte, "La formule d'ordination 'La grâce divine' dans les rites orientaux," *OS* 2 (1957), pp. 285–296.

————, "Les ordinations dans les rites orientaux," *BCES* 6 (1962), pp. 13–18.

Pierre Dib, *Étude sur la Liturgie Maronite* (Paris, 1919), pp. 169–224.

J. M. Hanssens, "Les oraisons sacramentalles des ordinations orientales," *OCP* 18 (1952), pp. 297–318 and in *idem, La liturgie d'Hippolyte: documents et études* (Rome, 1970), pp. 263–285.

G. Khouri-Sarkis, "Le rituel du sacre des évêques et des patriarches dans l'Église syrienne d'Antioche," *OS* 8 (1963), pp. 137–164.

E. Lanne, "Les ordinations dans le rite copte: leurs relations avec les Constitutions Apostoliques et la Tradition de saint Hippolyte," *OS* 5 (1960), pp. 89–106.

Alphonse Raes, "Les ordinations dans le Pontifical chaldéen," *OS* 5 (1960), pp. 63–80.

Jean Tchékan, "Elements d'introduction à l'étude de la liturgie byzantine des ordinations," *BCES* 10 (1968), pp. 190–208.

C. Vagaggini, "L'ordinazione delle diaconesse nella tradizione greca e bizantina," *OCP* 40 (1974), pp. 145–189.

WESTERN

Bernard Botte, "Le Rituel d'ordination des *Statuta Ecclesiae antiqua*," *Recherches de théologie ancienne et médiévale* 11 (1939), pp. 223–241.

————, "Le sacre épiscopal dans le rite romain," *Questions liturgiques et paroissiales* 25 (1940), pp. 22–32.

Select Bibliography of Secondary Literature

————, "Secundi meriti munus," *Questions liturgiques et paroissiales* 21 (1936), pp. 84–88.

Miquel S. Gros, "Les plus anciennes formules romaines de bénédiction des diacres," *Ecclesia Orans* 5 (1988) pp. 45–52.

Bruno Kleinheyer, *Die Priesterweihe in römischen Ritus* (Trier, 1962).

————, "Studien zur nichtromisch-westlichen Ordinationsliturgie," *ALW* 22 (1980), pp. 93–107; 23 (1981), pp. 313–366.

K. Richter, *Die Ordination des Bischofs von Rom* (Münster, 1976).

Antonio Santantoni, *L'ordinazione episcopale: storia e teologia dei riti dell'ordinazione nelle antiche liturgie dell'Occidente.* Studia Anselmiana 69 (Rome, 1976).

Notes

1. Critical edition by Bernard Botte, *La Tradition Apostolique de saint Hippolyte* (Münster, 1963; 4th Ed., 1972); English translation by G. J. Cuming, *Hippolytus. A Text for Students*, GLS 8 (Nottingham, 1976).

2. See especially J. M. Hanssens, *La Liturgie d'Hippolyte* I (Rome, 1959; 2nd Ed., 1965), II (Rome, 1970).

3. Paul F. Bradshaw, "Ordination," in G. J. Cuming (ed.), *Essays on Hippolytus*, GLS 15 (Nottingham, 1978), pp. 33–38; *idem*, "The participation of other bishops in the ordination of a bishop in the Apostolic Tradition of Hippolytus," *SP* 18 (forthcoming); E. C. Ratcliff, "Apostolic Tradition. Questions concerning the appointment of the Bishop," *SP* 8 (1966), pp. 266–270 and in A. H. Couratin and David Tripp (eds.), *E. C. Ratcliff. Liturgical Studies* (London, 1976), pp. 156–160; Eric Segelburg, "The ordination prayers in Hippolytus," *SP* 13 (1975), pp. 397–408; A. F. Walls, "The Latin version of Hippolytus' Apostolic Tradition," *SP* 3 (1961), pp. 155–162.

4. Critical edition by René-Georges Coquin, *Les Canons d'Hippolyte*, Patrologia Orientalis 31.2 (Paris, 1966); English translation in Paul F. Bradshaw, *The Canons of Hippolytus*, Alcuin/GROW Liturgical Study 2 (Nottingham, 1987).

5. Critical edition with French translation by Marcel Metzger, *Les Constitutions Apostoliques*, Sources Chrétiennes 320, 329, 336 (Paris, 1985–7); English translation by James Donaldson, *Constitutions of the Holy Apostles* (Edinburgh, 1886/New York, 1926).

6. P. Jounel, "Ordinations," in A. G. Martimort (ed.), *The Church at Prayer* III (Collegeville, MN, 1987), p. 147.

7. Syriac text with Latin translation by I. E. Rahmani, *Testamentum Domini nostri Jesu Christi* (Mainz, 1899; Hildesheim, 1968); English translation by James Cooper and A. J. Maclean, *The Testament of Our Lord Translated into English from the Syriac* (Edinburgh, 1902); critical edition of the Ethiopic, with French translation, by Robert Beylot, *Le Testamentum Domini éthiopien* (Louvain, 1984).

8. Text in F. E. Brightman, "The Sacramentary of Sarapion of Thmuis," *JTS* 1 (1900), pp. 88–113, 247–277; English translation by John Wordsworth, *Bishop Sarapion's Prayer-Book* (London, 1909, 2nd Ed., 1923; Hamden, CT, 1964).

9. Bernard Botte, "L'Euchologe de Serapion est-il authentique?" *OC* 48 (1964), pp. 50–56; G. J. Cuming, "Thmuis revisited: Another look at the prayers of Bishop Sarapion," *TS* 41 (1980), pp. 568–575.

10. "Ancient Ordination Prayers," *SL* 13 (1979), p. 73.

11. "Les oraisons sacramentalles des ordinations orientales," *OCP* 18 (1952), pp. 297–318 and in *idem, La liturgie d'Hippolyte* II, pp. 263–285.

12. See G. Winkler, "Zur Geschichte des armenischen Gottesdienstes im Hinblick auf den in mehreren Wellen erfolgten griechischen Einfluss," *OC* 58 (1974), pp. 154–172.

13. F. C. Conybeare, *Rituale Armenorum* (Oxford, 1905), p. xxx.

14. *Ibid.*, p. xxxiii.

15. Venice, San Lazzaro ms. 457 (320): English translation in Conybeare, *Rituale Armenorum*, pp. 228–235.

16. "Les ordinations dans les rites orientaux," *BCES* 6 (1962), p. 17.

17. Jean Morin, *Commentarius de sacris Ecclesiae ordinationibus* (Amsterdam, 1695, 2nd Ed.; Farnborough, 1969), pp. 52–73.

18. See further Miguel Arranz, "Les sacrements de l'ancien euchologe constantinopolitain, Pt. I: Etude préliminaire des sources," *OCP* 48 (1982), pp. 284–335.

19. Vat. copt. 44 (between A.D. 1305 and A.D. 1320); Coptic Museum, Cairo 253 *Lit.* (A.D. 1364); Vat. copt. 49 (the middle of the sixteenth century); Borgia copt. 26 and Vat. copt. 45 (seventeenth century). The other mss. (Borgia copt. 49, 77, 79, 80, 85, 99, 100; Paris BN 98; Vat. copt. 46 and 87) are all of the eighteenth century.

20. *Rituale Ecclesiae Aegyptiacae* (Coloniae Agrippinae, 1653), pp. 239ff.

21. Pp. 440–448. It was also included in Edmond Martène, *De antiquis ecclesiae ritibus* (Antwerp, 1737–1738, 2nd Ed.; Hildesheim, 1967), vol. 2, ch. 8, *Ordo* XXIII.

22. *Liturgiarum Orientalium Collectio* (Paris, 1716) I, pp. 467–490.

23. H. Denzinger, *Ritus Orientalium* (Würzburg, 1863; Graz, 1961), II, pp. 1–64.

24. V. Ermoni, "L'Ordinal copte," *ROC* 3 (1898), pp. 31–38, 191–199, 282–291, 425–434; 4 (1899), pp. 104–115, 416–427, 591–604; 5 (1900), pp. 247–253.

25. E. Lanne, "Les ordinations dans le rite copte: leurs relations avec les Constitutions Apostoliques et la Tradition de saint Hippolyte," *OS* 5

(1960), pp. 90–91. Ermoni, rather strangely, took his text from Paris BN 98 and not from the older mss.

26. *The Rite of Consecration of the Patriarch of Alexandria* (Cairo, 1960); *The Egyptian or Coptic Church: a detailed description of her liturgical services* (Cairo, 1967), pp. 154–187; *Ordination Rites of the Coptic Church* (Cairo, 1985).

27. P. Antoine, "L'ordination sacerdotale chez les coptes unis," *ROC* 28 (1931/1932), pp. 362–374.

28. "Les oraisons sacramentalles," p. 318; *La liturgie d'Hippolyte* I, pp. 376–394.

29. *Op. cit.*, pp. 89–106.

30. "Ancient Ordination Prayers," p. 72.

31. Berlin syr. 38. Others include Vat. syr. 45–46 (A.D. 1556), Cambridge add. 1988 (A.D. 1558), Mosul 55 (A.D. 1568), Diayrbakir 59 (A.D. 1569), Vat. syr. 43 (A.D. 1701).

32. Morin, pp. 364–401; J. S. Assemani, *Bibliotheca orientalis Clementino-vaticana* (Rome, 1719–1728), vol. 3, pt. 2, pp. 793ff.; J. A. Assemani, *Codex Liturgicus Ecclesiae Universae* (Rome, 1749–1766; Farnborough, 1968–1969), vol. 13. Morin's translation was reproduced in Martène, vol. 2., ch. 8, *Ordo XXI.*

33. *The Nestorians and their Rituals* (London, 1852; Farnborough, 1969), II, pp. 322–349.

34. *Pontificale iuxta ritum Ecclesiae Syrorum Orientalium*, 4 fascicles (Vatican City, 1937–1938).

35. "Les ordinations dans le Pontifical chaldéen," *OS* 5 (1960), pp. 63–80.

36. "Holy Orders in the Ordination Prayers," in *The Sacrament of Holy Orders* (London/Collegeville, MN, 1962), pp. 15–17.

37. Tiflis A 86: English translation in F. C. Conybeare and Oliver Wardrop, "The Georgian version of the Liturgy of St. James," *ROC* 19 (1914), pp. 155–173.

38. "Ancient Ordination Prayers," p. 78; see also p. 76 and n. 36.

39. For a translation of this note, see A. G. Martimort, *Deaconesses: An Historical Study* (San Francisco, 1986), p. 167.

40. The others are BN syr. 113 (written prior to 1579); BN syr. 110 and 114 (fifteenth century); and Borg. syr. 57, copied from Vat. syr. 51 in A.D. 1668.

41. Though a critical edition of the manuscripts of the rites for the diaconate and presbyterate used in the Jacobite communities of the East under the Metropolitan of Tagrit on the Tigris has recently been prepared by René Mouret and is forthcoming in *Patrologia Orientalis*.

42. *Op. cit.*, pp. 402–416. Morin's translation was reproduced in Martène, vol. 2., ch. 8, *Ordo XXII*.

43. "Ordination du prêtre dans le rite jacobite," *ROC* 1.2 (1896), pp. 1–36.

44. "Le rituel du sacre des évêques et des patriarches dans l'Église syrienne d'Antioche," *OS* 8 (1963), pp. 137–164.

45. *Op. cit.*, II, pp. 65–108.

46. J. M. Vosté, *Pontificale iuxta ritum Ecclesiae Syrorum occidentalium, id est Antiochae, versio latina* (Vatican City, 1941–1944), pp. 155–241.

47. "Le rituel du sacre des évêques et des patriarches dans l'Église syrienne d'Antioche," *OS* 8 (1963), pp. 165–212.

48. The oldest is Vat. syr. 309 (A.D. 1296); For later examples, see P.-E. Gemayel, *Avant-messe maronite: histoire et structure* (Rome, 1965), p. 125, n. 1.

49. *Étude sur la Liturgie Maronite* (Paris, 1919), pp. 169–224.

50. See Dib, pp. 169–174.

51. Morin, pp. 310–363: see Dib, p. 172, n. 1. Morin's translation was reproduced in Martène, vol. 2, ch. 8, *Ordo XX*.

52. *Op. cit.*, vols. 9–10.

53. *Op. cit.*, II, pp. 108–226.

54. British Museum Or. 4951: Matthew Black, *Rituale Melchitarum* (Stuttgart, 1938).

55. Text in C. L. Feltoe, *Sacramentarium Leonianum* (Cambridge, 1896), pp. 119–123, 139–140; L. C. Mohlberg, *Sacramentarium Veronese* (Rome, 1956), pp. 118–122, 138–139.

56. Text in H. A. Wilson, *The Gelasian Sacramentary* (Oxford, 1894), pp. 22–28, 151–152; L. C. Mohlberg, *Liber Sacramentorum Romanae Aeclesiae Ordini Anni Circuli* (Rome, 1960), pp. 24–28, 120–122.

57. L. C. Mohlberg, *Missale Francorum* (Rome, 1957), pp. 6–13.

58. See especially P. Cagin, *Le Sacramentaire Gélasien d'Angoulême* (Angoulême, 1919), pp. 148–152; P. Saint-Roch, *Liber sacramentorum Engolismensis* (Turnhout, 1987), pp. 313–325; A. Dumas, *Liber sacramentorum gellonensis* (Turnhout, 1981), pp. 381–395.

59. Text in H. A. Wilson, *The Gregorian Sacramentary* (London, 1915), pp. 5–8; D. H. Lietzmann, *Das Sacramentarium Gregorianum* (Münster, 1921), pp. 5–9; J. Deshusses, *Le sacramentaire grégorien* I (Fribourg, 1971; 2nd Ed., 1979), pp. 92–98.

60. *Ordines XXXIV–XL*: text in M. Andrieu, *Les Ordines Romani*, vols. III–IV (Louvain, 1951, 1956).

61. Text in Andrieu, III, pp. 616–619; G. Morin, *Caesari Opera Omnia* (Maredsous, 1942), II, pp. 90–96; C. Munier, *Les Statuta Ecclesiae Antiqua* (Paris, 1960), pp. 95–99, reproduced in his *Concilia Galliae A. 314—A. 506* (Turnhout, 1963), pp. 181–185. See also Bernard Botte, "Le Rituel d'ordination des *Statuta Ecclesiae antiqua*," *Recherches de théologie ancienne et médiévale* 11 (1939), pp. 223–241.

62. For the text of these, see nn. 56, 57, and 58 above.

63. "Studien zur nichtromisch-westlichen Ordinationsliturgie," *ALW* 23 (1981), pp. 313–366.

64. *Le Liber Ordinum* (Paris, 1904), col. 48–50, 54–55.

65. *De Eccl. Off.* 2.5 (*PL* 83.780–786); cf. also *Ep. I Leudefredo* (*PL* 83.893–898).

66. F. E. Warren, *The Leofric Missal* (Oxford, 1883), p. 217. On this book, see further Bruno Kleinheyer, "Studien zur nichtromisch-westlichen Ordinationsliturgie," *ALW* 22 (1980), pp. 93–107.

67. *Ibid.*, pp. xxvi-xxvii.

68. See H. Ménard, *Liber Sacramentorum* (*PL* 78.503D).

69. H. A. Wilson, *The Benedictional of Archbishop Robert* (London, 1902), p. 127.

70. H. A. Wilson, *The Pontifical of Magdalen College* (London, 1910), pp. 75–76.

71. See W. Maskell, *Monumenta Ritualia Ecclesiae Anglicanae* (Oxford, 1882, 2nd Ed.), pp. 281–282.

72. *L'ordinazione episcopale: storia e teologia dei riti dell'ordinazione nelle antiche liturgie dell'Occidente*, Studia Anselmiana 69 (Rome, 1976), pp. 98–106.

73. See p. 15.

Notes for Pages 14 to 17

74. See p. 15.

75. For editions of this, see n. 58.

CHAPTER 2

1. On this, see further Edward Schillebeeckx, *The Church with a Human Face* (London/New York, 1985), pp. 154–156; C. Vogel, "Vacua manus impositio: L'inconsistance de la chirotonie absolue en Occident," in *Mélanges liturgiques offerts au R. P. Dom Bernard Botte* (Louvain, 1972), pp. 511–524.

2. *Epp.* 6.6; 9.1; 10.6 (*PL* 54.620, 625–626, 634).

3. Cf. Acts 13:3; 14:23.

4. See the letter of Pope Pelagius I (555–560) to the bishop of Grumentum (*PL* 161.472), which also indicates that an episcopal ordination might even be performed at the end of the Lenten fast in the Easter vigil itself, following the baptismal rite.

5. For the *Apostolic Tradition*, see the articles by Bradshaw and Ratcliff cited above, ch. 1, n. 3; for the early Alexandrian practice, see A. Vilela, *La condition collégiale des prêtres au IIIe siècle* (Paris, 1971), pp. 173–179, and especially the works cited in n. 5 there.

6. See Roger Gryson, "Les élections ecclésiastiques au IIIe siècle," *RHE* 68 (1973), pp. 353–404; *idem*, "Les élections episcopales en Orient au IVe siècle," *RHE* 74 (1979), pp. 301–345; and the works cited therein, to which may be added: P. Stockmeier, "The election of bishops by clergy and people in the early church," *Concilium* 137 (1980), pp. 3–9.

7. See, for example, the statements of Cyprian cited by Gryson, "Les élections ecclésiastiques au IIIe siècle," p. 377.

8. See the ordination prayer for a presbyter in *Apostolic Constitutions*, where he is said to have been elected, but "by the vote and judgment of the whole clergy" rather than by the people (p. 115).

9. British Museum Add. 19,548: Conybeare, *Rituale Armenorum*, p. 237. The later episcopal rite also preserves the triple congregational response: see Denzinger, II, p. 361.

10. See further Bruno Kleinheyer, *Die Priesterweihe in römischen Ritus* (Trier, 1962), pp. 49–52.

11. Eusebius, *Hist. Eccl.* 6.29.2–4.

12. *Ep.* 213.

13. *Com. in Ps.* 105 (*PL* 53.485C); cf. G. Morin, *Études, Textes, Découvertes* (Maredsous/Paris, 1913), I, pp. 361–362.

14. *Hist. Franc.* 2.13 (*PL* 71.212A).

15. *De Eccl. Hier.* 5.2–3 (*PG* 3.509–516).

16. Philostorgius, *Hist. Eccl.* 9.10 (*PG* 65.576C).

17. See Jean Tchékan, "Elements d'introduction à l'étude de la liturgie byzantine des ordinations," *BCES* 10 (1968), p. 207.

18. Bernard Botte, "La formule d'ordination 'La grâce divine' dans les rites orientaux," *OS* 2 (1957), pp. 285–296. The formula also occurs in relation to the subdeacon in the Coptic and Jacobite rites, and both the reader and the subdeacon in the East Syrian and Melkite rites.

19. Botte includes the words "for him" in his rendering of the formula, but though this expression does occur in the later Byzantine texts, it is absent from the Barberini manuscript and also from the Coptic and Jacobite versions, and hence would appear to be a later addition.

20. Pseudo-Dionysius, *De Eccl. Hier.* 5.3.5 (*PG* 3.512).

21. *De Sacerdotio* 4.1 (*PG* 48.662).

22. *Or.* 18.15,35 (*PG* 35.1004,1032).

23. John Chrysostom, *Hom.* 1.4 (*PG* 48.700): Lanne, p. 81, n. 4; Eusebius, *Hist. Eccl.* 6.29.2; Theodoret, *Hist. Eccl.* 5.27.1: Gy, "Ancient Ordination Prayers," pp. 74, 77.

24. In the Jacobite rite for a bishop, however, it is said by one of the bishops (pp. 143, 145, 152, 178, 180, and 183).

25. Pp. 133, 156, 191, 194, and 197. Botte was in fact mistaken about the East Syrian rite, where the formulary is recited *before* the imposition of the hand.

26. Khouri-Sarkis, however, *op. cit.*, pp. 141ff., did make an unsatisfactory attempt to support it with regard to the Jacobite rite.

27. Gy, "Ancient Ordination Prayers," p. 75. See also Lanne, pp. 82–83; Tchékan, p. 201.

28. Strictly speaking, therefore, it is not exactly the Antiochene equivalent of the allocutions at the beginning of the Roman ordination rites (*pace* Gy, "Ancient Ordination Prayers," p. 77), since the latter permit objections from the people and are followed by distinct invitations to pray.

29. See Kleinheyer, *Die Priesterweihe*, pp. 59–60.

30. See pp. 52, 65, and 77.

31. John Chrysostom, *Jud. et Gent.* 9 (*PG* 48.826); see also *Hom in Matt.* 54 (*PG* 58.537).

32. *De Eccl. Hier.* 5.2.

33. The only exceptions are the ordination of a bishop in *Apostolic Constitutions* and some of the Roman *Ordines*, where it is not explicitly mentioned but nevertheless may still have been practiced: see pp. 113 and 219–221.

34. "Jewish Ordination on the Eve of Christianity," *SL* 13 (1979), pp. 11–41.

35. See further Tchékan, pp. 193–196.

36. See P. van Beneden, *Aux origines d'une terminologie sacramentelle: "ordo," "ordinare," "ordinatio" dans la littérature chrétienne avant 313* (Louvain, 1974).

37. See Justin Martyr, *Apology* 1.65.2; Tertullian, *De Oratione* 18.

38. *De Eccl. Hier.* 5.2 (*PG* 3.509).

39. Conybeare, *Rituale Armenorum*, p. 242.

40. No mention is made of a kiss in the case of a deaconess or subdeacon in this tradition, but it is recorded in the case of the reader, though here it is differently described, the word "peace" being used (p. 139).

41. *Op. cit.*, pp. 155–156.

CHAPTER 3

1. British Museum Or. 2615: *Rituale Armenorum*, p. 235.

2. *Ibid.*, pp. xxxiii, 53.

3. See Gemayel, pp. 125–133.

4. See *Ordo* XL A: Andrieu, IV, p. 297.

5. See p. 22.

6. 8.27.2–3.

7. *Dialogus Historicus* 16 (*PG* 47.53).

8. *PG* 125.533; cf. J. Lécuyer, "Note sur la liturgie du sacre des évêques," *EL* 66 (1952), pp. 369–372. K. Richter, "Zum Ritus der Bischofsordination in der 'Apostolischen Überlieferung' Hippolyts von Rom und davon abhängigen Schriften," *ALW* 17 (1975), p. 36, n. 205, erroneously cites the reference as *In genesim sermo* III (*PG* 56.533).

9. *De legislatore* (PG 56. 404). Munier, *Les Statuta Ecclesiae Antiqua*, p. 178, n. 41, mistakenly cites the reference as *PG* 54.404; and this error is repeated by Botte, "Les ordinations dans les rites orientaux," p. 14, and Richter, "Zum Ritus der Bischofsordination," p. 36, n. 204.

10. See Johannes Zellinger, *Studien zu Severian von Gabala*, Münsterische Beiträge zur Theologie 8 (Münster, 1926), pp. 60–64; J. A. de Aldama, *Repertorium Pseudochrysostomicum* (Paris, 1965), p. 182; A. M. Gila, *Severiano de Gabala* (Rome, 1965), pp. 56–57.

11. *De Eccl. Hier.* 5.3.7.

12. *Ordo* XL A: Andrieu, IV, p. 297.

13. W. Riedel, *Die Kirchenrechtsquellen des Patriarchats Alexandrien* (Leipzig, 1900; Aalen, 1968), p. 260.

14. "Holy Orders in the Ordination Prayers," p. 10.

15. *Les Statuta Ecclesiae Antiqua*, pp. 179–180.

16. See *Ordo* XXXV.64: Andrieu, IV, p. 44.

17. "Holy Orders in the Ordination Prayers," p. 14.

18. Ratcliff, p. 268 and in Couratin and Tripp, p. 158.

19. *Die Weihe der Bischöfe, Presbyter und Diakone in vornicänischer Zeit* (Munich, 1969), p. 179, n. 89.

20. While some would see a twofold imposition of hands in the *Apostolic Tradition*, first by all the bishops, and then by one bishop alone during the prayer, it seems more likely that the second should be understood merely as a continuation of the first; cf. the discussion in Richter, "Zum Ritus der Bischofsordination," pp. 15–19; W. Rordorf, "L'ordination de l'évêque selon la Tradition apostolique d'Hippolyte de Rome," *Questions Liturgiques* 55 (1974), pp. 143–150.

21. According to the text, this may be either a presbyter or a bishop: for the reason for this reading, see Paul F. Bradshaw, "The participation of other bishops in the ordination of a bishop in the Apostolic Tradition of Hippolytus," *SP* 18 (forthcoming).

22. Clarified further in *Ordo* XXXV.65: Andrieu, IV, p. 44.

23. See p. 15.

24. With regard to this suggestion, see further the articles by Bradshaw and Ratcliff cited in ch. 1, n. 3.

25. *De Eccl. Hier.* 5.2.

26. *Op. cit.*, p. 270, n. 13 and in Couratin and Tripp, p. 160, n. 13.

27. *Op. cit.*, pp. 397–402.

28. See, for example, Richter, "Zum Ritus der Bischofsordination," pp. 21–23, 30–31; Rordorf, p. 147.

29. "Early Christian liturgy in the light of contemporary historical research," *SL* 16.3/4 (1986/1987), p. 33.

30. There are some echoes of this latter part of the prayer in the intercession for the patriarch in the later Coptic eucharistic rite, which suggests that both may derive from a common euchological tradition: see F. E. Brightman, *Liturgies Eastern and Western* (Oxford, 1896, 1965), pp. 161, 171.

31. Gy, "Ancient Ordination Prayers," p. 76, did not take into account the significance of this change of sequence and suggested that the third prayer came from Jerusalem.

32. Though the Byzantine prayer attaches the phrase "laying down his life for the sheep" to the new bishop rather than to Christ.

33. See p. 64.

34. "La théologie des prières anciennes pour l'ordination des évêques et des prêtres," *Revue des sciences philosophiques et théologiques* 58 (1974), p. 604.

35. "Ancient Ordination Prayers," pp. 74–75.

36. See pp. 64 and 75.

37. See p. 31.

38. "La théologie des prières anciennes," pp. 604–605.

39. But it should be noted that the same verb also occurs in the second prayer for a presbyter and the second prayer for a deacon.

40. The same is also true of the second prayer for a deacon. Gy ("Ancient Ordination Prayers," p. 82) suggests that this is part of a general Byzantine tendency to direct to Christ those prayers which came to be said in a low voice.

41. Gy ("La théologie des prières anciennes," p. 604) considered that the description of God as unknowable that was added to the beginning of the Byzantine version was characteristic of the theology of the Greek fathers at the end of the fourth century.

42. "Ancient Ordination Prayers," p. 86.

43. On this, see Kleinheyer, "Studien zur nichtromisch-westlichen Ordinationsliturgie," *ALW* 23 (1981), pp. 335–338.

44. See further E. Stommel, "Die bischöfliche Kathedra im christlichen Altertum," *Münchener Theologische Zeitschrift* 3 (1952), pp. 17–32.

CHAPTER 4

1. See Conybeare, *Rituale Armenorum*, p. 242.

2. See Gemayel, pp. 125–127, 130.

3. See p. 38.

4. On this question, see ch. 5, n. 1.

5. See Conybeare, *Rituale Armenorum*, pp. 236–237.

6. See pp. 42 and 45.

7. *De Eccl. Hier.* 5.2.

8. "The Ordination of a Presbyter in the Church Order of Hippolytus," *JTS* 16 (1915), pp. 542–547.

9. "Early Forms of Ordination," in H. B. Swete (ed.), *Essays on the early history of the Church and the Ministry* (London, 1918), pp. 283–284.

10. *The Apostolic Tradition of St. Hippolytus* (London, 1937; 2nd Ed., 1968, with preface and corrections by Henry Chadwick), pp. 80–81.

11. "Ordo Presbyterii," *JTS* 26 (1975), p. 310.

12. *La Tradition Apostolique*, p. 21, n. 1.

13. In a review of Botte's edition of the text in *JTS* 15 (1964), p. 406.

14. *Op. cit.*, p. 159.

15. See p. 45.

16. *Op. cit.*, pp. 403–404.

17. Dix, *Apostolic Tradition*, p. 14, n. 4; see also *idem*, "The ministry in the early Church," in K. E. Kirk (ed.), *The Apostolic Ministry* (London, 1946), p. 218, n. 1.

18. See, for example, Botte, "Holy Orders in the Ordination Prayers," p. 7; J. Lécuyer, "Episcopat et Presbytérat dans les écrits d'Hippolyte de Rome," *Recherches de science religieuse* 41 (1953), pp. 42–43.

19. *Ministers of Christ and his Church* (London, 1969), pp. 33–36.

20. "The ministry in the early Church," p. 218.

21. *Eccl. Hist.* 5.22; see also Sozomen, *Eccl. Hist.* 7.19.

22. "Holy Orders in the Ordination Prayers," p. 14.

23. "Les ordinations dans les rites orientaux," p. 17.

24. See p. 51.

25. "La théologie des prières anciennes," p. 605.

26. See p. 52.

27. *Op. cit.*, p. 203.

28. See *Apostolic Constitutions* 2.57.9, and the evidence of John Chrysostom cited in F. van de Paverd, *Zur Geschichte der Messliturgie in Antiocheia und Constantinopel gegen Ende des vierten Jahrhunderts* (Rome, 1970), p. 131. According to the pilgrim Egeria (25.1; 26.1; 27.6–7; 42.1; 43.2,3), the same seems to have been true at Jerusalem.

29. PG 48.694,699; see Gy, "Ancient Ordination Prayers," p. 83.

30. See further Bernard Botte, "Secundi meriti munus," *Questions liturgiques et paroissiales* 21 (1936), pp. 84–88.

31. See ch. 3, n. 40.

32. For later developments of this ceremony, see Tchékan, pp. 204–205.

33. See p. 57.

34. See the extensive study by G. Ellard, *Ordination Anointings in the Western Church before 1000 A.D.* (Cambridge, MA, 1933).

CHAPTER 5

1. Although most commentators accept the whole passage as the work of the compiler, there are grounds for thinking that only the first sentence, and perhaps the second, are original, and that the rest may have been added in the fourth century in order to clarify the relationship between the orders, a subject of intense debate at that period: see Bradshaw, "Ordination," p. 36.

2. See p. 59.

3. *De Eccl. Hier.* 5.2.

4. See, for example, *Magnesians* 6; *Trallians* 3.

5. *Adv. Haer.* 3.12.10; 4.15.1.

6. See 2.19.3; 5.8.1; 6.30.10; 8.33.9; 8.46.16.

7. See pp. 51 and 65.

8. "Ancient Ordination Prayers," p. 74.

9. See, for example, Martimort, *Deaconesses*, p. 156.

10. For the reason for this, see ch. 3, n. 40.

11. See p. 72. The same phrase also occurs in one of the Maronite ordination prayers (p. 192).

12. *Hom. in Act.* 14.3 (*PG* 60.116).

13. *Baptismal homily* 2, in Edward Yarnold, *The Awe-Inspiring Rites of Initiation* (Slough, 1972), pp. 168–169.

14. "Ancient Ordination Prayers," p. 84.

15. *Op. cit.*, pp. 59–60.

16. "Ancient Ordination Prayers," p. 70.

CHAPTER 6

1. See Martimort, *Deaconesses*, pp. 195–200; Roger Gryson, *The Ministry of Women in the Early Church* (Collegeville, MN, 1976), pp. 101–108.

2. See Martimort, *Deaconesses*, pp. 202–206.

3. See, for example, Gryson, *Ministry of Women*, p. 24.

4. Chs. 9 and 16. English translation in Sebastian Brock and Michael Vasey, *The Liturgical Portions of the Didascalia*, GLS 29 (Nottingham, 1982), pp. 11, 22–23.

5. See Gryson, *Ministry of Women*, pp. 62–63, 115–120; Martimort, *Deaconesses*, p. 75, n. 66.

6. *Deaconesses*, p. 75.

7. 2.57.10; 2.58.4–6; 8.28.6. Cf. also Ps.-Ignatius, *Ad Antiochenœos* 12.2.

8. *Pace* Martimort, *Deaconesses*, p. 155.

9. 3.16.1–4.

10. Martimort, *Deaconesses*, p. 74.

11. See, for example, the regulations in *Apostolic Tradition* 20 concerning menstruation and female baptismal candidates, and those in *Canons of Hippolytus* 18 concerning midwives and women who have given birth.

12. 1.23.1.

13. Martimort, *Deaconesses*, p. 51, n. 65.

14. See p. 121.

15. *Ministry of Women*, p. 66.

16. 1.40.2; 2.8.12.

17. 1.40.2, as translated by Gryson (*Ministry of Women*, p. 69, n. 233) and Martimort (*Deaconesses*, p. 49, n. 55).

18. 1.23.14.

19. 1.19.7.

20. 1.36.1–4; 2.19.1.

21. 2.20.7.

22. On this development, see Martimort, *Deaconesses*, especially pp. 134ff.

23. Martimort, *Deaconesses*, p. 182, though noting some similarities, fails to recognize the extent of the relationship: "Such as they are, these three blessings were not simply borrowed from rituals known to the other churches."

24. P. Thomsen, *Die lateinischen und griechischen Inschriften der Stadt Jerusalem und ihrer nächsten Umgebung* (Leipzig, 1922), no. 130. The reference sometimes made to a second inscription that mentions another Jerusalem deaconess is based on a mistaken interpretation: see Martimort, *Deaconesses*, p. 145.

25. Though it is added in the margin of one ms.: see Vosté, *Pontificale iuxta ritum Ecclesiae Syrorum Orientalium*, p. 160, n. 1.

26. Martimort, *Deaconesses*, pp. 180–181.

27. See p. 100.

CHAPTER 7

1. See A. Faivre, *Naissance d'une hiérarchie: les premières étapes du cursus clérical* (Paris, 1977), pp. 57–58.

2. Though an allusion to a seemingly ancient practice of election to these offices is found in the Coptic rite, and this is also mentioned in the Gallican rite for a reader (pp. 141 and 223).

3. Cf. Luke 4:16; Paul F. Bradshaw, *Liturgical Presidency in the Early Church*, GLS 36 (Nottingham, 1983), pp. 4–5.

4. Sozomen, *Hist. Eccl.* 7.19; Cyprian states (*Ep.* 33.4) that in the third century in Africa the gospel might be proclaimed by a reader.

5. See p. 85.

6. See p. 85.

7. See p. 87.

8. *Sacramentary of Sarapion* 25. For other evidence for the office of interpreter, see Brightman, "The Sacramentary of Sarapion of Thmuis," pp. 254–255.

9. The Apostle, i.e., the Book of Acts and the Epistles of the New Testament, since he did not read the gospel.

10. See p. 91.

11. See p. 6.

12. Preserved in Eusebius, *Eccl. Hist.* 6.43.11.

13. With regard to these, see the works listed in Faivre, p. 182, n. 9.

14. *Ep. ad Senarium* 10 (*PL.* 59.404–405).

15. See pp. 42, 45, and 59–60.

16. Munier, *Les Statuta Ecclesiae Antiqua*, p. 172.

17. See Gryson, *The Ministry of Women*, pp. 116–117.

APOSTOLIC TRADITION OF HIPPOLYTUS

1. Translation reproduced from G. J. Cuming, *Hippolytus: A Text for Students*, pp. 8–10, 12–15.

2. Some versions read "from."

3. 2 Cor 1:3.

4. Ps 113:5–6.

5. Susanna 42.

6. Acts 20:32.

7. Ps 51:12.

8. This is the reading preserved in the Greek text of the *Epitome* of the *Apostolic Constitutions*, whereas the Latin translation of the *Apostolic Tradition* has "whom you gave to your beloved Son Jesus Christ, which he gave to your holy apostles:" see further Bradshaw, "Ordination," p. 37, n. 4.

9. Acts 1:24.

10. Is 42:1.

11. Jn 20:23.

12. Acts 1:26.

13. Mt 18:18.

14. Eph 5:2.

15. Cf. 1 Cor 12:28.

16. Nm 11:16–25.

17. The Latin version has a lacuna here, and remainder of the prayer after this point exists only in the Ethiopic version.

18. 1 Tm 3:13.

CANONS OF HIPPOLYTUS

1. Translation by Carol Bebawi, reproduced from Paul F. Bradshaw, *The Canons of Hippolytus*, pp. 11–16.

2. 1 Tm 3:2; Ti 1:6–7.

3. It seems unlikely that such an imprecise expression belongs to the original: Coquin (*Les Canons d'Hippolyte*, p. 83) suggested that the intermediate Coptic translation had intended it to be "Saturday," since the same word can have both meanings in that language, though whether the Greek itself spoke of "Saturday" or "Sunday," as in the *Apostolic Tradition* of Hippolytus, is an open question.

4. 2 Cor 1:3.

5. Ps 113:5–6.

6. Susanna 42.

7. Coquin (*op. cit.*, p. 83) suggested that this was probably the result of a copyist's error, the words for "Adam" and "beginning," as in the *Apostolic Tradition*, being very similar in Arabic.

8. Acts 1:24.

9. Eph 5:2.

10. The phrase "and the presbyters" is an addition to the text of the *Apostolic Tradition*, where the deacon is the servant of the bishop alone: a similar development can also be seen in *Apostolic Constitutions* 3.20.2; 8.46.10.

11. Jn 12:26.

12. Acts 6:5,8,10.

13. Cf. 1 Tm 5:17.

14. Cf. 1 Tm 5:3–15.

1. Translated from the Greek text in Metzger, *Les Constitutions Apostoliques* III, pp. 141–149, 217–225.

2. 1 Tm 3:2.

3. Cf. 1 Tm 3:4.

4. 1 Tm 3:2.

5. Mt 18:16.

6. Literally, "I AM:" cf. Ex 3:14.

7. Dn 2:22.

8. 2 Cor 1:3.

9. Ps 113:5–6.

10. Or "teachers of us," depending upon whether the designation "teachers" should be understood as referring to the apostles or to the bishops. see Metzger, III, p. 145.

11. Acts 1:24.

12. 2 Cor 13:14.

13. Jn 20:23.

14. Acts 1:26.

15. Mt 18:18.

16. Eph 5:2.

17. Cf. 1 Tm 5:17.

18. Cf. 1 Cor 12:28.

19. Nm 11:16–25.

20. Rom 10:12.

21. Ps 143:1.

22. Ps 31:16.

23. Acts 6:5,8.

24. Cf. 1 Tm 3:13.

25. 2 Cor 1:3.

26. The sister of Moses and Aaron, Ex 15:20–21.

27. Jgs 4–5.

28. Anna, the daughter of Phanuel (Lk 2:36–38), or, alternatively, Hannah, the mother of Samuel (1 Sm 1–2), may be meant here: cf. Martimort, p. 71, n. 51.

29. 2 Kgs 22:14–20.

30. Ex 38:8; 1 Sm 2:22.

31. 2 Cor 7:1.

32. Cf. 1 Chr 9:28.

33. Wis 7:17.

34. Neh 8.

TESTAMENTUM DOMINI

1. Translation by Grant Sperry-White from the Syriac text in Rahmani, *Testamentum Domini*, pp. 26–33, 68–71, 90–93, 98–99, 104–107.

2. Transliteration of the Greek word *cheirotonia*.

3. 2 Cor 1:3.

4. Susanna 42.

5. Cf. Rv 4:11.

6. Cf. Heb 11:8.

7. Cf. Gn 5:21–24; Heb 11:5.

8. Ps 51:12.

9. Or "oversight of the living/life."

10. Acts 1:24.

11. This sentence contains no main verb.

12. Mt 18:18.

13. The version of the *Testamentum Domini* in the West Syrian Synodicon has instead "those who suffer."

14. Eph 5:2.

15. Transliteration of the Greek word *cheirotonia*.

16. The Syriac here is very unclear.

17. Transliteration of the Greek word *cheirotonia*.

18. One ms. reads instead "has called."

19. Or simply "is."

1. Translated from the Greek text in F. E. Brightman, "The Sacramentary of Sarapion of Thmuis," *JTS* 1 (1900), pp. 266–267.

2. 1 Jn 4:10.

3. Greek: *leitourgia*.

4. Is 11:2; 1 Cor 12:10.

5. Neh 1:5.

6. Jn 15:26.

7. Lk 8:15.

8. 2 Cor 5:20.

9. Nm 11:16–25.

10. 1 Cor 12:8–9.

11. 1 Tm 3:9; 2 Tm 1:3

12. Cf. Jn 3:17.

13. Lk 6:13.

14. Est 9:28 (LXX).

15. Ps 31:5.

16. Literally "own," as distinct from those belonging to others.

17. Acts 20:28; 1 Pt 5:2.

ARMENIAN

1. Adapted from the English translation of the ninth/tenth-century ms., Venice San Lazzaro 457 (320), in Conybeare, *Rituale Armenorum*, pp. 228–235.

2. I.e., angels.

3. Cf. Eph 5:2.

4. Cf. Dt 6:4.

5. Cf. Jas 5:14.

6. Cf. 1 Tm 5:17.

7. Is 11:2.

8. Ps 110.

1. Translated from the eighth-century ms. Barberini 336; text in Morin, pp. 52–58.

2. 1 Cor 12:28.

3. Later mss. read instead "the yoke of the gospel."

4. Jn 10:15.

5. Rom. 2:19–20.

6. I.e., the pallium.

7. *Presbytatos*—a play on words with "elder," *presbyteros*.

8. Cf. Rom. 15:16; and see also the second prayer, n. 9.

9. *Ierourgein*: cf. Rom 15:16.

10. Ti 2:13.

11. I.e., stole.

12. The equivalent of the western chasuble.

13. 1 Tm 3:9.

14. Cf. Eph 4:12.

15. 1 Tm 3:13.

16. Mt 20:27.

17. The equivalent of the western chasuble, worn by all clergy.

18. I.e., stole.

19. This phrase also occurs in the first prayer for a deacon.

20. Rom 16:1–2.

21. Martimort, *Deaconesses*, p. 150, translates this phrase as "apply herself to household government," but this seems an improbably narrow interpretation.

22. I.e., stole.

23. I.e., veil.

24. I.e., sacristy.

25. I.e., assists him in performing the *lavabo*.

COPTIC

1. Translation by Dr. Harry Attridge from ms. 253 *Lit.*, Coptic Museum, Cairo (A.D. 1364); text in Burmester, *Ordination Rites of the Coptic Church*, pp. 23–44, 52–66.

2. This expression occurs frequently in the Coptic ordination rites, both in rubrics and in the text of the ordination prayers, and appears to be a technical term meaning, "to present for ordination." Lanne (*art. cit.*, p. 102) suggests on the basis of its occurrence in a similar sense in one of Chrysostom's homilies (*PG.* 48.700) that it was already used in this way in fourth-century Antioch.

3. I.e., the bishop.

4. Neh 8.

5. A version of the prayer for a reader in the *Apostolic Constitutions*: see p. 116.

6. Mk 13:14.

7. See n. 2.

8. This has some parallels with the exhortations in the Georgian and Melkite rites: see pp. 167 and 202.

9. This rubric is largely a repetition of that which preceded the catechesis and is omitted in the printed editions of the pontifical. It is obviously based on the final rubric of the Jacobite rite: see p. 175.

10. See n. 2.

11. Cf. the Jacobite version, p. 176.

12. Cf. 1 Chr 9:28.

13. See n. 2.

14. An amalgam of the prayers for a subdeacon from the *Apostolic Constitutions* and from the Jacobite rite: see pp. 116 and 176.

15. Cf. the conclusion of the Jacobite rite, p. 177.

16. I.e., stole.

17. Cf. the conclusion of the Jacobite rite, p. 177.

18. The original has "when," probably the result of textual corruption.

19. Cf. p. 112.

20. Cf. the Jacobite version, p. 178.

21. See n. 2.

22. Cf. the prayers for a deacon in the *Apostolic Constitutions* and in the Jacobite rite, pp. 115 and 178–179.

23. Cf. the conclusion of the Jacobite rite, p. 179.

24. I.e., stole.

25. Cf. the conclusion of the Jacobite rite, p. 180.

26. These words are supplied from the printed versions.

27. Jn 12:26.

28. 1 Tm 3:13.

29. An allusion to the deacon's function of administering the chalice.

30. Cf. the Jacobite version, pp. 180–181.

31. These words are found in the printed editions of the pontificals, but seem accidentally to have fallen out of this manuscript.

32. Cf. 1 Tm 5:17.

33. See n. 2.

34. Cf. 1 Cor 12:28.

35. The printed pontificals assign this bidding to a deacon, which is probably also the intention here.

36. Cf. the prayers for a presbyter in the *Apostolic Constitutions* and in the Jacobite rite, pp. 115 and 181–182.

37. Cf. the conclusion of the Jacobite rite, p. 182.

38. 1 Pt 5:1–4.

39. Cf. Mt 25:14ff. The same image also occurs in the preceding thanksgiving prayer.

40. Cf. 1 Thes 2:7.

41. I.e., A.D. 1364.

42. Cf. 1 Tm 3:2–3.

43. I.e., the Alexandrian patriarch.

44. Although this troparion is sung at all celebrations of the eucharist in the Byzantine tradition, it is only used in the Coptic tradition at the ordinations of bishops and patriarchs, at the consecration of the chrism and the holy oils, and on Good Friday (Burmester, *op. cit.*, p. 102, n. 3).

45. Ps 7:9.

46. Mt 25:21.

47. There appears to be a lacuna in the text here. The Arabic version inserts "what you asked."

48. See n. 2.

49. I.e., the previous bishop.

50. Cf. the Jacobite version, p. 183.

51. This first part of this prayer, as far as the archdeacon's interjected bidding, follows quite closely the text of the ordination prayer for a bishop in the *Apostolic Constitutions*: see pp. 113–114.

52. An interpretation of the Greek word *cleros*, "lot," found in the *Apostolic Constitutions*.

53. Whilst these last two functions are not mentioned in the corresponding prayer in the *Apostolic Constitutions*, they are found in the Jacobite ordination prayer: see p. 184.

54. Cf. a similar petition in the prayer for a presbyter, p. 146.

55. Rom 2:19–20.

56. 2 Tm 2:15.

57. Jn 10:15.

58. I.e., the pallium.

59. With regard to the preceding ceremonies, cf. the conclusion of the Jacobite rite, pp. 184–185.

60. See n. 2.

EAST SYRIAN

1. Translated from the Latin rendering in Vosté, *Pontificale iuxta ritum Ecclesiae Syrorum Orientalium*, pp. 8–71, 158–161.

2. I.e., stoles.

3. These are the lists of those for whom intercession is to be made, usually read by the deacon rather than the reader in the celebration of the liturgy.

4. I.e., stole.

5. Eph 4:11–12.

6. I.e., stole.

7. Ps 146:6.

8. Eph 4:11–12.

9. Cf. Eph 6:19.

10. Marginal note: *Here he holds their right hand.*

11. Cf. Jas 5:14.

12. I.e., stole.

13. Eph 3:20.

14. Rom 2:19–20.

15. Cf. Mt 16:19; 18:18.

16. Pss 79:13; 95:7; 100:3.

17. Episcopal vestments.

18. Cf. Ps 110:2.

GEORGIAN

1. Adapted from the English translation of the tenth/eleventh-century ms., Tiflis A 86, in F. C. Conybeare and Oliver Wardrop, "The Georgian version of the Liturgy of St. James," *ROC* 19 (1914), pp. 162–173.

2. This cross was said to have been set up in the time of St. Nino, the fourth-century slave who is credited with bringing Christianity to Georgia, and a festival was appointed in its honor, with many miracles attributed to it: see M. S. and J. O. Wardrop, *The Life of St. Nino* (Oxford, 1900), pp. 45–51.

3. This appears to be an expanded version of the exhortation in the *Testamentum Domini*, and also has some parallels with those in the Coptic and Melkite rites: see pp. 121, 140–141, and 202.

4. This designation treats the preceding charge as though it were a prayer.

5. Reading doubtful.

6. Based on the exhortation in the *Testamentum Domini*: see p. 121.

7. 2 Cor 1:3.

8. Literally, "a deacon," since there is no gender in the Georgian language.

9. Ex 15:20–21.

10. Jgs 4–5.

11. 1 Tm 3:8.

12. Rom 16:1–2.

13. Or "office," "service."

14. Cf. 1 Tm 3:2.

15. Cf. Dn 7:10; Rv 5:11.

16. Cf. Eph 5:27.

17. Ps 146:6.

18. Eph 4:11–12.

19. Cf. Eph 6:19.

20. Cf. Jas 5:14.

21. Eph 3:20.

22. Jn 10:15.

23. Cf. Eph 6:19.

24. Rom 2:19–20.

JACOBITE

1. Translated from the Latin rendering of ms. Vat. syr. 51 (A.D. 1172) in Vosté, *Pontificale iuxta ritum Ecclesiae Syrorum occidentalium*, pp. 157–189, 209–241.

2. Ps 7:9.

3. 2 Cor 7:1.

4. A version of this prayer is also found in the Coptic, Maronite, and Melkite rites: see pp. 141, 189, and 204, respectively.

5. I.e., stole.

6. The equivalent of the western chasuble.

7. Cf. Eph 4:12.

8. Rom 2:6.

9. Cf. 1 Tm 3:10.

10. Cf. Acts 6:7.

11. Cf. Mt 25:14ff.

12. A version of the thanksgiving prayer found in the rite for the subdiaconate: see p. 177.

13. I.e., stole.

14. The equivalent of the western chasuble.

15. Ps 7:9.

16. I.e., stole.

17. The equivalent of the western chasuble.

18. Although in this ms., the adjectives "holy" and "princely" are attached to God the Father, other mss. attribute them to the Spirit.

19. I.e., James/Jacob bar Addai (c. 500–578), the founder of the Jacobite church.

20. At the ordination of the patriarch, the prayer for a bishop from the *Testamentum Domini* was inserted here.

21. The equivalent of the western chasuble.

22. I.e., stole.

23. Jn 10:1–16.

24. Ps 110:2.

MARONITE

1. This synopsis was prepared with the assistance of Msgr. Hector Doueihi, Director of the Office of Liturgy in the Diocese of St. Maron, USA.

2. Ps 104:4; Heb 1:7.

3. 1 Cor 12:28.

4. Ps 110:2: cf. also the Jacobite rite, p. 186.

MELKITE

1. Translated from British Museum ms. Or. 4951, folios 43–69: text in Matthew Black, *Rituale Melchitarum*, pp. 58–71.

2. The preceding may alternatively be rendered: ". . . servant, adorning this church which is outstanding in its holiness: him also, O Lord, by the grace of your divinity make worthy. . . ."

3. Or "first."

4. Rom 1:1–3. Black (p. 60, n. 3) erroneously claims that this reading and the exhortation that follows are also found in the eighth-century Byzantine rite, whereas in reality they appear only in one sixteenth-century ms. of that rite, Barberini 390 ("Codex Allatianus"), from where they passed into the Russian pontificals: see Tchékan, p. 196.

5. The equivalent of the western chasuble.

6. This exhortation displays some similarity to those in the *Testamentum Domini*, and in the Coptic and Georgian rites: see pp. 121, 140–141, and 167, respectively.

7. Literally, "on whose giving of the imposition of hands reliance is placed."

8. I.e., stole.

9. 2 Cor 1:3.

10. See n. 3.

11. I.e., alb/tunic.

12. The word is uncertain.

13. This word is also uncertain.

14. Acts 6:5.

15. 1 Tm 3:9.

16. Cf. 1 Tm 3:13.

17. Jn 1:1–3.

18. Lk 12:42.

19. Cf. Dn 7:10; Rv 5.11.

20. Cf. Eph 5:27.

21. *Leitourgias*.

22. The equivalent of the western chasuble.

23. Jn 1:1–3.

24. The invitation to communion in the eucharistic rite.

25. Nm 11:24–25.

26. 1 Cor 12:28.

27. Cf. Eph 5:2.

28. Cf. Eph 6:19.

29. Cf. Jas 5:14.

30. Cf. Jas 1:27.

ROMAN

1. Translation adapted from Porter, pp. 19–35: text in Feltoe, *Sacramentarium Leonianum*, pp. 119–123, 139–140; Mohlberg, *Sacramentarium Veronese*, pp. 118–122, 138–139.

2. The use of two collects before the ordination prayer is a peculiar characteristic of the ancient Roman rite for a bishop. This collect appears consistently as the second one in all the sources, but the first is not always the same. In the Gelasian Sacramentary, the *Missale Francorum*, and the Sacramentary of Angoulême it is "Hear, Lord . . . ," whereas here in the Leonine Sacramentary, that prayer appears to be the opening collect of the eucharist, and "Assist [us] . . ." seems to be the first ordination collect, unless the latter is really intended to be the post-communion oration, as it is in the *Missale Francorum*. The Gregorian Sacramentary has a different text for the first ordination collect, which seems to have been formed by a fusion of the other two: "Assist our supplications, almighty God, and let what is carried out by our humble ministry be fulfilled by the working of your power; through. . . . "

3. This collect occurs in this preliminary position only in the Leonine Sacramentary: in the Gelasian Sacramentary and in the Sacramentary of Angoulême, it replaces the collect following the bidding; in the *Missale Francorum*, its construction is changed and it forms the conclusion of the bidding itself; and it does not appear at all in the Gregorian Sacramentary. Miquel Gros, "Les plus anciennes formules romaines de bénédiction des diacres," *Ecclesia Orans* 5 (1988), pp. 45–52, suggests that it was originally associated with the process of election.

4. The Gregorian Sacramentary considerably recasts this bidding.

5. As indicated in n. 3, this collect appears only in the Leonine Sacramentary: in the Gelasian Sacramentary and in the Sacramentary of Angoulême, it is replaced by the first collect; the *Missale Francorum* has no separate collect at all; and the Gregorian Sacramentary has a new and briefer collect, evidently inspired by the two collects of the earlier books. Gros (*art. cit.*) considers it to be older than the prayer that now follows it and to have been the original ordination prayer of the rite.

6. Cf. Is 11:2.

7. Nm 11:16–25.

8. Translated from the Latin text in Andrieu, *Les Ordines Romani*, III, pp. 603–613.

9. The *planeta*, or chasuble, was the common outer vestment of all Roman clerics.

10. A linen bag in which acolytes carried the consecrated bread or the holy oils: see Andrieu, II, pp. 70–71; III, p. 546, n. 3.

11. The candidate had to swear that he had never committed any of four capital sins: sodomy, violation of a consecrated virgin, bestiality, and adultery: see Andrieu, III, pp. 549–553.

12. I.e., into his bare hands, the chasuble being folded back, in contrast to the acolyte whose hands were covered by the chasuble when he received the *saccula*.

13. 1 Tm 3:8–14.

14. 1 Tm 3:1ff.

15. I.e., says the ordination prayer.

16. According to *Ordo* I, the bishops sat to the right of the Pope on the *subsellia*, or curved bench in the apse, and the newly consecrated bishop would thus have been assigned the first place on the Pope's right: see Andrieu, II, pp. 74–75.

17. I.e., his certificate of ordination: see Andrieu, III, p. 587.

18. *Ibid.*, pp. 587–591.

GALLICAN

1. For editions of the text, see Ch. 1, n. 61.

2. Some mss. read "neck."

3. This direction has close verbal parallels to the *Apostolic Tradition*: see p. 108.

4. Corrected in the light of the Gelasian Sacramentary and of the Sacramentary of Angoulême; for editions of the texts, see Ch. 1, nn. 56, 57, 58; translation adapted in part from Porter, pp. 40–57.

5. The text of the final words here has become so corrupt that it is impossible to restore its original meaning: later versions modify it so as to render it intelligible.

6. These words occur in all the sources, but seem superfluous.

7. Is 11:2.

8. The allocution is now terminated as if it were a prayer, but originally it must have been intended that the people should cry out, "He is worthy."

9. This title obviously derives from the position in which the formulary now occurs in the extant Gallican texts, directly after the Roman ordination prayer, but it is clearly the original bidding of the rite.

10. These words are omitted both in the *Missale Francorum* and in the Gelasian sacramentary, but they occur in the Sacramentary of Angoulême and are required by the sense. They are also supported by the Spanish version of this bidding: see p. 232.

11. Once again, the formulary has been terminated as if it were a prayer.

12. This word is omitted in the *Missale Francorum*, but is found in the other Gallican sources.

13. The singular here is in conflict with the plural reference in the prayers themselves.

14. Cf. Eph 2:10; Ti 2:7.

15. Cf. 1 Tm 4:12; 6:11.

16. This bidding only survives in the *Missale Francorum*, where it is labeled a collect!

17. Cf. Ps 107:32.

18. Cf. Ps 113:8.

19. Sir 32:1.

20. Cf. Ez 33:6.

21. This text is not known to us as a complete formulary, but only as a Gallican interpolation in the Roman ordination prayer in the *Missale Francorum* and other sources. It is cast in the plural (for the ordination of two or more bishops) in harmony with the Roman prayer, and in conflict with the preceding exhortation and bidding.

22. Is 52:7; Rom 10:15.

23. 2 Cor 5:18.

24. Rom. 15:19.

25. 1 Cor 2:4.

26. Mt 16:19.

27. 2 Cor 10:8.

28. Mt 16:19.

29. Jn 20:32.

30. Gn 27:29; Nm 24:9.

31. Mt 24:45.

32. Col 1:28.

33. Rom 12:11.

34. Is 5:20.

35. Cf. Rom 1:13–14.

MOZARABIC

1. Text in Férotin, *Le Liber Ordinum*, col. 46–50, 54–55; translation adapted in part from Porter, pp. 63–71.

2. I.e., the bidding, the prayer, and the completion; but note that in its present form, this rite has more than three formularies. Cf. the similar rubric in the rite for the presbyterate below.

3. In spite of this title, what follows is obviously a bidding.

4. I.e., the bidding, the prayer, and the completion. Cf. the similar rubric in the rite for the diaconate above.

AN ORDINATION PRAYER USED IN ENGLAND: THE LEOFRIC MISSAL

1. Text in Warren, *The Leofric Missal*, p. 217; translation adapted from Porter, pp. 75–77.

2. Cf. 1 Tm 2.7.

3. Cf. 1 Tm 3.2; Ti 1.8.

THE LATER COMPOSITE RITE: THE SACRAMENTARY OF ANGOULÊME

1. Text in P. Saint-Roch, *Liber sacramentorum Engolismensis*, pp. 313–325; adapted in part from Porter, pp. 85–93.

2. This prayer differs from that in the *Missale Francorum* (p. 223) but is found in the other eighth-century recensions of the Gelasian Sacramentary. Its text exhibits some confusion and is difficult to translate,

especially in its second half. An improved redaction of the prayer appears among the Gallican material in the tenth-century *Ordo Romanus* XXXV.10 (Andrieu, IV, p. 35), and from there passed into the Romano-German Pontifical.

3. This bidding is of uncertain origin: it first appears in the *Missale Francorum* and the Gelasian Sacramentary, and was presumably composed in order to harmonize the Roman formularies for a bishop with those for presbyter and deacon, which include biddings.

INDEX

Abbesses, 11, 14, 16
Abbots, 8, 11, 14, 16
Acolytes, 14, 101, 102, 218–219,
    222–223, 238
Ad-Doueihi, Stephen, patriarch,
    12
Al-Amchiti, Jeremiah, patriarch,
    12
Alexandrian patriarch, ordination
    of, 43
Ambrose of Milan, 22
Angoulême, Sacramentary of, 18,
    237–242
Anointing of bishops and pres-
    byters, 18, 227, 241, 242
Antoine, P., 9
Approbation by the people, 21–
    26
Apostolic Constitutions, 4, 5, 9, 11,
    13, 23, 27, 35, 38, 39–43, 48–
    49, 52, 55, 56, 61, 62, 68, 73,
    74, 75, 80, 84–86, 88, 93, 94,
    95, 96, 97, 99, 100, 113–116,
    243
Apostolic Tradition of Hippolytus,
    3–4, 5, 15, 17, 20, 21, 22, 23,
    25, 27, 30, 33, 34–35, 38, 44,
    45, 46–47, 48, 55, 56, 59, 60–
    62, 63, 64, 72, 73–74, 76, 83,
    87, 93, 98, 100, 101, 107–109
Archdeacons, 8, 10, 11, 16, 81,
    169–170
Archpresbyters, 16
Armenian Apostolic Church, 6
Armenian rite, 6–7, 23, 29, 32, 35,
    37, 58, 59, 67, 72, 79, 80, 89,
    91, 92, 96, 99, 100, 127–132,
    243
Arnobius the Younger, 24
Asolik, Stephanos, 6, 37
Assemani, J. A., 10, 13

Assemani, J. S., 10
Assyrian Church of the East, 9
Athanasius, metropolitan of Beni
    Suef and Bahnasa, 8
Athanasius of Alexandria, 5
Augustine of Hippo, 22, 24

Badger, G. Percy, 10
Bârlea, O., 43
Benedictional of Archbishop Rob-
    ert, 16
Berakah, 67
Bidding, 26–32
Black, Matthew, 13
Botte, Bernard, 5, 7, 10, 26, 27,
    41, 42, 51, 60, 64, 65, 75
Breve advocationis, 24
Burmester, O. H. E., 8
Byzantine rite, 7–8, 11, 13, 21, 25,
    26–29, 31, 35, 38, 41, 42, 44,
    51–53, 57, 58, 64–66, 69, 71,
    75–78, 81–82, 85, 88–89, 91,
    97–98, 133–139, 243, 245–247

Canons of Basil, 41
Canons of Hippolytus, 4, 9, 11, 23,
    32, 44, 47–48, 50, 54, 56, 61,
    73, 74–75, 83–84, 93, 110–112
Cantors, 11, 101, 139, 223
Chalcedon, Council of, 6, 8, 10,
    11
Chaldean Church, 9
    See also East Syrian rite
Charlemagne, emperor, 18
Cheirotonia, 34
    See also Imposition of hands
Chorepiscopos, 10, 11
Chrysostom, John, 26, 32, 40, 66,
    77
Clerics, rites for, 14, 16

Concluding ceremonies, 34–36,
  56–57, 69–70, 81–82
Conybeare, F. C., 37
Coptic Orthodox Church, 8
Coptic rite, 4, 8–9, 25, 27, 28, 31,
  35, 36, 38, 41, 44, 53–54, 58,
  68, 71, 80, 81, 97, 99, 101,
  140–155, 243, 245–247
Cornelius, pope, 101
Cross, sign of, 32
Cuming, Geoffrey, 5
Cyprian, bishop of Carthage, 22
Cyprian, bishop of Nisibis, 10

Deaconesses, rites for, 4, 7, 10,
  11, 14, 20, 83–92, 94, 116,
  137–139, 162–163, 168–169
Declaration of ordination, 36
Demophilus, bishop of Constanti-
  nople, 25
Denzinger, Henry, 8, 12, 13
Dib, Pierre, 12
Didache, 4
Didascalia Apostolorum, 4, 84, 86,
  87
"Divine Grace," 26–30
Dix, Gregory, 60, 61, 62
Doorkeepers, 14, 101, 102, 222–
  223, 237

Eastern ordination prayers, rela-
  tionship between, 243
Eastern texts, 125–212
East Syrian rite, 9–10, 11, 25, 27,
  29, 30, 36, 38, 41, 42, 44, 50,
  51, 53, 58, 66–67, 69, 71, 79,
  82, 89, 90, 92, 96, 99, 101,
  156–165, 243, 245–247
Election, 21–25, 57, 93
Ember seasons, 21
England, ordination prayer used
  in, 16–17, 236
Epaone, Council of, 83
Ephesus, Council of, 9
Ermoni, V., 8

Ethiopian Orthodox Church, 9
Eucharist, 20–21, 35, 38, 56–57,
  58, 69, 71, 82
Eusebius of Caesarea, 24
Exorcists, 14, 101, 102, 222, 224,
  237–38

Fabian, bishop of Rome, 24
Férotin, Marius, 16
Frere, W. H., 60

Gabriel, metropolitan of
  Bassorah, 10
Gallican rite, 14–15, 17–19, 24,
  30, 32, 42, 45, 56, 59–60, 69,
  70, 80–81, 82, 83, 101–103,
  222–230
Gelasian Sacramentary, 14, 15, 17,
  18, 32, 102
Gelasius I, pope, 11
Gennadius of Marseilles, 14
George, catholicos of Armenia, 37
Georgian rite, 10–11, 28, 29, 31,
  44, 50, 51, 53, 54, 57, 66–67,
  78–79, 81, 89–92, 96, 99, 100,
  166–173, 243, 245–247
Graffin, R., 12
Gregorian Sacramentary, 14, 18
Gregory of Nazianzus, 26
Gregory of Tours, 25
Gregory the Great, pope, 17
Gregory the Illuminator, 6, 100
Gryson, Roger, 84
Gy, P. M., 5, 9, 11, 27, 51, 52, 55,
  64, 66, 80, 81

Hadrian, pope, 18
Hanssens, J. M., 5, 9
Hippolytus, see Apostolic Tradition
Hoffman, Lawrence, 33

Ignatius of Antioch, 73
Imposition of the gospel book,
  39–44, 45
Imposition of hands, 10, 22, 27,

28, 32, 33–34, 36, 37, 38, 39,
  40, 41, 43, 44–46, 58, 59–60,
  71, 72–73, 83, 84, 87, 88, 89,
  94, 95, 96, 97
Irenaeus, 74
Isidore of Seville, 16
Iso'Yab III, 10

Jacob bar Addai, 11
Jacobite rite, 11–12, 13, 25, 27, 28,
  30–31, 36, 38, 41, 42, 44, 45,
  51, 53–54, 55, 58, 64, 65, 71,
  72, 75, 76, 78, 82, 96–97, 98,
  100, 174–187, 243, 245–247
John the Deacon, 101
Jounel, Pierre, 4

Khouri-Sarkis, G., 12, 36
Kircher, Athanasius, 8
Kiss, 34–36, 56–57, 69, 71, 81–82,
  88
Kleinheyer, Bruno, 15, 17
Kretschmar, Georg, 46

Lanne, Emmanuel, 8, 9, 27
Leo I, pope, 21, 55
Leofric Missal, 16, 236
Leonine Sacramentary, 14, 215–
  218
Liber Ordinum, 16, 17, 231–235
Librarians, 16
Litany, 31–32, 52
Liturgy of the Presanctified, 21,
  71

Magdalen College Pontifical, 16
Mandakuni, John, 6, 37
Marabas I, partriarch, 10
Maronite rite, 12–13, 14, 27, 36,
  38, 41, 44, 45, 54–55, 58, 67,
  69, 71, 72, 78, 80, 82, 97, 101,
  188–200
Martimort, A.-G., 84, 85, 86, 87
Melkite rite, 13–14, 21, 25, 29, 31,
  36, 37, 50, 58, 64, 65, 66, 67,

69, 71, 75–76, 77, 78, 79, 82,
  97, 98, 99, 100, 201–212, 243
Metropolitans, 10, 11
Michael the Great, patriarch, 11
Milanese ordination rites, 19
Minor orders, 93–104
Missale Francorum, 14, 15, 17, 102,
  103, 223–230
Morin, Jean, 7, 8, 10, 12, 13, 27
Mozarabic rite, 15–16, 18, 24, 30,
  35–36, 37, 60, 69, 70, 81, 82,
  103, 231–235
Munier, Charles, 42

Nestorian, see East Syrian rite
Nicea, Council of, 39
Nimes, Council of, 83

Omophorion, 57
Orange, Council of, 83
Orationes solemnes, 101
Ordinare, 34
Ordinatio, 34
Ordines Romani, 14, 30, 35, 44
Ordo XXXIV, 14, 32, 101, 218–221
Ordo XXXV, 101
Orleans, Council of, 83

Palladius, 40
Papal ordination, 42, 43–44
Patriarchs, 8, 10, 11, 12, 43
Patristic texts, 105–123
Philostorgius, 25
Porter, H. Boone, 81
Powell, Douglas, 60
Power, David, 62
Prayer of the people, 30–32
Proclamation/bidding, 26–30
Pseudo-Dionysius, 25, 26, 27, 32,
  35, 40, 42, 45, 60, 72
Psalmists, 14, 101–102, 223

Raes, Alphonse, 10
Ratcliff, E. C., 42, 46, 60
Ratold, Sacramentary of, 16

Readers, 3, 4, 6, 7, 8, 10, 11, 13,
    14, 83, 84, 85, 87, 88, 91, 93–
    103, 109, 111–112, 116, 121,
    127, 139, 140–141, 156, 167,
    174–175, 188–189, 201–203,
    222, 223, 237
Renaudot, Eusébe, 8, 12
Romano-German Pontifical, 18
Roman rite, 14, 17, 18, 19, 21, 24,
    30, 32, 35, 38, 41, 43, 44–45,
    55–56, 59, 68, 70, 71, 80, 82,
    101, 215–221

Sacristan, 16
Sahak, tenth Catholicos of Arme-
    nia, 6, 100
Santantoni, Antonio, 17
Sarapion, Sacramentary of, 5, 9, 46,
    49–50, 63–64, 75, 76, 96, 122–
    123
Scholtz, Antony, 8
Scribes, chief, 16
Segelberg, Eric, 46, 47, 61
Severian of Gabala, 40, 42
Shahare, 10
Sign of the cross, 32
Smet, Bernard de, 12
Spanish Church, see Mozarabic
    rite
Statuta Ecclesiae Antiqua, 14–15,
    33–34, 42, 45, 59–60, 98, 101–
    103, 222–223
Stephen, Saint, 74, 75, 76, 77, 78,
    79, 80

Subdeacons, 3, 4, 7, 8, 10, 11, 13,
    14, 16, 83, 84, 87, 88, 93–99,
    100, 101–103, 109, 111–112,
    116, 121, 127, 139, 141–143,
    157, 167–168, 175–177, 189–
    191, 203–205, 219, 222, 224–
    225, 231–232, 238–239
Sunday, 20–21
Symbols of office, bestowal of,
    36, 57, 69–70, 81–82, 88, 93,
    95, 101–103
Syrian Orthodox Church, 11

Tchékan, Jean, 65
Testamentum Domini, 4–5, 8, 11,
    25, 27, 35, 44, 49, 50, 55, 59,
    61, 62, 63, 69, 73, 74, 83, 86,
    87, 88, 89, 93, 95, 99, 100,
    117–121
Toledo, Council of, 103
Tuki, Raphaël, 8
Turner, C. H., 60

Vesting, 57, 69, 70, 81, 82, 88, 90
Vosté, J. M., 10, 12
Virgins, 3, 109
Visigothic rite, see Mozarabic rite
Visitors, in Jacobite rite, 11

Walls, A. F., 60
Western texts, 213–242
Widows, 3, 4, 83–84, 87, 109, 112,
    120–121